More than 250 Fresh, Fabulous Recipes for Every Day

weightwatchers

ultimate
chicken
cookbook

ST. MARTIN'S GRIFFIN ≋ NEW YORK

WEIGHT WATCHERS ULTIMATE CHICKEN COOKBOOK. Copyright © 2013 by Weight Watchers International, Inc. All rights reserved. Printed in the United States of America. For information, address St. Martin's Press, 175 Fifth Avenue, New York, N.Y. 10010.

On the cover: Crunchy Oven–Fried Chicken with Herb Gravy, page 274

www.stmartins.com

Editorial and art produced by W/W Twentyfirst Corp., 675 Avenue of the Americas, New York, NY 10010

WEIGHT WATCHERS is a trademark of Weight Watchers International, Inc. Printed in the USA.

Many recipes in this book were previously released in *Everyone Loves Chicken*, a Weight Watchers meeting room book.

Library of Congress Cataloging-in-Publication Data
    Weight watchers ultimate chicken cookbook : more than 250 fresh, fabulous recipes for every day /
        by Weight Watchers.—First US edition.
        pages cm
    ISBN 978-1-250-03820-3 (hardcover)
    ISBN 978-1-250-03821-0 (e-book)
      1. Reducing diets—Recipes.   2. Cooking (Chicken)   I. Weight Watchers International.
    RM222.2.W32835 2013
    641.5'635—dc23   2013013849

St. Martin's Griffin books may be purchased for educational, business, or promotional use. For information on bulk purchases, please contact Macmillan Corporate and Premium Sales Department at 1-800-221-7945, extension 5442, or write specialmarkets@macmillan.com.

First Edition: September 2013

10 9 8 7 6 5 4 3 2 1

About Weight Watchers

Weight Watchers International, Inc. is the world's leading provider of weight-management services, operating globally through a network of company-owned and franchise operations. Weight Watchers holds nearly 45,000 meetings each week worldwide, at which members receive group support and education about healthful eating patterns, behavior modification, and physical activity. Weight-loss and weight-management results vary by individual. We recommend that you attend Weight Watchers meetings to benefit from the supportive environment and follow the comprehensive Weight Watchers program, which includes a food plan, an activity plan, and a behavioral component.

WeightWatchers.com provides subscription weight-management products, such as eTools and Weight Watchers Mobile, and is the leading internet-based weight-management provider in the world. In addition, Weight Watchers offers a wide range of products, publications (including **Weight Watchers Magazine**, which is available on newsstands and in Weight Watchers meeting rooms), and programs for people interested in weight loss and control. For the Weight Watchers meeting nearest you, call **1-800-651-6000**. For information about bringing Weight Watchers to your workplace, call **1-800-8AT-WORK**.

WEIGHT WATCHERS PUBLISHING GROUP

VP, Editorial Director
Nancy Gagliardi

Creative Director
Ed Melnitsky

Photo Director
Deborah Hardt

Managing Editor
Diane Pavia

Assistant Editor
Katerina Gkionis

Food Editor
Eileen Runyan

Editor
Deborah Mintcheff

Nutrition Consultant
U. Beate Krinke

Production Manager
Alan Biederman

Photographers
Alan Richardson
Rita Maas (cover)

Food Stylist
Michael Pederson

Prop Stylist
Cathy Cook

Meatballs in Cinnamon-Tomato Sauce, page 205

Contents

About Our Recipes

While losing weight isn't only about what you eat, Weight Watchers realizes the critical role it plays in your success and overall good health. That's why our philosophy is to offer great-tasting, easy recipes that are nutritious as well as delicious. We make every attempt to use wholesome ingredients and to ensure that our recipes fall within the recommendations of the U.S. Dietary Guidelines for Americans for a diet that promotes health and reduces the risk for disease. If you have special dietary needs, consult with your health-care professional for advice on a diet that is best for you, then adapt these recipes to meet your specific nutritional needs.

To achieve these good-health goals and get the maximum satisfaction from the foods you eat, we suggest you keep the following information in mind while preparing our recipes:

Weight Watchers 360° and Good Nutrition

- Recipes in this book have been developed for Weight Watchers members who are following Weight Watchers 360°, as well as anyone else interested in smart weight loss. *PointsPlus*® values are given for each recipe. They're assigned based on the amount of protein, carbohydrates, fat, and fiber contained in a single serving of a recipe.

- Recipes include approximate nutritional information: they are analyzed for Calories (Cal), Total Fat, Saturated Fat (Sat Fat), Trans Fat, Cholesterol (Chol), Sodium (Sod), Carbohydrates (Carb), Dietary Fiber (Fib), Protein (Prot), and Calcium (Calc). The nutritional values are calculated by registered dietitians, using nutrition analysis software.

- Substitutions made to the ingredients will alter the per-serving nutritional information and may affect the *PointsPlus* value.

- Our recipes meet Weight Watchers Good Health Guidelines for eating lean proteins and fiber-rich whole grains and for having at least five servings of vegetables and fruits and two servings of low-fat or fat-free dairy products a day, while limiting your intake of saturated fat, sugar, and sodium.

- Health agencies recommend limiting sodium intake. To stay in line with this recommendation, we keep sodium levels in our recipes reasonably low; to boost flavor, we often include fresh herbs or a squeeze of citrus instead of salt. If you don't have to restrict your sodium, feel free to add a touch more salt as desired.

- For information about the science behind lasting weight loss and more, please visit WeightWatchers.com/science.

Calculations Not What You Expected?

- You might expect some of the *PointsPlus* values in this book to be lower when some of the foods they're made from, such as fruits and vegetables, have no *PointsPlus* values. Fruit and veggies have no *PointsPlus* values when served as a snack or part of a meal, like a cup of berries with a sandwich. But if these foods are part of a recipe, their fiber and nutrient content are incorporated into the recipe calculations. These nutrients can affect the *PointsPlus* value.

- Alcohol is included in our *PointsPlus* calculations. Because alcohol information is generally not included on nutrition labels, it's not an option to include when using the hand calculator or the online calculator. But since we include alcohol information that we get from our nutritionists, you might notice discrepancies between the *PointsPlus* values you see in our recipes, and the values you get using the calculator. The *PointsPlus* values listed for our recipes are the most accurate values.

Shopping for Ingredients

As you learn to eat healthier, remember these tips for choosing foods wisely:

Lean Meats and Poultry

Purchase lean meats and poultry, and trim them of all visible fat before cooking. When poultry is cooked with the skin on, we recommend removing the skin before eating. Nutritional information for recipes that include meat, poultry, and fish is based on cooked, skinless boneless portions (unless otherwise stated), with the fat trimmed.

Seafood

Whenever possible, our recipes call for seafood that is sustainable and deemed the most healthful for human consumption so that your choice of seafood is not only good for the oceans but also good for you. For more information about the best seafood choices and to download a pocket guide, go to environmentaldefensefund.org or montereybayaquarium.org. For information about mercury and seafood go to weightwatchers.com.

Produce

For best flavor, maximum nutrient content, and the lowest prices, buy fresh local produce, such as vegetables, leafy greens, and fruits, in season. Rinse them thoroughly before using, and keep a supply of cut-up vegetables and fruits in your refrigerator for convenient healthy snacks.

Whole Grains

Explore your market for whole grain products, such as whole wheat and whole grain breads and pastas, brown rice, bulgur, barley, cornmeal, whole wheat couscous, oats, and quinoa, to enjoy with your meals.

Preparation and Measuring

Before you start cooking any recipe, consider the following advice:

Read the Recipe

Take a couple of minutes to read through the ingredients and directions before you start to prepare a recipe. This will prevent you from discovering midway through that you don't have an important ingredient or that a recipe requires several hours of marinating. And it's also a good idea to assemble all ingredients and utensils within easy reach before you begin a recipe.

Weighing and Measuring

The success of any recipe depends on accurate weighing and measuring. The effectiveness of the Weight Watchers Program and the accuracy of the nutritional analysis depend on correct measuring as well. Use the following techniques:

- Weigh foods such as meat, poultry, and fish on a food scale.

- To measure liquids, use a standard glass or plastic measuring cup placed on a level surface. For amounts less than ¼ cup, use standard measuring spoons.

- To measure dry ingredients, use metal or plastic measuring cups that come in ¼-, ⅓-, ½-, and 1-cup sizes. Fill the appropriate cup, and level it with the flat edge of a knife or spatula. For amounts less than ¼ cup, use standard measuring spoons.

hearty salads

Grilled Chicken and Corn Salad with Creamy Lemon Dressing

Makes 4 Servings

¼ cup plain low-fat yogurt

Grated zest of ½ lemon

3 tablespoons lemon juice

1 tablespoon canola oil

1 teaspoon ground cumin

¾ teaspoon salt

⅛ teaspoon black pepper

2 large ears of corn, husks and
   silk removed

4 (5-ounce) skinless boneless
   chicken breasts

1 large tomato, seeded and
   coarsely chopped

½ sweet onion, thinly sliced

½ cup loosely packed fresh
   cilantro leaves

¼ cup loosely packed fresh
   mint leaves, torn

8 green leaf lettuce leaves

1. Spray the grill rack with nonstick spray; prepare the grill for a medium-hot fire.

2. To make the dressing, whisk together the yogurt, lemon zest and juice, oil, cumin, ½ teaspoon of the salt, and the pepper in a large bowl. Let stand at room temperature.

3. Place the corn on the grill rack and grill, turning, until softened and browned in spots, about 15 minutes. Sprinkle the chicken with the remaining ¼ teaspoon salt. Place the chicken on the grill rack and grill, turning once or twice, until cooked through, 8–10 minutes. Transfer the chicken and corn to a cutting board.

4. When cool enough to handle, cut the chicken on the diagonal into thin slices. Using a serrated knife, cut the kernels from the corn. Add the chicken, corn, tomato, onion, cilantro, and mint to the dressing. Toss until mixed well and coated evenly with the dressing. Place 2 lettuce leaves on each of 4 plates; top evenly with the chicken salad.

PER SERVING (1¾ cups chicken salad and 2 lettuce leaves): 275 Cal, 8 g Total Fat, 2 g Sat Fat, 0 g Trans Fat, 79 mg Chol, 531 mg Sod, 20 g Total Carb, 6 g Total Sugar, 3 g Fib, 33 g Prot, 60 mg Calc. *PointsPlus* value: *7*.

COOK'S TIP

To make this tasty main dish even more satisfying, serve it with grilled slices of reduced-calorie whole wheat bread (1 slice of reduced-calorie whole wheat bread per serving will increase the *PointsPlus* value by *1*). End the meal with a refreshing salad of mixed berries tossed with some thinly sliced fresh mint.

Bistro Chicken Salad

Makes 4 Servings

½ pound skinless boneless
    chicken breast halves,
    lightly pounded

3 cups crusty Italian bread
    cubes (about ¾ inch)

1 cup grape or cherry tomatoes,
    halved

1 cup yellow pear tomatoes,
    halved

½ cucumber, peeled, seeded,
    and diced

1½ cups chopped fresh basil

10 Kalamata olives, pitted and
    coarsely chopped

3 tablespoons red-wine vinegar

4 teaspoons extra-virgin
    olive oil

1. Spray a nonstick ridged grill pan with nonstick spray and set over medium-high heat. Add the chicken and cook until browned on the outside and cooked through, about 4 minutes on each side. Transfer the chicken to a cutting board; let rest about 5 minutes. Cut the chicken, on the diagonal, into ¼-inch-thick slices.

2. Meanwhile, combine the bread, grape and yellow pear tomatoes, cucumber, basil, and olives in a large bowl. Drizzle with the vinegar and oil; toss well to coat. Stir in the chicken and serve at once.

PER SERVING (1¾ cups): 217 Cal, 9 g Total Fat, 2 g Sat Fat, 0 g Trans Fat, 34 mg Chol, 280 mg Sod, 19 g Carb, 2 g Fib, 16 g Prot, 52 mg Calc.
PointsPlus value: *6.*

COOK'S TIP

Similar to the classic Italian bread salad panzanella, this dish becomes a satisfying supper with the addition of chicken. Grape tomatoes and yellow pear tomatoes combined with strips of grilled chicken, toasted Italian bread cubes, fresh basil, and olives provide vibrant color and great flavor.

Corn and Salsa Chicken Salad

Makes 4 Servings

½ cup salsa

2 tablespoons balsamic vinegar

1 teaspoon brown mustard

2 tablespoons plus ¼ cup chopped fresh cilantro

4 (¼-pound) skinless boneless chicken breast halves

1 tablespoon Cajun seasoning

2 cups fresh corn kernels, cut from the cob

1 tomato, chopped

½ avocado, halved, pitted, peeled, and chopped

4 scallions, finely chopped

8 fat-free tortilla chips, coarsely crushed (about ¼ cup)

1. To make the dressing, combine the salsa, vinegar, mustard, and 2 tablespoons of the cilantro in a medium bowl; set aside.

2. Sprinkle the chicken with the Cajun seasoning. Spray a large nonstick skillet with nonstick spray and set over medium-high heat. Add the chicken and cook until browned on the outside and cooked through, about 5 minutes on each side. Transfer the chicken to a cutting board; let rest for about 5 minutes. Cut each breast, on the diagonal, into 4 or 5 slices, keeping the slices together at one end.

3. Combine the corn, tomato, avocado, scallions, and the remaining ¼ cup cilantro in a large bowl. Add the dressing and toss well to coat. Divide the salad evenly among 4 plates. Top each salad with a chicken breast with slices fanned open, then sprinkle with the chips.

PER SERVING (1½ cups salad, 1 chicken breast half, and 1 tablespoon chips): 269 Cal, 8 g Total Fat, 2 g Sat Fat, 0 g Trans Fat, 68 mg Chol, 646 mg Sod, 24 g Carb, 4 g Fib, 29 g Prot, 43 mg Calc. *PointsPlus* value: *7.*

COOK'S TIP

Fresh sweet corn makes this Southwestern chicken salad special. The corn is delicious raw, but you can use boiled or grilled corn on the cob, if you like. To easily remove the kernels, stand a cob upright on a cutting board. Using a serrated knife, cut off the kernels. One medium ear of corn yields about ½ cup of kernels.

Grilled Chicken Salad with Green Goddess Dressing

Makes 4 Servings

½ cup fat-free sour cream

¼ cup fat-free mayonnaise

1 bunch fresh chives, chopped

2 tablespoons coarsely
   chopped fresh tarragon

1 tablespoon tarragon vinegar

1 teaspoon Worcestershire
   sauce

4 (¼-pound) skinless boneless
   chicken breast halves

½ teaspoon salt

¼ teaspoon black pepper

1 (16-ounce) bag iceberg
   salad mix

1. Puree the sour cream, mayonnaise, chives, tarragon, vinegar, and Worcestershire sauce in a blender.

2. Spray a grill rack with extra-virgin olive oil nonstick spray; prepare the grill for a medium-hot fire. Lightly spray the chicken with nonstick spray; sprinkle with the salt and pepper.

3. Place the chicken on the grill rack and grill until cooked through, about 6 minutes on each side. Transfer to a cutting board.

4. Transfer 2 tablespoons of the dressing to a small bowl; set aside. Combine the salad mix and the remaining dressing in a large bowl; mix well. Divide the salad among 4 plates. Cut each chicken breast on the diagonal into ¼-inch-thick slices; arrange 1 breast half on top of each salad. Drizzle the chicken evenly with the reserved 2 tablespoons dressing.

PER SERVING (1 chicken breast half with ½ tablespoon dressing and about 1¾ cups salad): 183 Cal, 4 g Total Fat, 1 g Sat Fat, 0 g Trans Fat, 64 mg Chol, 540 mg Sod, 11 g Carb, 2 g Fib, 26 g Prot, 92 mg Calc.
PointsPlus value: *4.*

COOK'S TIP

This oh-so-tasty salad features grilled chicken breast atop crunchy iceberg lettuce and a creamy Green Goddess dressing. If you don't have any fresh tarragon on hand, substitute ¼ cup fresh basil leaves, chopped, but don't use dried tarragon, as it lacks any flavor resemblance to fresh.

Glossary of Salad Greens

It's so easy to serve inspiring salads with all of the beautiful, flavorful salad greens available in super-markets, specialty food stores, farmers' markets, and produce stores. Look for firm, unblemished leaves without any wilting or brown spots. At home, loosely wrap the greens in a paper towel and place in a zip-close plastic bag; store in the crisper drawer.

Arugula: The elongated leaves are slightly peppery. Also look for baby, or micro arugula.

Try with: Italian-inspired salads and with citrus fruits

Butterhead Lettuce: Bibb is miniature butterhead lettuce, while Boston is a larger version that has soft pale green leaves.

Try with: salads dressed with a light dressing or in sandwiches

Endive: Also called Belgian chicory, the leaves of this ivory and pale yellow–edged vegetable are oval with a satiny, crunchy texture and mild bitterness. Use whole or sliced.

Try with: sliced or diced apple or pear, toasted walnuts, and blue cheese or goat cheese

Escarole: Also called broad-leaved endive, this slightly bitter green has long crisp leaves.

Try with: white beans, garlic, and tomatoes in soups or salads

Frisée: Also called curly endive, chicory, and curly chicory, frisée's tender curly edges are pale to medium green with a slightly bitter taste.

Try with: crisp turkey bacon, a mustardy dressing, croutons, and poached egg for a classic French salad

Lollo Rosso: Small loose heads of delicately flavored ruffle-edged red lettuce.

Try with: other greens in a mixed salad

Mâche: Also called field salad, lamb's lettuce, corn salad, and field lettuce, this green is usually sold in bunches with its soil attached. It is sweet and mild with tender leaves that easily bruise.

Try with: other baby greens in a mixed salad

Oak Leaf: Small loose heads of deep red-brown lettuce with tender, delicately flavored oak leaf–shaped leaves.

Try with: other baby greens in a mixed salad

Radicchio: Also known as chiogga, red chicory, and red Italian chicory, this deep burgundy lettuce is sold as small solid round heads or in elongated heads that resemble Belgian endive.

Try with: arugula and Belgian endive for a classic Italian salad known as *salade tri colore*

Tatsoi: An Asian green that is mild and peppery. Its leaves are dark green and spoon-shaped. Tatsoi grows in clusters that resemble compact rosettes.

Try with: other baby greens in a mixed salad

Watercress: Also called cress, this dark green is sold in bunches and in clear plastic bags. A beautiful purple variety is sometimes available in specialty food stores. This green is pleasantly peppery; be sure to rinse it well to remove any sand.

Try with: almost any other green, but it makes an excellent addition to sandwiches

Chicken, Mango, and Black Bean Salad

Makes 4 Servings

3 tablespoons lime juice

2 teaspoons extra-virgin
olive oil

½ teaspoon salt

¼ teaspoon chili powder

2 cups shredded cooked
chicken breast

1 small jicama (about 1 pound),
peeled and diced

1 (15½-ounce) can black beans,
rinsed and drained

1 mango, peeled, pitted, and
cut into ¾-inch chunks

½ cup diced red onion

⅓ cup chopped fresh cilantro

1 jalapeño pepper, seeded and
minced

Combine the lime juice, oil, salt, and chili powder in a large bowl. Add the chicken, jicama, beans, mango, onion, cilantro, and jalapeño; mix well. Let stand for 10 minutes to allow the flavors to blend.

PER SERVING (1½ cups): 283 Cal, 6 g Total Fat, 1 g Sat Fat, 0 g Trans Fat, 60 mg Chol, 482 mg Sod, 30 g Carb, 11 g Fib, 27 g Prot, 58 mg Calc.
PointsPlus value: *6.*

COOK'S TIP

If you prefer to cook the chicken yourself, here's how: Bring 1 cup water to a boil in a medium saucepan; add ½ pound skinless boneless chicken breast. Reduce the heat to low and simmer, covered, until cooked through, about 10 minutes. Let the chicken cool in the pot, then shred it and proceed with the recipe.

Tandoori-Style Chicken Salad

Tandoori-Style Chicken Salad

Makes 4 Servings

¾ cup plain fat-free yogurt

1½ teaspoons ground cumin

1 teaspoon minced peeled fresh ginger

1 garlic clove, minced

½ teaspoon salt

1 pound thin-sliced chicken breast cutlets

4 cups shredded red cabbage

¾ cup shredded carrots

¼ cup plus 2 tablespoons chopped fresh cilantro

3 tablespoons red-wine vinegar

1 tablespoon extra-virgin olive oil

½ teaspoon black pepper

1. Combine the yogurt, cumin, ginger, garlic, and ¼ teaspoon of the salt in a large zip-close plastic bag; add the chicken. Squeeze out the air and seal the bag; turn to coat the chicken. Refrigerate, turning the bag occasionally, for at least 1 hour or up to overnight.

2. Combine the cabbage, carrots, the ¼ cup cilantro, the vinegar, oil, pepper, and the remaining ¼ teaspoon salt in a large bowl; toss well to coat.

3. Remove the chicken from the yogurt marinade; discard the marinade. Spray a large nonstick ridged grill pan with nonstick spray and set over medium-high heat. Add the chicken and cook until browned on the outside and cooked through, about 3 minutes on each side. Transfer the chicken to a cutting board; let rest for about 5 minutes. Cut the chicken, on the diagonal, into thin slices.

4. Arrange the cabbage mixture on a large serving platter; top with the chicken and sprinkle with the remaining 2 tablespoons cilantro.

PER SERVING (1½ cups)**:** 207 Cal, 7 g Total Fat, 2 g Sat Fat, 0 g Trans Fat, 69 mg Chol, 271 mg Sod, 8 g Carb, 2 g Fib, 27 g Prot, 81 mg Calc.
PointsPlus value: *5.*

COOK'S TIP

You can prepare most of this salad the day before you plan to serve it. Set the chicken to marinate (step 1) and toss the cabbage and carrots with the seasonings (step 2); refrigerate, separately, overnight. The next day, cook the chicken and serve with the cabbage mixture and extra cilantro.

Chicken Salad Provençal

Makes 4 Servings

2 tablespoons apple cider vinegar

1 tablespoon extra-virgin olive oil

1 tablespoon chopped fresh tarragon

1 teaspoon Dijon mustard

½ teaspoon black pepper

¾ teaspoon salt

1 pound fingerling potatoes, scrubbed and cut into ¼-inch-thick slices

½ pound haricots verts, trimmed

1 pound thin-sliced chicken breast cutlets

1 teaspoon dried oregano

½ fennel bulb, trimmed and thinly sliced

½ cup grape or cherry tomatoes, halved

½ red onion, thinly sliced

6 Kalamata olives, pitted and coarsely chopped

1. To make the dressing, combine the vinegar, oil, tarragon, mustard, pepper, and ¼ teaspoon of the salt in a small bowl; set aside.

2. Place the potatoes and enough water to cover in a large saucepan; bring to a boil. Reduce the heat and simmer, covered, until the potatoes are tender, about 15 minutes. Using a slotted spoon, transfer the potatoes (reserving the water in the pot) to a large bowl.

3. Add the beans to the boiling water in the pot and cook until crisp-tender, about 4 minutes. Drain the beans and rinse under cold running water, then drain on layers of paper towels. Add the beans to the potatoes.

4. Sprinkle the chicken with the oregano and the remaining ½ teaspoon salt. Spray a large nonstick skillet with nonstick spray and set over medium-high heat. Add the chicken and cook until browned on the outside and cooked through, about 3 minutes on each side. Transfer the chicken to a cutting board; let rest about 5 minutes. Cut the chicken, on the diagonal, into ¼-inch-thick slices.

5. Add the chicken, fennel, tomatoes, onion, and olives to the potato mixture. Add the dressing and toss gently to coat.

PER SERVING (1 cup): 311 Cal, 8 g Total Fat, 2 g Sat Fat, 0 g Trans Fat, 68 mg Chol, 617 mg Sod, 32 g Carb, 5 g Fib, 28 g Prot, 76 mg Calc.
PointsPlus value: *8.*

COOK'S TIP

Blanching—a technique where food is cooked briefly in boiling water, then quickly cooled—is an excellent method for cooking tender vegetables, such as green beans, haricots verts, asparagus, sugar snap peas, and snow peas. Blanching both heightens their color and preserves their flavor.

Jerk Chicken and Sweet Potato Salad

Makes 4 Servings

2 medium sweet potatoes, peeled and cut into 1½-inch pieces

1 (15¼-ounce) can pineapple chunks, drained (¼ cup juice reserved)

1 red bell pepper, diced

¼ cup chopped fresh cilantro

1 pound thin-sliced chicken breast cutlets

1 tablespoon Caribbean jerk seasoning

1 tablespoon reduced-sodium soy sauce

1 tablespoon packed light brown sugar

1 teaspoon minced peeled fresh ginger

1 teaspoon Asian (dark) sesame oil

1. Place the potatoes and enough water to cover in a large saucepan; bring to a boil. Reduce the heat and simmer, covered, until the potatoes are tender, 12–15 minutes. Drain the potatoes and transfer to a large bowl; let cool about 10 minutes. Add the pineapple, bell pepper, and cilantro.

2. Sprinkle the chicken with the jerk seasoning. Spray a large nonstick skillet with nonstick spray and set over medium-high heat. Add the chicken and cook until browned on the outside and cooked through, about 3 minutes on each side. Transfer the chicken to a cutting board; let rest for about 5 minutes. Cut the chicken, on the diagonal, into thin slices.

3. Meanwhile, to make the dressing, whisk together the reserved ¼ cup pineapple juice, the soy sauce, sugar, ginger, and oil in a small bowl until blended; set aside.

4. Add the chicken to the potato mixture; drizzle with the dressing and toss gently to coat.

PER SERVING (scant 2 cups): 309 Cal, 5 g Total Fat, 1 g Sat Fat, 0 g Trans Fat, 68 mg Chol, 208 mg Sod, 39 g Carb, 4 g Fib, 27 g Prot, 61 mg Calc.
PointsPlus value: *8.*

COOK'S TIP

In the fall and winter, roast the sweet potatoes instead of boiling them, as it intensifies their flavor: Arrange the sweet potato pieces in one layer on a baking sheet that has been sprayed with nonstick spray. Spray them lightly and roast in a preheated 375°F oven until tender and browned, about 25 minutes.

Sesame Chicken Fingers and Pickled Ginger–Rice Salad

Makes 4 Servings

3 tablespoons cornflake crumbs

2 tablespoons sesame seeds

1 tablespoon honey

4 teaspoons reduced-sodium soy sauce

½ pound skinless boneless chicken breasts, cut into 2 × ½-inch strips

2 tablespoons seasoned rice vinegar

1 tablespoon pickled ginger, drained and chopped

1 tablespoon pickled ginger juice

3 tablespoons chopped fresh cilantro

2 cups cooked white rice

1 red bell pepper, diced

¼ pound snow peas, trimmed

½ carrot, cut into matchstick-thin strips

¼ cup chopped scallions

1. Preheat the oven to 450°F. Spray a small baking pan with nonstick spray.

2. Combine the cornflake crumbs and sesame seeds on a sheet of wax paper.

3. Combine the honey and 2 teaspoons of the soy sauce in a medium bowl; add the chicken and toss to coat. Dip the chicken, 1 piece at a time, into the crumb mixture, coating all sides. Place the chicken in the baking pan in one layer; lightly spray the chicken with nonstick spray. Bake, turning once, until the chicken is browned on the outside and cooked through, about 10 minutes.

4. Meanwhile, to make the dressing, whisk together the vinegar, ginger, ginger juice, cilantro, and the remaining 2 teaspoons soy sauce in a small bowl until blended; set aside.

5. Combine the rice, bell pepper, snow peas, carrots, and scallions in a large bowl. Add the chicken, drizzle with the dressing, and toss well to coat.

PER SERVING (1½ cups): 265 Cal, 5 g Total Fat, 1 g Sat Fat, 0 g Trans Fat, 34 mg Chol, 261 mg Sod, 36 g Carb, 3 g Fib, 18 g Prot, 43 mg Calc.
PointsPlus value: 7.

COOK'S TIP

Want to save time making this crunchy and colorful salad? Buy packaged cut or salad bar–cut veggies. Mix and match them: Choose yellow bell pepper instead of red, broccoli florets instead of snow peas, and chopped red onion instead of scallions.

Sesame Chicken Fingers and
Pickled Ginger–Rice Salad

**Mustard Chicken
with Watercress and
Belgian Endive**

Mustard Chicken with Watercress and Belgian Endive

Makes 4 Servings

½ cup plain dry bread crumbs

1 pound skinless boneless chicken breasts, cut into 2 × ½-inch strips

1 tablespoon plus 2 teaspoons Dijon mustard

3 tablespoons lemon juice

1 tablespoon extra-virgin olive oil

1 tablespoon capers, drained

½ teaspoon black pepper

¼ teaspoon salt

1 bunch watercress, tough stems discarded

1 head Belgian endive, cored and cut into matchstick-thin strips

½ red onion, thinly sliced

1. Preheat the oven to 450°F. Spray a small baking pan with nonstick spray.

2. Place the bread crumbs on a sheet of wax paper.

3. Combine the chicken and the 1 tablespoon mustard in a medium bowl. Dip the chicken, one piece at a time, into the crumbs, coating all sides. Place the chicken in the baking pan in one layer; lightly spray the chicken with nonstick spray. Bake, turning once, until the chicken is browned on the outside and cooked through, about 10 minutes.

4. Meanwhile, to make the dressing, whisk together the lemon juice, oil, capers, pepper, salt, and the remaining 2 teaspoons mustard in a small bowl; set aside.

5. Place the watercress, endive, and onion in a large bowl. Add the dressing and toss well to coat. Add the chicken and toss lightly. Serve at once.

PER SERVING (1 cup): 250 Cal, 9 g Total Fat, 2 g Sat Fat, 0 g Trans Fat, 68 mg Chol, 556 mg Sod, 14 g Carb, 2 g Fib, 28 g Prot, 96 mg Calc.
PointsPlus value: *6.*

COOK'S TIP

Dijon mustard does double duty here—it flavors up the chicken and helps the bread crumbs adhere. To save time, look for 4-ounce bags of trimmed watercress. Even though the package may say it has been triple-washed, we recommend washing it at home.

Chicken, Penne, and Asparagus Salad

Makes 4 Servings

½ pound skinless boneless chicken breasts, cut into 2 × ½-inch strips

2 teaspoons seasoning for poultry and meat

¼ (1-pound) box penne pasta (about 1⅓ cups)

1 pound asparagus, trimmed and cut diagonally into thirds

2 tomatoes, chopped

1 cup chopped fresh basil

¼ cup (1 ounce) grated Pecorino Romano cheese

2 garlic cloves, minced

1 tablespoon extra-virgin olive oil

¼ teaspoon salt

1. Sprinkle the chicken with the seasoning. Spray a large nonstick skillet with nonstick spray and set over medium-high heat. Add the chicken and cook, turning occasionally, until browned on the outside and cooked through, about 8 minutes.

2. Meanwhile, cook the pasta according to the package directions omitting the salt, if desired. Using a small strainer or slotted spoon, transfer the pasta (reserving the water in the pot) to a colander. Rinse the pasta under cold running water; drain and transfer to a large bowl.

3. Add the asparagus to the same pot of boiling water and cook until crisp-tender, about 3 minutes. Rinse under cold running water to stop the cooking; drain and add to pasta. Add the chicken, tomatoes, basil, cheese, garlic, oil, and salt; toss well to coat. Serve at once.

PER SERVING (1½ cups): 273 Cal, 8 g Total Fat, 2 g Sat Fat, 0 g Trans Fat, 39 mg Chol, 411 mg Sod, 29 g Carb, 3 g Fib, 21 g Prot, 136 mg Calc.
PointsPlus value: 7.

COOK'S TIP

Fresh basil—and lots of it—is a key component in this simple yet delicious meal. Use whatever green vegetable is fresh and in season. If asparagus is not available, sugar snap peas, snow peas, or broccoli florets are good alternatives.

Chicken, Penne, and Asparagus Salad

Chunky Chicken Gazpacho Salad

Makes 4 Servings

½ cup vegetable juice cocktail
  or tomato juice

1 tablespoon balsamic vinegar

1 tablespoon extra-virgin
  olive oil

1 jalapeño pepper, seeded and
  minced

1 garlic clove, minced

1 pound skinless boneless
  chicken breasts, cut into
  ¾-inch pieces

⅛ teaspoon salt

½ teaspoon black pepper

½ large seedless cucumber,
  peeled and cut into ½-inch
  pieces

1 cup cherry tomatoes, halved

½ red bell pepper, diced

½ yellow bell pepper, diced

½ red onion, diced

½ cup chopped fresh cilantro

1. To make the dressing, whisk together the juice, vinegar, oil, jalapeño pepper, and garlic in a small bowl until blended; set aside.

2. Spray a large nonstick skillet with nonstick spray and set over medium-high heat. Add the chicken and sprinkle with the salt and black pepper. Cook, turning occasionally, until browned on the outside and cooked through, about 8 minutes.

3. Combine the cucumber, tomatoes, red and yellow bell peppers, onion, and cilantro in a large bowl. Add the chicken, drizzle with the dressing, and toss to coat.

PER SERVING (1¾ cups): **206 Cal, 7 g Total Fat, 2 g Sat Fat, 0 g Trans Fat, 68 mg Chol, 222 mg Sod, 8 g Carb, 2 g Fib, 26 g Prot, 33 mg Calc.**
PointsPlus value: *5.*

COOK'S TIP

For a fun variation, serve this salad with low-fat baked tortilla chips and use them as scoopers to eat this crunchy, colorful salad. One ounce of low-fat baked tortilla chips per serving will up the *PointsPlus* value by *3.*

Lots-of-Vegetables Chicken Panzanella Salad

Makes 4 Servings

12 ounces day-old crusty whole-grain bread, lightly toasted and cut into 1-inch chunks

½ pound cooked skinless boneless chicken breast, cut into bite-size pieces

2 large tomatoes, cut into ¾-inch chunks

1 large yellow bell pepper, cut into ¾-inch chunks

1 large red bell pepper, cut into ¾-inch chunks

1 small onion, very thinly sliced

½ cup coarsely chopped fresh flat-leaf parsley

8 large fresh basil leaves, torn

1 teaspoon capers, rinsed, drained, and chopped

½ cup fat-free Italian dressing

¼ teaspoon black pepper

Combine the bread, chicken, tomatoes, bell peppers, onion, parsley, basil, and capers in a serving bowl and toss until mixed well. Drizzle with the dressing and sprinkle with the black pepper; toss until coated evenly.

PER SERVING (2 cups): 367 Cal, 6 g Total Fat, 2 g Sat Fat, 0 g Trans Fat, 49 mg Chol, 971 mg Sod, 47 g Carb, 9 g Fib, 31 g Prot, 148 mg Calc.
PointsPlus value: *9.*

COOK'S TIP

Tossing thick slices of peeled and halved cucumber into this flavorful summer salad will add both crunch and a bit of fresh flavor. Here's how to easily seed a cucumber: After cutting the cucumber lengthwise in half, use the tip of a teaspoon or a melon baller and scrape down along the length of the cucumber; remove and discard the seeds.

Moroccan Chicken Salad

Makes 6 Servings

¼ cup orange juice

2 tablespoons lemon juice

1 tablespoon honey

2 teaspoons Dijon mustard

2 teaspoons extra-virgin
olive oil

1¼ teaspoons garam masala

¾ pound skinless boneless
chicken thighs

2 cups water

1 cup couscous

1 (15½-ounce) can chickpeas,
rinsed and drained

½ cucumber, peeled and diced

½ cup shredded carrot

½ cup dried currants or raisins

3 tablespoons finely chopped
scallions

1. To make the dressing, whisk together the orange juice, lemon juice, honey, mustard, oil, and ½ teaspoon of the garam masala in a small bowl until blended; set aside.

2. Sprinkle the chicken with the remaining ¾ teaspoon garam masala. Spray a large nonstick skillet with nonstick spray and set over medium-high heat. Add the chicken and cook, turning occasionally, until browned and cooked through, about 10 minutes. Transfer the chicken to a cutting board; let rest for about 5 minutes. Cut the chicken into 1-inch pieces.

3. Bring the water to a boil in a medium saucepan. Stir in the couscous; cover and remove from the heat. Let stand until all of the liquid is absorbed, about 5 minutes. Transfer the couscous to a large bowl; fluff with a fork and let cool. Add the chicken, chickpeas, cucumber, carrot, currants, and scallions. Drizzle with the dressing and toss well to coat.

PER SERVING (1⅓ cups): 357 Cal, 8 g Total Fat, 2 g Sat Fat, 0 g Trans Fat, 35 mg Chol, 154 mg Sod, 52 g Carb, 6 g Fib, 21 g Prot, 63 mg Calc.
PointsPlus value: *9.*

COOK'S TIP

Garam masala is an aromatic Indian blend that includes sweet spices and hot pepper. If you can't find it, you can easily make your own by combining 1 teaspoon each of ground cinnamon, ground cumin, ground coriander, and ground cardamom with ½ teaspoon black pepper or a pinch of cayenne.

Chicken Salad Adobo

Makes 6 Servings

1 tablespoon grated orange
    zest

2 tablespoons orange juice

1 tablespoon white-wine
    vinegar

2 teaspoons extra-virgin
    olive oil

1 teaspoon honey

1 teaspoon Dijon mustard

1 garlic clove, minced

⅛ teaspoon salt

1 pound skinless boneless
    chicken thighs, cut into
    1-inch pieces

1 tablespoon adobo seasoning

1 (15½-ounce) can black beans,
    rinsed and drained

1 ripe mango, peeled, pitted,
    and diced

1 red bell pepper, diced

½ red onion, finely chopped

½ cup chopped fresh cilantro

1 jalapeño pepper, seeded and
    minced

1. To make the dressing, whisk together the orange zest, orange juice, vinegar, oil, honey, mustard, garlic, and salt in a small bowl until blended; set aside.

2. Sprinkle the chicken with the adobo seasoning. Spray a large nonstick skillet with nonstick spray and set over medium-high heat. Add the chicken and cook, turning occasionally, until browned on the outside and cooked through, about 8 minutes. Transfer the chicken to a large bowl. Stir in the beans, mango, bell pepper, onion, cilantro, and jalapeño pepper. Drizzle with the dressing and toss well to coat.

PER SERVING (scant 1 cup): 248 Cal, 8 g Total Fat, 2 g Sat Fat, 0 g Trans Fat, 47 mg Chol, 321 mg Sod, 23 g Carb, 4 g Fib, 21 g Prot, 63 mg Calc.
PointsPlus value: *6.*

COOK'S TIP

You can transform this salad into delicious sandwich wraps by enclosing the chicken mixture in 3 (10-inch) whole wheat tortillas. Cut each wrap in half on the diagonal and serve half a wrap to each person (½ whole wheat tortilla per person will increase the *PointsPlus* value by *3*).

**Grilled Chicken Sausage with
Roasted Potato Salad**

Grilled Chicken Sausage with Roasted Potato Salad

Makes 6 Servings

2 tablespoons apple cider vinegar

1 tablespoon country-style mustard

1 tablespoon extra-virgin olive oil

1 garlic clove, minced

½ teaspoon salt

¾ teaspoon black pepper

1 pound small red potatoes, scrubbed and halved

1 large red onion, cut into ½-inch-thick wedges

1 tablespoon chopped fresh rosemary

1 (12-ounce) package fully cooked chicken sausage

1 (10-ounce) box frozen peas, thawed

1 yellow bell pepper, thinly sliced

10 Kalamata olives, pitted and chopped

¼ cup chopped fresh flat-leaf parsley

3 tablespoons crumbled reduced-fat goat cheese

1. Preheat the oven to 425°F. Spray a nonstick roasting pan with nonstick spray.

2. To make the dressing, whisk together the vinegar, mustard, oil, garlic, ¼ teaspoon of the salt and ¼ teaspoon of the black pepper in a small bowl until blended; set aside.

3. Combine the potatoes, onion, rosemary, and the remaining ¼ teaspoon salt and ½ teaspoon black pepper in a large bowl. Lightly spray the potato mixture with extra-virgin olive oil nonstick spray; toss to coat. Arrange the potato mixture in the roasting pan in one layer. Roast, stirring occasionally, until the potatoes are tender and browned, about 40 minutes. Transfer the potatoes to a large bowl; set aside.

4. Spray a large nonstick skillet with nonstick spray and set over medium heat. Add the sausages and cook, covered, until lightly browned and just heated through, about 7 minutes. When the sausages are cool enough to handle, cut them diagonally into 1-inch pieces; add to the potatoes.

5. Add the peas, bell pepper, olives, and parsley to the potato mixture. Drizzle with the dressing and toss well to coat. Sprinkle with the cheese and serve at once.

PER SERVING (1⅓ cups): 241 Cal, 10 g Total Fat, 2 g Sat Fat, 0 g Trans Fat, 31 mg Chol, 909 mg Sod, 26 g Carb, 5 g Fib, 13 g Prot, 50 mg Calc.
PointsPlus value: *6.*

COOK'S TIP

Chicken sausages are readily found in supermarkets. They are available low in fat, fully cooked, and in a variety of flavors, ranging from sweet and mild to spicy and hot. If you happen to have regular-size red potatoes on hand, use them here by cutting them into 1-inch pieces.

Layered Chicken Taco Salad

Makes 6 Servings

2 teaspoons canola oil

1 pound ground skinless
    chicken breast

1 onion, chopped

2 tablespoons taco or chili
    seasoning mix

1 (8-ounce) can no-salt-added
    tomato sauce

¼ cup water

¼ cup (1 ounce) shredded
    reduced-fat Cheddar cheese

¼ cup chopped fresh cilantro

1 cup fat-free refried beans

3 cups shredded iceberg
    lettuce

½ cup salsa verde (green salsa)

¼ cup fat-free sour cream

12 reduced-fat tortilla chips

1. Heat the oil in a large nonstick skillet over medium-high heat. Add the chicken, onion, and taco seasoning. Cook, breaking up the chicken with a wooden spoon, until browned, about 8 minutes. Stir in the tomato sauce and water; bring to a boil. Reduce the heat and simmer, uncovered, until the flavors are blended and the liquid has evaporated, about 6 minutes. Remove the skillet from the heat; stir in the cheese and cilantro.

2. Spread the beans in the bottom of a 7 × 11-inch baking dish; top with a layer of the lettuce, then with the chicken mixture, salsa, and finally a layer of sour cream. Tuck the chips around the dish. Serve at once.

PER SERVING (¾ cup salad with 2 tortilla chips): 207 Cal, 5 g Total Fat, 1 g Sat Fat, 0 g Trans Fat, 47 mg Chol, 540 mg Sod, 19 g Carb, 4 g Fib, 22 g Prot, 109 mg Calc.
PointsPlus value: *5.*

COOK'S TIP

Show off this colorful layered salad by serving it in a glass dish or layer the ingredients on a large round platter. If you like to cook Mexican food, you might consider buying taco or chili seasoning in cans, which are a better buy. Otherwise, it's available in individual packets.

Creole Chicken and Spicy Potato Salad

Makes 4 Servings

¼ cup honey-Dijon mustard

3 tablespoons fat-free mayonnaise

4 teaspoons Creole seasoning

1 tablespoon apple cider vinegar

4 drops hot pepper sauce

1 pound red potatoes, cut into 1½-inch pieces

4 (¼-pound) thin-sliced chicken breast cutlets

1 green bell pepper, chopped

1 celery stalk, finely chopped

1 small red onion, finely chopped

¼ cup chopped fresh flat-leaf parsley

2 slices bacon, crisp-cooked, drained, and crumbled

1. To make the dressing, whisk together the mustard, mayonnaise, Creole seasoning, vinegar, and hot pepper sauce in a small bowl until blended; set aside.

2. Place the potatoes and enough water to cover in a large saucepan; bring to a boil. Reduce the heat and simmer, covered, until the potatoes are tender, about 20 minutes. Drain the potatoes and transfer to a large bowl; let cool about 10 minutes.

3. Spray a large nonstick skillet with nonstick spray and set over medium-high heat. Add the chicken and cook until browned on the outside and cooked through, about 4 minutes on each side. Transfer the chicken to a cutting board; let rest for about 5 minutes. Cut the chicken into 1-inch pieces.

4. Add the chicken, bell pepper, celery, onion, and parsley to the potatoes. Drizzle with the dressing and toss well to coat. Serve at once, sprinkled with the bacon.

PER SERVING (1¾ cups salad with 2 teaspoons bacon): 294 Cal, 4 g Total Fat, 1 g Sat Fat, 0 g Trans Fat, 78 mg Chol, 489 mg Sod, 35 g Carb, 4 g Fib, 31 g Prot, 54 mg Calc.
PointsPlus value: 7.

COOK'S TIP

Spicy and delicious, this salad is great served with steamed green beans or asparagus sprinkled with grated lemon zest.

Chicken Cobb Salad

Makes 6 Servings

2 tablespoons white-wine
   vinegar

1 tablespoon lemon juice

1 tablespoon Dijon mustard

4 teaspoons extra-virgin
   olive oil

¼ teaspoon black pepper

⅛ teaspoon salt

6 cups mesclun greens

2 cups bite-size pieces cooked
   chicken breast

2 tomatoes, diced

1 Hass avocado halved, pitted,
   peeled, and cut into ½-inch
   pieces

2 hard-cooked large egg
   whites, finely chopped

3 slices bacon, crisp-cooked,
   drained, and crumbled

2 tablespoons crumbled blue
   cheese

1. To make the dressing, whisk together the vinegar, lemon juice, mustard, oil, pepper, and salt in a small bowl until blended; set aside.

2. Place the greens on a large serving platter. Arrange the chicken, tomatoes, and avocado in rows on top of the greens. Sprinkle the salad with the cooked egg whites, bacon, and cheese. Drizzle with the dressing and serve at once.

PER SERVING (generous 1 cup): **191 Cal, 11 g Total Fat, 2 g Sat Fat, 0 g Trans Fat, 44 mg Chol, 265 mg Sod, 6 g Carb, 3 g Fib, 18 g Prot, 57 mg Calc.**
PointsPlus value: *5.*

COOK'S TIP

Cobb salad originated at the Brown Derby restaurant in Hollywood in 1937, when owner Bob Cobb used the ingredients he had on hand to create what was to become a famous and delectable main-course salad.

Chicken Cobb Salad

Rice Noodle Salad with Chicken and Green Beans

Makes 6 Servings

4 ounces rice stick noodles

2 tablespoons apple cider vinegar

Grated zest and juice of 1 lime

1 tablespoon packed light brown sugar

2 teaspoons Asian fish sauce

1 teaspoon Sriracha

2 teaspoons canola oil

1 pound ground skinless chicken breast

½ teaspoon five-spice powder

¼ teaspoon salt

½ pound green beans, trimmed and cut into 2-inch lengths

3 large garlic cloves, minced

¼ cup chopped fresh cilantro

3 tablespoons unsalted dry-roasted peanuts, chopped

1. Cook the rice noodles according to the package directions; drain. Rinse the noodles under cold running water and drain again. Transfer the noodles to a large bowl.

2. To make the dressing, whisk together the vinegar, lime zest and juice, brown sugar, fish sauce, and Sriracha in a small bowl until the brown sugar has dissolved.

3. Heat 1 teaspoon of the oil in a large nonstick skillet over medium heat. Add the chicken, five-spice powder, and salt. Cook, breaking up the chicken with a wooden spoon, until no longer pink and most of the liquid has evaporated, about 5 minutes. Add the chicken mixture to the noodles.

4. Heat the remaining 1 teaspoon oil in the same skillet over medium heat. Add the green beans and garlic and cook, tossing constantly, just until the beans turn bright green, 1–2 minutes. Add the beans to the chicken mixture in the bowl. Add the dressing and toss until mixed well. Transfer the salad to a serving platter; sprinkle with the cilantro and peanuts.

PER SERVING (1 cup): 198 Cal, 5 g Total Fat, 0 g Sat Fat, 0 g Trans Fat, 23 mg Chol, 346 mg Sod, 25 g Total Carb, 2 g Fib, 17 g Prot, 33 mg Calc.
PointsPlus value: *5.*

COOK'S TIP

Sriracha is a very tasty hot sauce that can be used any time you want to add a bit of a kick to a dish. It is made of chile peppers, white vinegar, garlic, sugar, and salt. There are several brands available, but the one most readily found is Huy Fong. It comes in a tall clear plastic bottle with a bright green top.

Smoked Chicken and Crunchy Fruit Slaw

Makes 4 Servings

½ cup plain fat-free yogurt

3 tablespoons apricot preserves

2 teaspoons lemon juice

1 teaspoon Dijon mustard

½ pound piece cooked smoked chicken, cut into bite-size pieces or strips

1 small jicama, peeled and cut into matchstick-thin strips

1 apple, cored and chopped

1 cup seedless red or green grapes, halved

1 carrot, cut into matchstick-thin strips

1 celery stalk, diced

¼ cup golden raisins

4 large red or green leaf lettuce leaves

1. Combine the yogurt, preserves, lemon juice, and mustard in a large bowl. Add the chicken, jicama, apple, grapes, carrot, celery, and raisins; toss well to coat. Let stand for 10 minutes to allow flavors to blend.

2. Place a lettuce leaf on each of 4 plates. Divide the chicken-slaw mixture evenly (about 1½ cups) onto each lettuce leaf. Serve at once.

PER SERVING (1 plate): 246 Cal, 2 g Total Fat, 1 g Sat Fat, 0 g Trans Fat, 28 mg Chol, 753 mg Sod, 45 g Carb, 7 g Fib, 13 g Prot, 106 mg Calc.
PointsPlus value: **6.**

COOK'S TIP

Can't find jicama? Substitute an extra apple, a pear, or even fresh pineapple chunks. If you like, sprinkle each serving of this tasty no-cook salad with a tablespoon of sunflower seeds and increase the *PointsPlus* value by **1.**

Curried Chicken–Stuffed Tomatoes

Makes 4 Servings

2 cups bite-size pieces cooked chicken

2 celery stalks, finely diced

1 Granny Smith apple, cored and finely chopped

½ cup raisins

¼ cup fat-free mayonnaise

2 tablespoons mango chutney

1 tablespoon fat-free sour cream

1 tablespoon lime juice

1½ teaspoons curry powder

½ teaspoon ground cumin

4 medium tomatoes

4 large red or green leaf lettuce leaves

1. Combine the chicken, celery, apple, raisins, mayonnaise, chutney, sour cream, lime juice, curry powder, and cumin in a large bowl; toss well to coat.

2. Cut each tomato horizontally in half. Scoop out the seeds and pulp leaving a ¼-inch border all around. Spoon the chicken mixture evenly (scant ½ cup) into each of the tomato halves.

3. Place a lettuce leaf on each of 4 plates; arrange 2 tomato halves on each lettuce leaf. Serve at once.

PER SERVING (2 stuffed tomato halves): 266 Cal, 6 g Total Fat, 2 g Sat Fat, 0 g Trans Fat, 60 mg Chol, 220 mg Sod, 34 g Carb, 4 g Fib, 22 g Prot, 61 mg Calc.
PointsPlus value: *7.*

COOK'S TIP

Cut a thin slice from the bottoms of the tomato halves before stuffing them so they can securely stand upright.

Curried Chicken–Stuffed Tomatoes

Chicken with Farfalle and Roasted Vegetable Salad

Makes 6 Servings

1 (1-pound) eggplant, cut into 1-inch pieces

1 zucchini, cut into 1-inch pieces

1 yellow squash, cut into 1-inch pieces

1 red onion, cut into 1-inch pieces

½ (1-pound) box farfalle (bow tie) pasta

2 cups shredded cooked chicken breast

½ cup cherry tomatoes, halved

½ cup chopped fresh basil

3 tablespoons grated Pecorino Romano cheese

1 tablespoon extra-virgin olive oil

½ teaspoon black pepper

1. Preheat the oven to 450°F. Spray a large shallow roasting pan with nonstick spray.

2. Spread out the eggplant, zucchini, yellow squash, and onion in the pan. Lightly spray the vegetables with nonstick spray. Roast, stirring occasionally, until the vegetables are tender and browned, about 45 minutes. Let cool slightly.

3. Cook the pasta according to the package directions omitting the salt, if desired; drain. Rinse under cold running water and drain again. Transfer the pasta to a large bowl. Add the roasted vegetables, chicken, tomatoes, basil, cheese, oil, and pepper; toss well to coat. Serve at once.

PER SERVING (generous 1⅓ cups): 306 Cal, 7 g Total Fat, 2 g Sat Fat, 0 g Trans Fat, 42 mg Chol, 230 mg Sod, 39 g Carb, 5 g Fib, 22 g Prot, 80 mg Calc.
PointsPlus value: *8.*

COOK'S TIP

Roasting intensifies the flavor of vegetables by caramelizing their natural sugars. Be sure to use a roasting pan large enough to accommodate the vegetables in one layer so the vegetables brown and don't steam. And, to ensure they cook in the same amount of time, cut the vegetables about the same size.

Chicken Sausage, Mushroom, and Barley Salad

Makes 6 Servings

4 teaspoons extra-virgin olive oil

1 pound Italian chicken sausage

1 onion, thinly sliced

1 garlic clove, minced

½ pound fresh shiitake mushrooms, stems discarded, caps thinly sliced

¼ cup dry white wine

1 tablespoon chopped fresh thyme

3 tablespoons white-wine vinegar

2 teaspoons Dijon mustard

2 cups water

1 cup quick-cooking barley

1. Heat 1 teaspoon of the oil in a large nonstick skillet over medium heat. Add the sausages and cook, covered, turning occasionally, until browned and cooked through, about 15 minutes. Transfer the sausages to a cutting board; let rest for about 5 minutes. Cut the sausages into ¾-inch pieces.

2. Heat another 1 teaspoon oil in the same skillet over medium heat. Add the onion and garlic; cook, stirring occasionally, until softened and fragrant, about 5 minutes. Add the mushrooms and cook, stirring occasionally, until tender, about 5 minutes. Add the wine and bring to a boil. Reduce the heat and simmer, uncovered, until the liquid has evaporated, about 3 minutes longer. Remove the skillet from the heat; stir in the thyme and set aside.

3. To make the dressing, whisk together the vinegar, mustard, and the remaining 2 teaspoons oil in a large bowl until blended; set aside.

4. Meanwhile, bring the water to a boil in a medium saucepan; add the barley. Reduce the heat and simmer, covered, until the barley is tender and the liquid has evaporated, 10–12 minutes.

5. Add the barley, sausages, and onion mixture to the dressing; toss well to coat.

PER SERVING (1 cup): 310 Cal, 12 g Total Fat, 1 g Sat Fat, 0 g Trans Fat, 45 mg Chol, 535 mg Sod, 35 g Carb, 7 g Fib, 17 g Prot, 24 mg Calc.
PointsPlus value: *8.*

COOK'S TIP

Traditionally known as a long-cooking grain, barley is now available in a quick-cooking form, which means this hearty salad can be made in minutes. You can serve this salad while it is still warm, or cover and refrigerate it for up to a day and serve it right out of the fridge.

sandwiches and wraps

Chicken, Salsa Verde, and Avocado in Ciabatta

Makes 4 Servings

4 (3-ounce) skinless boneless chicken breast halves

¼ teaspoon salt

⅛ teaspoon coarsely ground black pepper

2 tablespoons salsa verde (green salsa)

1 tablespoon fat-free sour cream

1 (½-pound) loaf ciabatta bread

1 Hass avocado, halved, pitted, peeled, and cut into 12 slices

1. Spray a nonstick ridged grill pan with nonstick spray and set over medium heat. Sprinkle the chicken with the salt and pepper. Add the chicken to the pan and cook, turning occasionally, until browned on the outside and cooked through, 12–14 minutes.

2. Meanwhile, combine the salsa and sour cream in a small bowl; set aside.

3. Slice the bread horizontally in half. Pull out some of the bread from the center, if desired. Spread the sour cream mixture on both sides of the bread. Cut the bread crosswise into quarters. Arrange a piece of chicken and 3 slices of avocado on each of the bottom halves of the bread. Close the bread and serve the sandwiches at once while still warm.

PER SERVING (1 sandwich): 333 Cal, 11 g Total Fat, 2 g Sat Fat, 0 g Trans Fat, 51 mg Chol, 568 mg Sod, 32 g Carb, 4 g Fib, 25 g Prot, 69 mg Calc.
PointsPlus value: *8.*

COOK'S TIP

It isn't always possible to find ripe avocados. Plan ahead and set one aside on the countertop, and allow a few days for it to ripen. Once ripened, refrigerate the avocado in the crisper drawer so it doesn't overripen.

Chicken, Salsa Verde, and Avocado in Ciabatta

Chicken Panzanella Sandwiches

Makes 4 Servings

4 (¼-pound) skinless boneless
    chicken breasts

¼ teaspoon salt

⅛ teaspoon black pepper

4 teaspoons extra-virgin
    olive oil

1 teaspoon red-wine vinegar

1 teaspoon brined capers,
    drained and chopped

8 slices rustic Italian bread

1 garlic clove, halved

8 large slices tomato

8 large fresh basil leaves

1. Spray a nonstick ridged grill pan with nonstick spray and set over medium heat. Sprinkle the chicken with the salt and pepper. Add the chicken to the pan and cook, turning occasionally, until browned on the outside and cooked through, 12–14 minutes.

2. Meanwhile, combine the oil, vinegar, and capers in a small bowl; set aside.

3. Rub 4 slices of the bread with the cut sides of the garlic. Brush the oil mixture on the garlic-rubbed sides of the bread. Arrange the chicken, tomato, and basil evenly on the bread. Top with the remaining 4 slices of bread then cut each sandwich in half. Serve at once, or wrap in plastic wrap and refrigerate for up to 4 hours.

PER SERVING (1 sandwich): 320 Cal, 10 g Total Fat, 2 g Sat Fat, 0 g Trans Fat, 68 mg Chol, 507 mg Sod, 27 g Carb, 4 g Fib, 30 g Prot, 56 mg Calc.
PointsPlus value: *8.*

COOK'S TIP

Panzanella—the classic tomato and bread salad—is deconstructed here and turned into a great sandwich using the same classic ingredients plus juicy grilled chicken. You can toast the bread before assembling the sandwich, if you like.

Grilled Portobello, Chicken, and Mozzarella Heroes

Makes 4 Servings

1 tablespoon extra-virgin olive oil

1 tablespoon finely chopped sun-dried tomatoes (not oil-packed)

¼ teaspoon salt

¼ teaspoon black pepper

3 (¼-pound) skinless boneless chicken breasts

2 (3-ounce) portobello mushroom caps, sliced

2 seeded hero rolls

8 arugula or spinach leaves

¼ cup shredded part-skim mozzarella cheese

1. Combine the oil, sun-dried tomatoes, salt, and pepper in a medium bowl.

2. Spray a ridged grill pan with nonstick spray and set over medium heat. Add the chicken and mushrooms and cook, turning occasionally, until the chicken is browned on the outside and cooked through and the mushrooms are tender, 12–14 minutes.

3. Transfer the chicken to a cutting board; let rest for about 5 minutes. Put the mushrooms in the bowl with the sun-dried tomato mixture. Cut the chicken, on the diagonal, into slices. Add to the mushroom mixture and toss until well combined.

4. Slice the rolls horizontally almost all the way through; spread open. Pull out some of the bread from the center, if desired. Place the warm chicken mixture on the bottoms of the rolls and top evenly with the arugula and cheese. Close the rolls and cut each sandwich in half.

PER SERVING (½ **sandwich): 241 Cal, 8 g Total Fat, 2 g Sat Fat, 0 g Trans Fat, 55 mg Chol, 388 mg Sod, 16 g Carb, 1 g Fib, 24 g Prot, 95 mg Calc.**
PointsPlus value: *6.*

COOK'S TIP

These warm sandwiches are a tempting combination of textures and flavors. If you want, assemble them ahead of time, wrap in foil, and refrigerate until the next day. Remove the foil, place them on a baking sheet, and re-warm in a 350°F oven until the cheese has melted and the sandwiches are heated through, about 8 minutes.

Chicken with Caramelized Onion and Tomato on Rye

Makes 4 Servings

2 teaspoons extra-virgin olive oil

1 large onion, thinly sliced

½ teaspoon fresh thyme leaves

¼ teaspoon salt

⅛ teaspoon black pepper

2 (¼-pound) skinless boneless chicken breasts

4 teaspoons light sour cream

4 slices rye or pumpernickel bread

4 large slices tomato

1. Heat the oil in a large nonstick skillet over medium heat. Add the onion, thyme, salt, and pepper. Cook, stirring frequently, until the onion turns deep golden brown, about 10 minutes. Transfer to a bowl and cover to keep warm.

2. Put the same skillet over medium heat. Add the chicken and cook, turning occasionally, until browned on the outside and cooked through, 12–14 minutes.

3. Spread 1 teaspoon of the sour cream on each slice of bread. Divide the onion between 2 of the bread slices, top with the tomato and warm chicken, then top each with a slice of the remaining bread. Cut each sandwich in half and serve while warm.

PER SERVING (½ sandwich): 184 Cal, 6 g Total Fat, 1 g Sat Fat, 0 g Trans Fat, 36 mg Chol, 356 mg Sod, 17 g Carb, 2 g Fib, 15 g Prot, 40 mg Calc.
PointsPlus value: *5.*

COOK'S TIP

Consider making a double batch of the onions, so you can make these sandwiches at a later date in short time. You can also save time by getting two skillets going at the same time—one for the onion and one for the chicken.

Chicken Burgers with Scallions and Ginger

Makes 4 Servings

2 scallions, thinly sliced

1 tablespoon chopped peeled fresh ginger

1 large garlic clove, peeled

1 pound skinless boneless chicken breasts, cut into chunks

½ plus ⅓ cup plain dried bread crumbs

⅓ cup fat-free egg substitute

⅓ cup chopped fresh cilantro

½ teaspoon Sriracha plus additional for serving

¼ teaspoon salt

¼ teaspoon black pepper

4 multigrain hamburger buns, toasted

16 very thin slices peeled cucumber

8 very thin slices sweet onion

1. With the motor running, drop the scallions, ginger, and garlic through the feed tube of a food processor and process until finely minced. Stop the food processor and add the chicken; pulse until coarsely chopped. Transfer to a medium bowl and stir in ½ cup of the bread crumbs, the egg substitute, cilantro, Sriracha, salt, and pepper.

2. Place the remaining ⅓ cup bread crumbs on a sheet of wax paper. With damp hands, form the chicken mixture into 4 (¾-inch-thick) patties. Coat the patties with the bread crumbs, pressing gently so they adhere. Transfer the patties to a plate; cover and refrigerate for at least 30 minutes or up to several hours.

3. Spray a large nonstick skillet with nonstick spray and set over medium heat. Add the patties; cover and cook, turning occasionally, until an instant-read thermometer inserted into the side of a burger registers 165°F for well done, about 6 minutes per side. Place a burger in each bun and top evenly with the cucumber and onion. Serve with Sriracha sauce.

PER SERVING (1 burger): 209 g, 347 Cal, 7 g Total Fat, 2 g Sat Fat, 0 g Trans Fat, 63 mg Chol, 662 mg Sod, 39 g Total Carb, 3 g Fib, 32 g Prot, 104 mg Calc.
PointsPlus value: *9.*

COOK'S TIP

Top each burger with one or two thin slices of tomato and a Boston lettuce leaf.

Chicken Chat and Choices

Chicken is one of America's most popular and versatile foods. It is easy to prepare, economical, and delicious when made in a myriad of ways, including alone or paired with other foods, such as grains, vegetables, and fruit. Poultry can be enjoyed as an appetizer, in soups, salads, sandwiches, and main dishes—and some cuts only take minutes to prepare and cook.

Did you know that chicken—with the skin removed—is an excellent source of lean protein, iron, zinc, and B vitamins? According to the U.S. Department of Agriculture National Nutrient Database, a 3½-ounce serving provides 31 grams of protein, a great way to get a portion of your daily dose of lean protein. And you can remove the skin before or after cooking.

Here are some of the various types of chicken—and its cousins—that are available in supermarkets, specialty food stores, butcher shops, and online:

Broiler-Fryer

A young, tender whole chicken about 7 weeks old, weighing from 2½ to 4½ pounds. The choices include: whole, cut into eighths or quarters, legs, thighs, drumsticks, whole breasts, breast halves, wings, and ground. Whole broiler-fryers can be roasted in the oven, cooked in an outdoor smoker, or grilled using the indirect method. Broiler-fryer parts lend themselves to a variety of cooking methods, including baked, broiled, sautéed, grilled, braised, and stewed.

Roaster

A chicken 3 to 5 months old, weighing between 5 and 7 pounds. It is usually cooked whole, making it a good choice for a crowd. Whole roasters can be roasted in the oven, cooked in an outdoor smoker, or grilled using the indirect method.

Capon

A castrated rooster from 4 to 8 months old and weighing between 8 and 10 pounds. Its meat is very plump and juicy, making it a good choice for a holiday dinner. A capon can be roasted whole in the oven or on a grill using the indirect method.

Stewing Hen

A mature laying hen 10 months to 1½ years old. Its meat is not as tender as other birds, making it an excellent choice for a rich chicken soup or broth. Flavorful stewing hens can also be stewed or slowly braised.

Cornish Game Hen

This bird used to be called a Rock Cornish Game Hen and is a cross between a Cornish Game Hen and a Plymouth or White Rock Chicken. Although it is called a hen, it can be male or female. Cornish Game Hens weigh between 1¼ and 2 pounds. A small hen can serve one and a larger hen can serve two diners nicely. Whole game hens can be roasted or baked in the oven, cooked in an outdoor smoker, or grilled either directly or indirectly. Butterflied or split game hens can be broiled, baked, or grilled.

Poussin

French for "baby chicken," poussin is a plump, tender bird that weighs between 14 ounces and 1¼ pounds. Depending on its size, it can serve one or two. It is excellent roasted, grilled, or broiled, either split, butterflied, or whole. Whole poussin can be roasted or baked in the oven, cooked in an outdoor smoker, or grilled either directly or indirectly. When butterflied or split, it can be broiled, baked or grilled.

Open-Faced Greek Chicken Sandwiches

Makes 4 Servings

¾ cup plain low-fat yogurt

¼ cup finely chopped
  cucumber

1 tablespoon chopped fresh dill

¼ teaspoon salt

⅛ teaspoon black pepper

2 (7-inch) pocketless whole
  wheat pita breads

1½ cups chopped cooked
  chicken

12 grape tomatoes, halved

¾ cup finely shredded romaine
  lettuce

¼ cup crumbled reduced-fat
  feta cheese

1. Combine the yogurt, cucumber, dill, salt, and pepper in a small bowl. Cover and refrigerate for at least 10 minutes to allow the flavors to develop, or until ready to use, up to several hours.

2. Spread each pita bread with about 2 tablespoons of the cucumber mixture. Top with the chicken, tomatoes, lettuce, and cheese. Drizzle with the remaining cucumber mixture, cut each sandwich in half, and serve at once.

PER SERVING (½ sandwich): 252 Cal, 7 g Total Fat, 3 g Sat Fat, 0 g Trans Fat, 56 mg Chol, 560 mg Sod, 26 g Carb, 3 g Fib, 22 g Prot, 151 mg Calc.
PointsPlus value: *6*.

COOK'S TIP

Shredded romaine makes a great crunchy addition to sandwiches. You can prepare it ahead: Wash and dry the romaine leaves, then shred and store them in a paper towel–lined zip-close plastic bag. The paper towels will absorb the moisture that accumulates, keeping the lettuce fresh and crunchy for at least 2 days.

Barbecued Chicken and Tangy Coleslaw Sandwiches

Makes 4 Servings

1½ cups finely shredded green cabbage

3 tablespoons fat-free sour cream

2 teaspoons apple cider vinegar

½ teaspoon sugar

¼ teaspoon salt

¼ teaspoon black pepper

2 cups shredded cooked chicken breast

⅓ cup barbecue sauce

4 kaiser rolls, split

1. Combine the cabbage, sour cream, vinegar, sugar, salt, and pepper in a medium bowl. Cover and refrigerate for at least 10 minutes to allow the flavors to develop or until ready to use, up to 6 hours.

2. Meanwhile, combine the chicken and barbecue sauce in a medium nonstick saucepan and cook over medium heat, stirring occasionally, until heated through, about 4 minutes.

3. Pull out some of the bread from the center of the rolls, if desired. Place the warm chicken mixture then the coleslaw on the bottoms of the rolls. Close the rolls, cut in half, if desired, and serve while warm.

PER SERVING (1 sandwich): 308 Cal, 5 g Total Fat, 1 g Sat Fat, 1 g Trans Fat, 58 mg Chol, 692 mg Sod, 37 g Carb, 2 g Fib, 27 g Prot, 102 mg Calc.
PointsPlus value: *8.*

COOK'S TIP

Here are some pantry items you can stir into the coleslaw if you want a little extra zing: a big pinch of freshly grated lemon zest, a handful of shredded carrots, a dash of hot red pepper sauce, your favorite chopped fresh herbs, or a finely chopped scallion.

Barbecued Chicken and
Tangy Coleslaw Sandwiches

Chicken and White Bean Salad in Pita Pockets

Makes 4 Servings

1½ cups finely shredded cooked chicken

½ cup rinsed and drained canned small white beans

¼ cup finely chopped red onion

¼ cup chopped fresh flat-leaf parsley

2 teaspoons extra-virgin olive oil

¾ teaspoon grated lemon zest

1 tablespoon lemon juice

¼ teaspoon salt

⅛ teaspoon black pepper

2 (6-inch) whole wheat pita breads

4 tomato slices

8 watercress sprigs, tough stems discarded

1. Combine the chicken, beans, onion, parsley, oil, lemon zest, lemon juice, salt, and pepper in a medium bowl. Let stand for 10 minutes to allow the flavors to blend.

2. Cut each pita bread crosswise in half to form 2 pockets. Spoon the chicken mixture evenly into the pita pockets, then add the tomato and watercress.

PER SERVING (½ pocket): 230 Cal, 7 g Total Fat, 1 g Sat Fat, 0 g Trans Fat, 45 mg Chol, 344 mg Sod, 23 g Carb, 4 g Fib, 20 g Prot, 45 mg Calc.
PointsPlus value: *6.*

COOK'S TIP

This is a great high-protein, bold-flavored combination of chicken and beans that can be put together quickly. The ingredients are similar to those found in a classic tuna and white bean salad. If you prefer, substitute minced shallots, chopped fresh chives, or chopped scallions for the onion.

Hoisin Chicken and Scallion Wraps

Makes 4 Servings

2 cups shredded cooked
   chicken breast

3 tablespoons hoisin sauce

2 scallions, thinly sliced

⅛ teaspoon black pepper

4 (8-inch) spinach or whole
   wheat tortillas

8 watercress sprigs, tough
   stems discarded

1. Combine the chicken, hoisin sauce, scallions, and pepper in a medium bowl, and toss until mixed well. Let stand for 10 minutes to allow the flavors to blend.

2. Toast the tortillas in a dry large nonstick skillet over medium heat, about 1 minute on each side.

3. Divide the chicken mixture evenly onto the tortillas, top with the watercress, and roll up. Cut the rolls in half on a slight diagonal.

PER SERVING (1 wrap): 230 Cal, 5 g Total Fat, 1 g Sat Fat, 0 g Trans Fat, 57 mg Chol, 425 mg Sod, 22 g Carb, 4 g Fib, 25 g Prot, 38 mg Calc.
PointsPlus value: *6.*

COOK'S TIP

Hoisin sauce is a great condiment—it adds lots of rich flavor and complex sweetness. Buy a good-quality brand, such as Lee Kum Kee, for truly authentic Asian taste and texture. It is available in most supermarkets and in Asian markets. Hoisin sauce keeps almost indefinitely in the refrigerator.

Curried Chicken and Mango Wraps

Curried Chicken and Mango Wraps

Makes 4 Servings

¾ pound skinless boneless
chicken breasts

1 teaspoon canola oil

1 red onion, thinly sliced

1 teaspoon curry powder

½ teaspoon ground coriander

½ teaspoon salt

¼ teaspoon black pepper

1 ripe mango, peeled, pitted,
and cut into ½-inch pieces

2 (about 12 × 18-inch) pieces
lavash or 2 (10-inch, burrito-
size) fat-free flour tortillas

½ cup finely shredded romaine
lettuce

1. Cut the chicken into ⅜-inch-wide slices on a slight diagonal.

2. Heat the oil in a large nonstick skillet over medium heat. Add the onion and cook, stirring occasionally, until softened, about 4 minutes. Add the curry powder and coriander; cook, stirring constantly, until fragrant, about 1 minute. Increase the heat to medium-high; add the chicken, salt, and pepper. Cook, stirring occasionally, until the chicken is cooked through and most of the liquid has evaporated, about 7 minutes. Remove the pan from the heat, stir in the mango, and let stand for about 10 minutes to cool.

3. Spoon half of the chicken filling onto each lavash, top with the lettuce, and roll up. Cut each roll in half on a slight diagonal.

PER SERVING (½ wrap): 277 Cal, 6 g Total Fat, 1 g Sat Fat, 0 g Trans Fat, 42 mg Chol, 694 mg Sod, 36 g Carb, 3 g Fib, 19 g Prot, 65 mg Calc.
PointsPlus value: *7.*

COOK'S TIP

It's easy to roll a wrap. Place the filling in the center of the wrap, fold two opposite sides in towards the center overlapping them, then fold the bottom up and roll to enclose the filling.

substantial soups and stews

Homemade Chicken Broth

Makes 11 Servings

1 (4½-pound) chicken, skinned, giblets discarded

12 cups water

4 carrots, cut into 2-inch pieces

2 onions, cut into eighths

2 celery stalks, cut into 2-inch pieces

2 garlic cloves, minced

Handful fresh parsley sprigs

10 whole black peppercorns

4 whole cloves

3 bay leaves

1 teaspoon salt

1. Bring the chicken, water, carrots, onions, celery, garlic, parsley, peppercorns, cloves, bay leaves, and salt to a boil in a large soup pot. Reduce the heat and simmer, covered, until the chicken is very tender and cooked through, about 2 hours.

2. Lift the chicken from the broth and set aside until cool enough to handle. Pull the chicken meat from the bones, then tear or cut it into bite-size pieces.

3. Strain the broth through a large strainer (or a colander lined with cheesecloth) into a large bowl or pot. Discard the vegetables and spices and bay leaves in the strainer.

4. Cool the broth quickly, then cover and refrigerate until chilled, for at least 4 hours or overnight. Remove any fat from surface of broth, then pack and refrigerate or freeze the broth.

PER SERVING (1 cup): 32 Cal, 0 g Total Fat, 0 g Sat Fat, 0 g Trans Fat, 0 mg Chol, 270 mg Sod, 4 g Carb, 0 g Fib, 3 g Prot, 12 mg Calc.
PointsPlus value: *1.*

COOK'S TIP

You'll get about 11 cups broth and 5 cups cooked chicken from this recipe. Pack the broth in 2-cup containers, and refrigerate for up to 3 days or freeze for up to 3 months. Wrap the chicken and refrigerate for up to 3 days or freeze for up to 4 months. Use the broth and chicken in any of our recipes that call for broth or cooked chicken.

Old-Fashioned Chicken Noodle Soup

Makes 6 Servings

1 (3-pound) chicken, cut into 8 pieces and skinned, giblets discarded

7 cups water

6 carrots, cut into 1-inch pieces

3 celery stalks, cut into 1-inch pieces

2 onions, cut into eighths

2 bay leaves

2 teaspoons salt

½ teaspoon coarsely ground black pepper

2 cups broad egg noodles

1 large tomato, chopped

2 teaspoons dried thyme, crumbled

¼ cup chopped fresh flat-leaf parsley

1. Bring the chicken, water, carrots, celery, onions, bay leaves, salt, and pepper to a boil in a large soup pot. Reduce the heat and simmer, covered, until the chicken is tender and cooked through, about 45 minutes.

2. Lift the chicken from the soup and set aside until cool enough to handle. Pull the chicken meat from the bones, then tear or cut it into bite-size pieces.

3. Discard the bay leaves. Add the noodles and return the soup to a boil. Reduce the heat and simmer, uncovered, until the noodles are tender, about 5 minutes. Add the tomato and thyme; simmer 5 minutes longer. Add the parsley and return 2 cups of the chicken to the soup; heat through, about 3 minutes.

PER SERVING (2 cups): 175 Cal, 4 g Total Fat, 1 g Sat Fat, 0 g Trans Fat, 47 mg Chol, 672 mg Sod, 21 g Carb, 4 g Fib, 15 g Prot, 58 mg Calc.
PointsPlus value: *4.*

COOK'S TIP

When a little TLC is needed, this homey soup fits the bill. You'll get about 4 cups of cooked chicken from the recipe, but you only need 2 cups for this soup. Use the remaining chicken to make one of the tempting chicken salads in this book.

Paella Soup

Makes 4 Servings

1 tablespoon extra-virgin
    olive oil

1 large red onion, chopped

1 red bell pepper, chopped

3 garlic cloves, minced

6 cups reduced-sodium
    chicken broth

1 (14½-ounce) can diced
    tomatoes

½ cup long-grain white rice

½ pound skinless boneless
    chicken breast, cut into
    2 × ¼-inch strips

½ pound large shrimp, peeled
    and deveined

1 cup frozen peas

1 teaspoon dried oregano

½ teaspoon saffron threads,
    lightly crushed

⅛ teaspoon black pepper

1 ounce chorizo or other hard
    cured or fully cooked
    sausage, cut into very thin
    slices

¼ cup chopped fresh flat-leaf
    parsley

1. Heat the oil in a nonstick soup pot or large Dutch oven over medium-high heat. Add the onion, bell pepper, and garlic; cook, stirring occasionally, until softened, about 8 minutes. Add the broth, tomatoes, and rice; bring to a boil, stirring once or twice. Reduce the heat and simmer, partially covered, until the rice is tender, about 20 minutes.

2. Add the chicken, shrimp, peas, oregano, saffron, and black pepper to the pot; bring to a boil. Reduce the heat and simmer, uncovered, until the chicken is just cooked through and the shrimp are just opaque in the center, about 4 minutes. Stir in the chorizo and parsley; return to a boil. Reduce the heat and simmer about 3 minutes.

PER SERVING (2½ cups): 379 Cal, 10 g Total Fat, 3 g Sat Fat, 0 g Trans Fat, 122 g Chol, 590 mg Sod, 38 g Carb, 4 g Fib, 34 g Prot, 85 mg Calc.
PointsPlus value: *9.*

COOK'S TIP

We've used all the flavorful ingredients found in a traditional Spanish paella to make this delicious and hearty soup, including tomatoes, rice, chicken, shrimp, chorizo, and saffron. For some added freshness, sprinkle the soup with chopped fresh cilantro.

Paella Soup

Asian Chicken and Noodle Bowl

Asian Chicken and Noodle Bowl

Makes 4 Servings

6 cups reduced-sodium
  chicken broth

¾ pound skinless boneless
  chicken breast, cut into
  2 × ¼-inch strips

1 (6¾-ounce) package rice
  stick noodles

¼ pound fresh snow peas,
  trimmed and sliced
  diagonally in half

¼ pound fresh shiitake
  mushrooms, stems
  discarded, caps sliced

½ cup sliced radishes

2 tablespoons rice wine vinegar

1 tablespoon reduced-sodium
  soy sauce

2 teaspoons dark (Asian)
  sesame oil

1 teaspoon minced peeled
  fresh ginger

1 garlic clove, minced

½ cup fresh bean sprouts

3 scallions (white and light
  green portion only), thinly
  sliced

1. Bring the broth to a boil in a Dutch oven. Add the chicken, noodles, snow peas, mushrooms, radishes, vinegar, soy sauce, oil, ginger, and garlic; return to a boil. Reduce the heat and simmer, stirring occasionally, until the chicken and noodles are cooked through, about 5 minutes.

2. Add the bean sprouts; return to a boil. Reduce the heat and simmer, about 1 minute. Serve the soup sprinkled with the scallions.

PER SERVING (generous 1½ cups): 400 Cal, 8 g Total Fat, 2 g Sat Fat, 0 g Trans Fat, 51 mg Chol, 942 mg Sod, 48 g Carb, 3 g Fib, 31 g Prot, 62 mg Calc.
PointsPlus value: *10.*

COOK'S TIP

If "dinner in a flash" sounds good to you, you must try this recipe. You can prepare the chicken and vegetables in the time it takes to bring the broth to a boil. Add them to the soup along with a few other ingredients, cook for 6 minutes, and you're done. Look for rice stick noodles in Asian markets and supermarkets, but you can use capellini or thin spaghetti instead.

Safely Storing Soups and Stews

With a variety of soups and stews in your freezer, you can have lunch or dinner on the table in record time. Soups and stews can be stored in the refrigerator or freezer. Use a refrigerator thermometer to check that your refrigerator is set at 40°F or below. Use a freezer thermometer to check that your freezer is set at 0°F or below. At this temperature, bacteria, yeasts, and molds that may be present in food are inactivated. Freezer burn, which sometimes appears on the surface of frozen food as grayish-brown areas, does not make food unsafe to eat. It is caused by air coming in contact with the surface of the food. Cut freezer-burned portions away, keeping in mind that heavily freezer-burned foods should be thrown away.

STORAGE

Soups and stews can be refrigerated up to 4 days or frozen up to 4 months.

Cool It

Place the pot of soup or stew in a sink filled with ice water and let it stand, adding more ice if needed and stirring to quickly cool it until tepid. Or ladle the hot soup or stew into small (one-meal size) freezer-safe containers and let cool on the counter for about 30 minutes or until tepid.

Pack It

Ladle the cooled soup or stew into small freezer-safe containers, leaving ½ inch of headspace to allow for expansion. Label and date the containers. Or ladle the cooled soup or stew into 1-quart zip-close plastic freezer bags. Squeeze out the air and seal the bags, then label and date. Place the bags flat on a rimmed baking sheet and freeze until hard, then stack in the freezer—a great space saver.

And Remember

Soups and stews that contain potatoes, pasta, or cream do not freeze well, as freezing turns pasta and potatoes grainy and mushy and can curdle cream.

FOUR WAYS TO THAW AND REHEAT

On the Stovetop

Place the frozen soup or stew in a saucepan and set over low heat; cook, covered, stirring frequently, until thawed. Bring to a rolling boil.

In the Refrigerator

Thaw soups and stews overnight in the refrigerator.

In the Sink

Place a container of soup or stew in a sink half-filled with cold water and let stand, changing the water every 30 minutes, until thawed.

In the Microwave

Transfer the frozen soup or stew to a microwavable bowl and thaw according to the manufacturer's instructions.

For more information on the safe freezing and thawing of food, go to the USDA Web site and check out their Safe Food Handling section.

Mexicali Chicken Soup with Lime

Makes 4 Servings

1 pound skinless boneless chicken breast, cut into ½-inch pieces

2 onions, chopped

2 carrots, chopped

2 garlic cloves, minced

1 serrano pepper, seeded and minced

4½ cups reduced-sodium chicken broth

2 plum tomatoes, seeded and chopped

½ medium ripe Hass avocado, halved, pitted, peeled, and diced

3 tablespoons lime juice

3 tablespoons chopped fresh cilantro

¼ teaspoon salt

⅛ teaspoon black pepper

1. Spray a nonstick Dutch oven with canola nonstick spray and set over medium-high heat. Add the chicken and cook, stirring occasionally, until browned, about 4 minutes. Transfer the chicken to a plate.

2. Add the onions, carrots, garlic, and chile pepper to the saucepan. Cook, stirring occasionally, until lightly browned, 5–6 minutes. Add the broth and bring to a boil. Reduce the heat and simmer, covered, until the flavors are blended, about 20 minutes. Return the chicken to the saucepan and simmer until cooked through, about 8 minutes.

3. Stir in the tomatoes, avocado, lime juice, cilantro, salt, and pepper; cook, stirring occasionally, until heated through, about 1 minute.

PER SERVING (1¾ cups): 244 Cal, 6 g Total Fat, 1 g Sat Fat, 0 g Trans Fat, 67 mg Chol, 924 mg Sod, 17 g Carb, 5 g Fib, 31 g Prot, 44 mg Calc.
PointsPlus value: *6.*

COOK'S TIP

Serve this soup with toasted tortilla wedges for even more satisfaction. Preheat the broiler. Stack 4 (6-inch) corn tortillas and cut in quarters. Arrange the wedges on a baking sheet and broil, 5 inches from the heat until golden, about 45 seconds on each side. Four tortilla wedges per serving will increase the *PointsPlus* value by *1.*

**Caramelized Onion and
Chicken Soup au Gratin**

Caramelized Onion and Chicken Soup au Gratin

Makes 4 Servings

1 teaspoon unsalted butter

1 teaspoon canola oil

3 Vidalia onions, halved lengthwise, then thinly sliced crosswise

6 cups reduced-sodium chicken broth

¼ cup dry white wine

1 teaspoon chopped fresh thyme, or ¼ teaspoon dried

⅛ teaspoon black pepper

1½ cups chopped cooked chicken breast

½ (10-ounce) French baguette, cut into 16 rounds

½ cup shredded Comté, Gruyère, or Jarlsberg cheese

1. Melt the butter and oil in a nonstick Dutch oven over medium-high heat. Add the onions and cook, stirring occasionally, until translucent, about 8 minutes. Reduce the heat to medium-low and cook, stirring occasionally, until golden brown and well softened, about 12 minutes.

2. Add the broth, wine, thyme, and pepper; bring to a boil. Reduce the heat and simmer, uncovered, about 25 minutes. Add the chicken and simmer until heated through, about 2 minutes.

3. Preheat the broiler. Place the bread rounds on a baking sheet and broil 5 inches from the heat until toasted, about 2 minutes on each side.

4. Place 4 bread rounds in each of 4 ovenproof soup bowls. Add the soup (a generous 2 cups in each bowl) and sprinkle evenly with the cheese.

5. Place the bowls on the baking sheet and broil 5 inches from the heat until the cheese melts and is golden brown, about 3 minutes.

PER SERVING (1 bowl): 413 Cal, 11 g Total Fat, 5 g Sat Fat, 0 g Trans Fat, 62 mg Chol, 449 mg Sod, 44 g Carb, 3 g Fib, 34 g Prot, 225 mg Calc.
PointsPlus value: *11.*

COOK'S TIP

Though much like a classic French onion soup, ours is made heartier with the addition of chicken. Comté cheese, from the Gruyère family, is the perfect finishing touch for the soup. If you don't have ovenproof soup bowls, use small casserole dishes instead.

Mulligatawny Soup

Makes 4 Servings

2 teaspoons canola oil

1 onion, chopped

3 garlic cloves, minced

2 teaspoons curry powder

5 cups reduced-sodium
   chicken broth

2 Yukon Gold potatoes, peeled
   and diced (about 1½ cups)

2 carrots, diced (about 1 cup)

2 cups small cauliflower florets

¾ pound skinless boneless
   chicken thighs, cut into
   ½-inch chunks

¼ cup chopped fresh cilantro
   or flat-leaf parsley

1 teaspoon garam masala

¼ teaspoon salt

¼ cup plain fat-free yogurt

1. Heat the oil in a Dutch oven over medium heat. Add the onion and garlic; cook, stirring occasionally, until golden, 7–10 minutes. Add the curry powder and cook, stirring constantly, until fragrant, about 1 minute.

2. Stir in the broth, potatoes, carrots, and cauliflower; bring to a boil. Reduce the heat and simmer, uncovered, until the vegetables are tender, about 15 minutes.

3. Add the chicken, cilantro, garam masala, and salt; return to a boil. Reduce the heat and simmer, covered, until the chicken is cooked through, about 5 minutes. Serve with the yogurt.

PER SERVING (scant 2 cups soup with 1 tablespoon yogurt): 309 Cal, 11 g Total Fat, 3 g Sat Fat, 0 g Trans Fat, 53 mg Chol, 835 mg Sod, 24 g Carb, 4 g Fib, 28 g Prot, 88 mg Calc. *PointsPlus* value: *8.*

COOK'S TIP

Heavy cream is often stirred into mulligatawny, but plain yogurt makes a healthy—and flavorful—alternative.

Matzo Ball Soup

Makes 6 Servings

½ cup matzo meal

¼ teaspoon salt

⅛ teaspoon black pepper

2 large eggs, lightly beaten

⅓ cup seltzer water or water

2 teaspoons canola oil

6 cups Homemade Chicken Broth (page 52) or canned reduced-sodium chicken broth

2 carrots, very thinly sliced

1 shallot, finely chopped

1 cup fresh or frozen peas, thawed

1½ cups shredded cooked chicken breast

2 tablespoons chopped fresh flat-leaf parsley

1. To make the matzo balls, combine the matzo meal, salt, and pepper in a medium bowl. Combine the eggs, seltzer water, and oil in a small bowl. Add the egg mixture to the matzo meal mixture and stir until just blended. Cover and refrigerate for about 20 minutes.

2. Bring the broth, carrots, and shallot to a boil in a Dutch oven or large pot. Reduce the heat and simmer, covered, until the carrots are partially tender, about 5 minutes.

3. With wet hands, shape the matzo mixture into 12 balls. Carefully drop the balls, one at a time, into the simmering soup. Simmer, covered, until the matzo balls are cooked through and tender, 20–30 minutes, stirring in the peas during the last 5 minutes. Stir in the chicken and simmer until heated through, about 2 minutes. Stir in the parsley just before serving.

PER SERVING (1 cup soup with 2 matzo balls): 207 Cal, 6 g Total Fat, 2 g Sat Fat, 0 g Trans Fat, 99 mg Chol, 654 mg Sod, 16 g Carb, 2 g Fib, 20 g Prot, 40 mg Calc.
PointsPlus value: *5*.

COOK'S TIP

Matzo ball soup is a favorite first course at Passover. For this special occasion—if you have the time—we highly recommend making our Homemade Chicken Broth. To lend the soup a bit of additional color, add 1 or 2 cooked sliced carrots just before serving.

Tuxedo Meatball Soup with Escarole

Makes 6 Servings

2 teaspoons extra-virgin olive oil

1 large onion, chopped

3 garlic cloves, minced

5 cups reduced-sodium chicken broth

1 (28-ounce) can peeled tomatoes, broken up

1 cup small egg bow ties or small elbow macaroni

1 pound ground skinless chicken breast

⅓ cup seasoned dry bread crumbs

1 large egg, lightly beaten

¼ teaspoon salt

¼ teaspoon black pepper

1 small bunch escarole, cleaned and chopped (about 8 cups)

¼ cup coarsely chopped fresh basil

6 tablespoons shredded Parmesan cheese

1. Heat the oil in a nonstick Dutch oven over medium heat. Add the onion and garlic; cook, stirring frequently, until softened, about 5 minutes. Transfer half of the onion mixture to a medium bowl; set aside.

2. Add the broth, tomatoes, and pasta to the remaining onion mixture in the Dutch oven; bring to a boil. Reduce the heat and simmer, uncovered, about 2 minutes.

3. Meanwhile, add the chicken, bread crumbs, egg, salt, and pepper to the onion mixture in the bowl; mix well. Shape into 24 meatballs.

4. Add the meatballs to the simmering mixture in the Dutch oven; return to a boil, stirring occasionally. Reduce the heat and simmer, partially covered, until the meatballs and pasta are cooked through, about 10 minutes. Gently stir in the escarole and basil; return to a simmer and cook, partially covered, about 3 minutes. Serve with the cheese.

PER SERVING (1½ cups soup with 1 tablespoon cheese): 329 Cal, 9 g Total Fat, 3 g Sat Fat, 0 g Trans Fat, 86 mg Chol, 920 mg Sod, 32 g Carb, 4 g Fib, 30 g Prot, 191 mg Calc.
PointsPlus value: *8*.

COOK'S TIP

Adding small bow-tie pasta to this everyday soup is an easy way to make it a bit special. Lots of tender meatballs, dark leafy escarole, and fresh basil add great color, texture, and flavor to this comforting Italian favorite.

Tuxedo Meatball Soup with Escarole

Chicken and Barley Soup

Makes 6 Servings

1 red onion, thinly sliced

1 garlic clove, minced

¾ pound (2 small) sweet
   potatoes, peeled and
   chopped

2 small carrots, halved
   lengthwise and thinly sliced

2 small celery stalks with
   leaves, thinly sliced

½ cup quick-cooking barley

¾ teaspoon fresh thyme leaves

8 cups reduced-sodium
   chicken broth

¼ teaspoon salt

¼ teaspoon black pepper

2 cups small broccoli florets

½ pound skinless boneless
   chicken breast, cut into
   2 × ¼-inch strips

1. Spray a nonstick Dutch oven with canola nonstick spray and set over medium heat. Add the onion and cook, stirring frequently, until softened, about 4 minutes. Add the garlic and cook, stirring frequently, until fragrant, about 30 seconds.

2. Stir in the potatoes, carrots, celery, barley, and thyme; cook, stirring occasionally, until the vegetables begin to soften, about 4 minutes. Add the broth, salt, and pepper; bring to a boil. Reduce the heat and simmer until the vegetables are softened and the barley is cooked through, about 15 minutes.

3. Stir in the broccoli and chicken; return to a boil. Reduce the heat and simmer until the broccoli is fork-tender and the chicken is cooked through, about 5 minutes.

PER SERVING (about 1½ cups): 163 Cal, 1 g Total Fat, 0 g Sat Fat, 0 g Trans Fat, 21 mg Chol, 960 mg Sod, 24 g Carb, 5 g Fib, 15 g Prot, 38 mg Calc.
PointsPlus value: *4.*

COOK'S TIP

This lovely concoction has the goodness of lots of fresh vegetables, comforting, earthy barley, and fragrant fresh thyme. Consider making a double batch, as this soup freezes well.

Chicken Scotch Broth

Makes 6 Servings

1 teaspoon canola oil

1 large onion, chopped

6 cups reduced-sodium
   chicken broth

¾ cup pearl barley, rinsed

3 carrots, thinly sliced

2 parsnips, peeled and diced

½ teaspoon salt

¼ teaspoon black pepper

1¼ pounds skinless bone-in
   chicken thighs

1 (10-ounce) package cremini
   or baby bella mushrooms,
   halved or quartered if large

1½ cups frozen peas

1½ tablespoons chopped fresh
   thyme, or 1½ teaspoons
   dried

1. Heat the oil in a nonstick Dutch oven over medium heat. Add the onion and cook, stirring occasionally, until golden, 7–10 minutes. Add the broth, barley, carrots, parsnips, salt, and pepper; bring to a boil. Add the chicken; return to a boil. Reduce the heat and simmer, covered, until the chicken is cooked through and the barley is tender, about 40 minutes.

2. Lift the chicken from the soup and set aside until cool enough to handle. Pull the chicken meat from the bones, then tear or cut it into bite-size pieces.

3. Add the mushrooms, peas, and thyme to the pot; return to a boil. Reduce the heat and simmer, covered, until the vegetables are tender, about 10 minutes. Return the chicken to the soup and heat through.

PER SERVING (1½ cups): 372 Cal, 10 g Total Fat, 3 g Sat Fat, 0 g Trans Fat, 59 mg Chol, 777 mg Sod, 39 g Carb, 9 g Fib, 31 g Prot, 77 mg Calc.
PointsPlus value: *9.*

COOK'S TIP

Most soups containing grains, such as barley, tend to thicken upon standing, so add a little water when reheating. Scotch broth is traditionally made with lamb, barley, and a variety of vegetables, but chicken is a tasty and satisfying alternative to the lamb.

Gingered Chicken and Sweet Potato Soup

Makes 6 Servings

2 teaspoons extra-virgin olive oil

1 large Vidalia onion, chopped

3 garlic cloves, minced

1½ tablespoons minced peeled fresh ginger

1 small jalapeño pepper, seeded and chopped

3 large (about 2 pounds) sweet potatoes, peeled and cut into 1-inch chunks

6 cups reduced-sodium chicken broth

1 (10-ounce) package carved roasted skinless chicken breast pieces

2 teaspoons lime juice

6 tablespoons fat-free half-and-half

2 tablespoons chopped fresh cilantro or flat-leaf parsley

1. Heat the oil in a nonstick Dutch oven or large saucepan over medium-high heat. Add the onion and cook, stirring frequently, until softened, about 8 minutes. Add the garlic, ginger, and jalapeño pepper; cook, stirring constantly, until fragrant, about 2 minutes.

2. Add the sweet potatoes and 3 cups of the broth to the Dutch oven; bring to a boil. Reduce the heat and simmer, covered, until the potatoes are tender, about 20 minutes. Remove the pan from the heat and let the mixture cool for about 15 minutes.

3. Transfer the mixture in batches, if necessary, to a food processor or blender and puree. Return the soup to the Dutch oven. Stir in the remaining 3 cups broth, the chicken, and lime juice; bring to a boil. Reduce the heat and simmer until heated through, about 3 minutes. Divide the soup among 6 bowls, swirl a tablespoon of the half-and-half on top of each bowl, and sprinkle with the cilantro.

PER SERVING (1¾ cups soup with 1 tablespoon half-and-half): 275 Cal, 6 g Total Fat, 2 g Sat Fat, 0 g Trans Fat, 42 mg Chol, 112 mg Sod, 36 g Carb, 4 g Fib, 19 g Prot, 79 mg Calc. *PointsPlus* value: 7.

COOK'S TIP

A package of carved cooked chicken parts—available in most supermarkets in a variety of flavors, such as Southwestern, lemon-pepper, and oven-roasted—makes this recipe especially easy. For a refreshing start, begin your meal with an orange, radish, and watercress salad drizzled with fat-free dressing.

Gingered Chicken and
Sweet Potato Soup

Tex Mex–Style Chicken and Corn Soup

Makes 4 Servings

2 teaspoons canola oil

1 onion, chopped

1 red bell pepper, chopped

1 jalapeño pepper, seeded and minced

3 garlic cloves, minced

3 cups reduced-sodium chicken broth

1 (14½-ounce) can fire-roasted diced tomatoes

1 (10-ounce) box frozen corn kernels

2 teaspoons chili powder

1 teaspoon ground cumin

½ teaspoon dried oregano

1½ cups shredded cooked chicken breast

¼ cup coarsely chopped fresh cilantro

1. Heat the oil in a large saucepan over medium-high heat. Add the onion, bell pepper, jalapeño, and garlic; cook, stirring, until softened, about 5 minutes.

2. Add the broth, tomatoes, corn, chili powder, cumin, and oregano; bring to a boil. Stir in the chicken; reduce the heat and simmer, stirring occasionally, until heated through, about 3 minutes. Stir in the cilantro.

PER SERVING (generous 1 cup): 258 Cal, 6 g Total Fat, 1 g Sat Fat, 0 g Trans Fat, 40 mg Chol, 333 mg Sod, 29 g Total Carb, 4 g Fib, 23 g Prot, 54 mg Calc.
PointsPlus value: *6.*

COOK'S TIP

To retain all the tempting fresh flavor of the delicate cilantro leaves, stir them in just before serving.

South-of-the-Border Bean and Chicken Soup

Makes 4 Servings

1 teaspoon canola oil

1 large onion, chopped

2 garlic cloves, minced

2 cups reduced-sodium chicken broth

1 (15½-ounce) can pinto beans, rinsed and drained

1 (14½-ounce) can diced tomatoes with green chiles

2 cups fresh or frozen corn kernels

1 teaspoon chipotle chile powder

1 teaspoon ground cumin

1 cup chopped cooked chicken

3 tablespoons chopped fresh cilantro

2 teaspoons lime juice

¼ cup fat-free sour cream

1. Heat the oil in a nonstick Dutch oven over medium heat. Add the onion and garlic; cook, stirring occasionally, until golden, about 8 minutes.

2. Add the broth, beans, tomatoes, corn, chili powder, and cumin; bring to a boil. Reduce the heat and simmer, covered, until the flavors are blended, about 10 minutes.

3. Add the chicken, cilantro, and lime juice; simmer, stirring frequently, until heated through, about 3 minutes. Serve the soup with the sour cream.

PER SERVING (1¾ **cups soup with 1 tablespoon sour cream**): **305 Cal, 5 g Total Fat, 1 g Sat Fat, 0 g Trans Fat, 30 mg Chol, 569 mg Sod, 44 g Carb, 10 g Fib, 23 g Prot, 130 mg Calc.** *PointsPlus* value: 7.

COOK'S TIP

For really fresh cumin flavor, toast and grind your own cumin seeds. Here's how: Toast 2 tablespoons cumin seeds in a small dry skillet over medium heat, tossing them frequently, until fragrant, 3–4 minutes. Immediately transfer the cumin seeds to a plate to cool, then grind them in a spice grinder or coffee grinder.

Thai Chicken with Spinach

Thai Chicken with Spinach

Makes 4 Servings

1 cup light (reduced-fat)
    coconut milk

2 garlic cloves, minced

2 tablespoons minced peeled
    fresh ginger

1 tablespoon paprika

1 tablespoon reduced-sodium
    soy sauce

1 tablespoon Asian fish sauce

1 teaspoon grated lime zest

¼ teaspoon red pepper flakes

4 (¼-pound) skinless boneless
    chicken breasts

1 (6-ounce) bag washed baby
    spinach leaves

3 tablespoons chopped fresh
    basil or cilantro

1 teaspoon Asian (dark)
    sesame oil

1 tablespoon packed brown
    sugar

½ teaspoon salt

2 cups hot cooked white rice

4 teaspoons unsweetened
    shredded coconut, toasted

1. Bring the coconut milk, garlic, ginger, paprika, soy sauce, fish sauce, lime zest, and pepper flakes to a boil in a large saucepan. Cook, stirring occasionally, over medium-high heat until the flavors are blended and the mixture thickens slightly, about 8 minutes.

2. Add the chicken; reduce the heat and simmer, covered, until just cooked through, about 10 minutes. Add the spinach, basil, oil, sugar, and salt; return to a boil. Reduce the heat and simmer, uncovered, stirring occasionally, until the spinach wilts, about 2 minutes. Serve with the rice and sprinkle with the coconut.

PER SERVING (1 piece chicken, scant ½ cup sauce, ½ cup rice, and 1 teaspoon coconut): 355 Cal, 10 g Total Fat, 6 g Sat Fat, 0 g Trans Fat, 68 mg Chol, 991 mg Sod, 36 g Carb, 4 g Fib, 31 g Prot, 78 mg Calc.
PointsPlus value: *9.*

COOK'S TIP

Here's an easy way to enjoy some exotic Thai flavors at home. The tasty ingredients, which include coconut milk, ginger, fish sauce, lime zest, and basil make a subtly flavored but distinctly Thai dish that you will turn to again and again. Finish the meal with sliced ripe mango and strawberries.

Braised Chicken with Peanut Sauce

Makes 6 Servings

2 teaspoons extra-virgin
   olive oil

6 (¼-pound) skinless boneless
   chicken breasts

1 large onion, chopped

2 garlic cloves, minced

1 yellow bell pepper, chopped

½ teaspoon ground cumin

½ teaspoon curry powder

½ teaspoon dried oregano

¼ teaspoon red pepper flakes

1 cup reduced-sodium chicken
   broth

½ (6-ounce) can tomato paste

¼ cup reduced-fat creamy
   peanut butter

2 teaspoons lemon juice

3 cups hot cooked white rice

3 tablespoons chopped
   unsalted dry-roasted
   peanuts

1. Heat the oil in a nonstick Dutch oven over medium-high heat. Add the chicken and cook until lightly browned, about 2 minutes on each side. Transfer to a plate.

2. Add the onion and garlic to the Dutch oven and cook, stirring occasionally, until golden, about 7 minutes. Add the bell pepper, cumin, curry powder, oregano, and pepper flakes; cook, stirring occasionally, until fragrant, about 2 minutes.

3. Add the broth and tomato paste; bring to a boil, stirring to scrape any browned bits from the bottom of the pan. Add the chicken; reduce the heat and simmer, covered, until the chicken is cooked through, about 15 minutes.

4. Combine the peanut butter with some of the liquid from the Dutch oven; mix to form a smooth paste. Stir the peanut butter mixture into the Dutch oven and bring to a simmer, stirring constantly. Stir in the lemon juice. Serve with the rice and sprinkle with the peanuts.

PER SERVING (1 piece chicken, scant ½ cup sauce, ½ cup rice, and ½ tablespoon peanuts): 391 Cal, 12 g Total Fat, 2 g Sat Fat, 0 g Trans Fat, 68 mg Chol, 734 mg Sod, 38 g Carb, 3 g Fib, 33 g Prot, 55 mg Calc.
PointsPlus value: *10*.

COOK'S TIP

Peanut butter stews are very popular in Africa, where they vary greatly in their spiciness depending on the cook. Ours is quite mild with just a little heat coming from crushed red pepper and curry powder. You might like to add a package of frozen cut green beans to the stew along with the peanut butter to make it a complete meal.

Creamy Green Curry Chicken

Makes 4 Servings

1 cup light (reduced-fat) coconut milk

4 scallions, thinly sliced

2 tablespoons Thai green curry paste

2 cups reduced-sodium chicken broth

1 tablespoon Asian fish sauce

2 teaspoons packed brown sugar

Pinch salt

¾ pound chicken cutlets, cut on the diagonal into long, thin strips

3 cups hot cooked basmati or jasmine rice

⅓ cup loosely packed fresh mint leaves

1. Heat the coconut milk in a large heavy saucepan over medium heat. Stir in the scallions and curry paste and cook, stirring, until heated through and smooth, about 3 minutes.

2. Stir in the broth and bring to a boil, stirring constantly. Reduce the heat to a simmer. Add the fish sauce, brown sugar, and salt; cook stirring occasionally, about 2 minutes.

3. Add the chicken to the curry sauce and cook, stirring occasionally, until cooked through, about 2 minutes. Divide the rice among 4 large bowls. Top evenly with the curry and sprinkle with the mint.

PER SERVING (1¼ cups curry and ¾ cup rice): **312 Cal, 7 g Total Fat, 3 g Sat Fat, 0 g Trans Fat, 51 mg Chol, 931 mg Sod, 39 g Carb, 2 g Fib, 24 g Prot, 54 mg Calc.** *PointsPlus* value: *8*.

COOK'S TIP

To make this curry even more delicious, stir 1 cup of halved cherry tomatoes into the pot along with the chicken in step 3. Green curry paste, sold in small cans and available in many supermarkets, Asian markets, and online, is a bold blend of green chiles, garlic, lemongrass, and ginger.

Brunswick Drumstick Stew

Makes 6 Servings

2 slices thick-cut bacon, chopped

6 (5-ounce) skinless chicken drumsticks

1 Vidalia onion, chopped

1 tablespoon all-purpose flour

1 (14½-ounce) can diced tomatoes

1 cup reduced-sodium chicken broth

1 tablespoon Worcestershire sauce

½ teaspoon salt

⅛ teaspoon black pepper

1 (10-ounce) package frozen baby lima beans

1 (10-ounce) package frozen corn kernels

1 cup frozen cut okra

1 slice whole wheat bread, made into crumbs

1 teaspoon melted unsalted butter

1. Cook the bacon in a nonstick Dutch oven over medium heat until crisp, about 3 minutes. Drain the bacon on paper towels and set aside. Add the drumsticks to the Dutch oven and cook until lightly browned, about 2 minutes on each side; transfer the drumsticks to a plate.

2. Add the onion to the Dutch oven and cook over medium heat, stirring occasionally, until softened, about 8 minutes. Add the flour and cook, stirring constantly, until lightly browned, about 1 minute. Add the tomatoes, broth, Worcestershire sauce, salt, and pepper; bring to a boil, stirring constantly, until the sauce thickens slightly. Add the chicken. Reduce the heat and simmer, covered, about 20 minutes.

3. Add the lima beans, corn, and okra; return to a boil. Reduce the heat and simmer, covered, until the chicken is cooked through and the vegetables are tender, about 10 minutes. Stir in the bacon.

4. Meanwhile, toss the bread crumbs with the butter in a small bowl. Serve the stew sprinkled with the buttered crumbs.

PER SERVING (1 drumstick, scant 1 cup vegetables and sauce, and 1 tablespoon buttered crumbs): 284 Cal, 9 g Total Fat, 3 g Sat Fat, 0 g Trans Fat, 71 mg Chol, 570 mg Sod, 28 g Carb, 6 g Fib, 24 g Prot, 79 mg Calc.
PointsPlus value: 7.

COOK'S TIP

Brunswick Stew originated in Brunswick County, Virginia in the early 1800s, where it was first made with rabbit, onions, tomatoes, lima beans, corn, and okra. We've substituted skinless chicken for the rabbit and used convenient frozen vegetables and canned tomatoes to cut down on your kitchen time.

Brunswick Drumstick Stew

Country Captain Chicken

Makes 6 Servings

2 teaspoons extra-virgin
olive oil

2¼ pounds skinless boneless
chicken thighs, cut into
1-inch pieces

1 large onion, chopped

1 green bell pepper, chopped

3 garlic cloves, minced

2 tablespoons all-purpose flour

2–3 teaspoons Madras curry
powder

¼ teaspoon salt

¼ teaspoon ground cinnamon

¼ teaspoon ground allspice

1 (14½-ounce) can diced
tomatoes

1 cup reduced-sodium
chicken broth

¼ cup dried currants

3 tablespoons unsweetened
shredded coconut

2 tablespoons chopped fresh
flat-leaf parsley

2 tablespoons toasted sliced
almonds

1. Heat 1 teaspoon of the oil in a nonstick Dutch oven over medium-high heat. Add the chicken and cook, turning occasionally, until browned, about 6 minutes; transfer to a bowl.

2. Add the remaining 1 teaspoon oil to the Dutch oven and set over medium-high heat. Add the onion, bell pepper, and garlic; cook, stirring frequently, until lightly browned, about 8 minutes. Add the flour, curry powder, salt, cinnamon, and allspice; cook, stirring constantly, until fragrant, about 1 minute.

3. Add the tomatoes, broth, currants, coconut, and the browned chicken; bring to a boil. Reduce the heat and simmer, covered, stirring once or twice, until the chicken is cooked through and the flavors are blended, about 15 minutes. Stir in the parsley and serve sprinkled with the almonds.

PER SERVING (scant 1 cup stew with 1 teaspoon almonds): 261 Cal, 12 g Total Fat, 4 g Sat Fat, 0 g Trans Fat, 59 mg Chol, 337 mg Sod, 15 g Carb, 3 g Fib, 23 g Prot, 69 mg Calc.
PointsPlus value: 7.

COOK'S TIP

This spicy favorite of the American South is believed to have been introduced to America by a sea captain involved in the spice trade. Serve it with basmati rice (½ cup cooked rice per serving will up the *PointsPlus* value by *3*), and mango chutney (2 tablespoons per serving will up the *PointsPlus* value by *1*).

Big Easy Chicken and Okra Gumbo

Makes 4 Servings

2 teaspoons canola oil

¼ pound turkey kielbasa, thinly sliced

1 onion, chopped

3 celery stalks, chopped

1 green bell pepper, chopped

3 large garlic cloves, minced

2 tablespoons all-purpose flour

2 cups reduced-sodium chicken broth

1 cup diced cooked chicken breast

1 (14½-ounce) can diced tomatoes

1 cup sliced fresh or frozen sliced okra

2 cups hot cooked brown rice

2 scallions, thinly sliced

¼ cup chopped fresh flat-leaf parsley

1. Heat the oil in a large saucepan over medium-high heat. Add the kielbasa, onion, celery, bell pepper, and garlic; cook, stirring, until the vegetables are softened, about 5 minutes. Add the flour and cook, stirring constantly, 1 minute.

2. Stir in the broth, chicken, tomatoes, and okra; bring to a boil. Reduce the heat and simmer until slightly thickened, about 15 minutes. Divide the gumbo among 4 bowls. Top each serving with ½ cup rice and sprinkle with the scallions and parsley.

PER SERVING (1¼ cups gumbo with ½ cup rice): 307 Cal, 8 g Total Fat, 2 g Sat Fat, 0 g Trans Fat, 43 mg Chol, 874 mg Sod, 39 g Carb, 7 g Fib, 22 g Prot, 131 mg Calc. *PointsPlus* value: *8*.

COOK'S TIP

The "holy trinity" of chopped onion, celery, and green bell pepper is a must for gumbo, a mainstay of New Orleans cuisine. Gumbo can be made with chicken, shellfish, sausage, ham, or a combination. It is thickened from the addition of either okra or filé powder, a spicy herb made from the dried and ground leaves of the sassafras tree.

**Chicken Stew
with Dumplings**

Chicken Stew with Dumplings

Makes 4 Servings

STEW

1 pound skinless boneless
chicken thighs, cut into
1-inch chunks

¼ teaspoon salt

¼ teaspoon black pepper

1 onion, chopped

1 tablespoon all-purpose flour

2 cups reduced-sodium
chicken broth

1 large (about 10-ounce) Yukon
Gold potato, diced

1 cup frozen peas and carrots

1 teaspoon dried tarragon

DUMPLINGS

¾ cup all-purpose flour

1½ teaspoons baking powder

¼ teaspoon salt

½ cup fat-free milk

2 teaspoons melted unsalted
butter

2 tablespoons chopped fresh
flat-leaf parsley

1. To make the chicken stew, spray a nonstick Dutch oven with nonstick spray and set over medium-high heat. Add the chicken; sprinkle with the salt and pepper and cook, turning occasionally, until browned, about 6 minutes. Add the onion; cook, stirring frequently, until softened, about 4 minutes. Add the flour and cook, stirring constantly, until lightly browned, about 1 minute. Stir in the broth and potato; bring to a boil. Reduce the heat and simmer, covered, until the chicken and potato are cooked through, about 15 minutes. Stir in the peas and carrots and the tarragon; return to a boil. Reduce the heat and simmer 2 minutes.

2. Meanwhile, to make the dumplings, combine the flour, baking powder, and salt in a medium bowl. Add the milk, butter, and parsley; stir until a soft dough forms.

3. Drop the dough, by 8 rounded tablespoonfuls onto the simmering stew. Cover the Dutch oven and simmer about 8 minutes. Uncover and simmer until the dumplings have doubled in size and are cooked through, about 3 minutes longer.

PER SERVING (scant 1 cup stew with 2 dumplings): 414 Cal, 12 g Total Fat, 4 g Sat Fat, 0 g Trans Fat, 76 mg Chol, 986 mg Sod, 42 g Carb, 4 g Fib, 33 g Prot, 202 mg Calc. *PointsPlus* value: *10.*

COOK'S TIP

Nothing is as likely to please and comfort the whole family as much as this delicately flavored chicken, dumpling, and vegetable stew. Tarragon goes particularly well with chicken, but you can substitute an equal amount of oregano or ½ teaspoon thyme, if you prefer.

stir-fries
and skillet
meals

Honey-Balsamic Chicken

Makes 4 Servings

4 (¼-pound) skinless boneless
  chicken breasts, lightly
  pounded to even thickness

1 tablespoon balsamic vinegar

1 tablespoon lemon juice

1 tablespoon honey

4 teaspoons extra-virgin
  olive oil

1 garlic clove, minced

½ teaspoon salt

¼ teaspoon black pepper

½ cup reduced-sodium
  chicken broth

½ cup dry white wine

⅓ cup golden raisins

1. Combine the chicken, vinegar, lemon juice, honey, and 2 teaspoons of the oil in a bowl; toss well to coat and set aside for 15 minutes.

2. Heat the remaining 2 teaspoons oil in a large nonstick skillet over medium-high heat. Add the garlic and cook, stirring constantly, until fragrant, about 15 seconds. Add the chicken and sprinkle with ¼ teaspoon of the salt and ⅛ teaspoon of the pepper. Cook until lightly browned, 1–2 minutes on each side.

3. Add the broth, wine, raisins, and the remaining ¼ teaspoon salt and ⅛ teaspoon pepper to the skillet; bring to a boil. Reduce the heat and simmer, covered, until the chicken is cooked through, 10–12 minutes. Transfer the chicken to a serving plate and keep warm. Bring the mixture in the skillet to a boil over high heat and cook until the sauce has reduced to about ½ cup, about 4 minutes. Serve the chicken with the sauce.

PER SERVING (1 piece chicken with 2 tablespoons sauce): 256 Cal, 7 g Total Fat, 1 g Sat Fat, 0 g Trans Fat, 63 mg Chol, 359 mg Sod, 17 g Carb, 1 g Fib, 24 g Prot, 23 mg Calc.
PointsPlus value: *7.*

COOK'S TIP

Lightly pounding chicken breasts helps to tenderize them and indirectly adds flavor by exposing more surface area to the honey-balsamic marinade. To save on the cleanup, sandwich the chicken breast halves between pieces of plastic wrap or sheets of wax paper before pounding with a meat mallet or a heavy saucepan.

Chipotle-Marinated Chicken Breasts with Chimichurri

Makes 4 Servings

3 garlic cloves, minced

2 chipotles en adobo, finely chopped

2 tablespoons honey

1 teaspoon ground cumin

2 (¾-pound) bone-in chicken breast halves, skinned and cut crosswise in half

¾ teaspoon salt

4 teaspoons extra-virgin olive oil

1 cup reduced-sodium chicken broth

¼ cup white-wine vinegar

3 tablespoons chopped fresh cilantro

1. Combine 2 of the garlic cloves, the chipotles, honey, and cumin in a zip-close plastic bag; add the chicken. Squeeze out the air and seal the bag; turn to coat the chicken. Refrigerate, turning the bag occasionally, for at least 4 hours or up to overnight.

2. Sprinkle the chicken with ½ teaspoon of the salt. Heat 1 teaspoon of the oil in a large nonstick skillet over medium-high heat. Add the chicken and cook until browned, 3–4 minutes on each side. Add the broth and bring to a boil. Reduce the heat and simmer, covered, about 10 minutes. Uncover the chicken and increase the heat to medium. Cook, turning twice, until the chicken is cooked through, 12–15 minutes. Discard any liquid left in the skillet.

3. Meanwhile, to make the chimichurri sauce, combine the remaining 1 garlic clove, 3 teaspoons oil, and ¼ teaspoon salt with the vinegar and cilantro; mix well. Serve the chimichurri with the chicken.

PER SERVING (1 piece chicken with 2 tablespoons chimichurri): 237 Cal, 8 g Total Fat, 2 g Sat Fat, 0 g Trans Fat, 76 mg Chol, 545 mg Sod, 11 g Carb, 0 g Fib, 29 g Prot, 25 mg Calc. *PointsPlus* value: *6.*

COOK'S TIP

To store the leftover chipotle chiles, transfer them to a small jar or airtight container and refrigerate for up to a month.

Simmered Chicken with Soy-Ginger Sauce

Makes 4 Servings

3 teaspoons Asian (dark) sesame oil

2 (¾-pound) bone-in chicken breast halves, skinned and cut crosswise in half

5 scallions, finely chopped

1 tablespoon plus 2 teaspoons grated peeled fresh ginger

1 cup reduced-sodium chicken broth

3 tablespoons reduced-sodium soy sauce

3 tablespoons rice vinegar

5 teaspoons honey

1. Heat 2 teaspoons of the oil in a large nonstick skillet over medium-high heat. Add the chicken and cook until browned, 3–4 minutes on each side. Transfer the chicken to a plate.

2. Add 4 of the scallions and the 1 tablespoon ginger to the skillet and cook, stirring constantly, until fragrant, about 1 minute. Add the broth and 2 tablespoons of the soy sauce; bring to a boil. Reduce the heat and simmer, covered, about 4 minutes. Add the chicken and return to a gentle simmer; cook, covered, about 12 minutes. Turn off the heat and let the chicken sit in the liquid about 10 minutes longer. Using a slotted spoon, transfer the chicken from the liquid to a serving plate. Discard the liquid.

3. Combine the remaining 1 teaspoon oil, 1 scallion, 2 teaspoons ginger, 1 tablespoon soy sauce, the vinegar, and honey in a small bowl; mix well. Serve with the chicken.

PER SERVING (1 piece chicken with 1½ tablespoons sauce): 205 Cal, 6 g Total Fat, 1 g Sat Fat, 0 g Trans Fat, 74 mg Chol, 299 mg Sod, 10 g Carb, 0 g Fib, 28 g Prot, 22 mg Calc. *PointsPlus* value: *5*.

COOK'S TIP

Gently simmering chicken breasts in an Asian-influenced broth infuses them with all the flavors. Serve this dish with a steaming bowl of brown rice (½ cup cooked brown rice per serving will increase the *PointsPlus* value by *3*).

Chicken Sauté with Lemon-Caper Sauce

Makes 4 Servings

4 (¼-pound) skinless boneless chicken breasts, pounded to a ⅛-inch thickness

½ teaspoon salt

¼ teaspoon black pepper

1 tablespoon plus 1 teaspoon unsalted butter

½ cup reduced-sodium chicken broth

¼ cup lemon juice

1 tablespoon drained capers

½ teaspoon dried oregano

1. Sprinkle the chicken with ¼ teaspoon of the salt and ⅛ teaspoon of the pepper.

2. Melt the 1 tablespoon of butter in a large nonstick skillet over medium heat. Add the chicken and cook until lightly browned, about 4 minutes on each side. Add the broth, lemon juice, capers, and oregano; bring to a simmer. Reduce the heat and simmer, turning the chicken once to coat with the sauce, until the chicken is cooked through, about 2 minutes.

3. Remove the skillet from the heat and swirl in the remaining 1 teaspoon butter, ¼ teaspoon salt, and ⅛ teaspoon pepper.

PER SERVING (1 piece chicken with generous 1 tablespoon sauce): 182 Cal, 8 g Total Fat, 3 g Sat Fat, 0 g Trans Fat, 79 mg Chol, 477 mg Sod, 1 g Carb, 0 g Fib, 26 g Prot, 19 mg Calc. *PointsPlus* value: *5.*

COOK'S TIP

This delicately flavored chicken and sauce is delicious served over wide egg noodles (½ cup cooked egg noodles per serving will increase the *PointsPlus* value by *3*). If you don't have a large enough skillet to brown the chicken in one batch without crowding it, brown it in two batches.

Cajun Chicken and Okra Stir-Fry

Makes 4 Servings

2 teaspoons extra-virgin
   olive oil

1 pound skinless boneless
   chicken thighs, cut into
   1-inch pieces

¼ teaspoon salt

⅛ teaspoon black pepper

1 green bell pepper, chopped

1 onion, chopped

1 celery stalk, chopped

2 garlic cloves, minced

1 cup frozen okra, cut into
   ½-inch pieces

1 (14½-ounce) can diced
   tomatoes with jalapeños

1 teaspoon dried oregano

1. Heat a large nonstick skillet or wok over medium-high heat until a drop of water sizzles. Pour in 1 teaspoon of the oil and swirl to coat the pan. Add the chicken, salt, and black pepper; stir-fry until the chicken is browned and cooked through, 4–5 minutes. Transfer the chicken to a plate.

2. Add the remaining 1 teaspoon oil to the same skillet and swirl to coat the pan. Add the bell pepper, onion, celery, and garlic; stir-fry until crisp-tender, about 2 minutes. Add the okra and stir-fry until tender, about 4 minutes. Add the chicken, tomatoes, and oregano; bring to a boil. Reduce the heat and simmer until the mixture thickens slightly, about 4 minutes longer.

PER SERVING (1 cup): 222 Cal, 6 g Total Fat, 2 g Sat Fat, 0 g Trans Fat, 94 mg Chol, 508 mg Sod, 15 g Carb, 4 g Fib, 27 g Prot, 111 mg Calc.
PointsPlus value: *5.*

COOK'S TIP

Okra plants were brought to the New World during the slave trade. It is a Southern staple that is frequently battered and deep-fried or used in gumbos or stir-fries as both a thickening agent and a vegetable. Enjoy this stir-fry with warm corn bread. A 2-ounce wedge of corn bread per serving will up the *PointsPlus* value by *4.*

Cajun Chicken and Okra Stir-Fry

Chicken Veronique

Makes 4 Servings

2 (¾-pound) bone-in chicken breast halves, skinned and cut crosswise in half

¼ teaspoon salt

Pinch of black pepper

1 tablespoon extra-virgin olive oil

1 cup reduced-sodium chicken broth

½ pound seedless green grapes, halved

2 teaspoons chopped fresh tarragon

1. Sprinkle the chicken with the salt and pepper. Heat the oil in a large nonstick skillet over medium heat. Add the chicken and cook until browned, 5–6 minutes on each side. Add the broth and bring to a boil. Reduce the heat and simmer, covered, until the chicken is almost cooked through, about 8 minutes. Add the grapes and tarragon; simmer, covered, until the grapes are slightly softened, about 2 minutes longer.

2. Divide the chicken and tarragon among 4 plates. Spoon the pan juices over.

PER SERVING (1 piece chicken with about ½ cup grapes): 208 Cal, 7 g Total Fat, 1 g Sat Fat, 0 g Trans Fat, 68 mg Chol, 363 mg Sod, 11 g Carb, 1 g Fib, 26 g Prot, 24 mg Calc. *PointsPlus* value: *5.*

COOK'S TIP

Serve this delicately flavored dish with wild rice (½ cup cooked wild rice per serving will increase the *PointsPlus* value by *2*).

Buying and Safe Handling Hints

Like all fresh meats, chicken is perishable, so it should be handled with care. Proper handling also helps to eliminate the risk of bacterial infection. Follow these easy steps to safeguard your family's health:

HOW TO SHOP IN THE STORE

- When shopping, poultry should be the last thing you put into your cart to help keep it cold. Never leave chicken or other perishables in a hot car. Instead place it in a cooler bag or small cooler and surround it with a few ice packs.

- Buy raw poultry by the sell-by date on the label. If you purchase it before the sell-by date, make sure you use it or freeze it within 2 days.

- Chicken is sometimes on sale on its sell-by date, making it easy on the wallet. Buy and use fully cooked poultry by the use-by date. If you purchase it before that, be sure to cook it or freeze it by that date.

HOW TO HANDLE AT HOME

- When you get home, immediately refrigerate raw chicken. Do not leave it on a countertop at room temperature for any length of time.

- Place packaged raw chicken in its original wrapping on a plate to prevent any juices from dripping onto other foods. Store it in the coldest part of the refrigerator (40°F or lower), which is usually the back.

- Any raw chicken that is not used within 2 days should be frozen at 0°F. Chicken that is frozen continuously at 0°F or less will be safe to eat for at least 9 months.

- When handling raw chicken, always wash your hands, countertops, cutting boards, knives, and other utensils with hot, soapy water before they come in contact with other raw or cooked foods.

HOW TO WRAP AND STORE

- Chicken may be frozen in its original wrapping for up to 2 months.

- When freezing chicken for more than 2 months, overwrap the store wrapping with heavy-duty aluminum foil, plastic wrap, or freezer paper. Be sure to date and label each package. Alternatively, you can place the store-wrapped chicken in a large zip-close plastic freezer bag. Before sealing the bag, be sure to remove all the excess air.

HOW TO THAW

- Thaw chicken in the refrigerator—not on the countertop. It takes about 24 hours to thaw a 4-pound chicken in the refrigerator, while cut-up parts take from 3 to 9 hours.

- Chicken may be safely thawed in cold water. Place the chicken in its original wrapping or in a zip-close plastic bag in a sink filled with cold water, changing the water every 30 minutes to keep it cold. It takes about 2 hours to thaw a whole chicken.

- For quick thawing of raw or cooked chicken, use a microwave oven, following the manufacturer's directions. The thawing time will vary.

Poached Chicken with Asparagus and Hoisin Sauce

Makes 4 Servings

¼ cup hoisin sauce

¼ cup rice wine or dry sherry

¼ cup water

1 tablespoon low-sodium soy sauce

2 large garlic cloves, thinly sliced

Pinch of red pepper flakes

4 (5-ounce) skinless boneless chicken breasts

1 pound slender asparagus, trimmed and cut into 2-inch lengths

1 teaspoon Asian (dark) sesame oil

1. Stir together the hoisin sauce, rice wine, water, soy sauce, garlic, and pepper flakes in a large skillet; bring to a boil. Add the chicken; reduce the heat and simmer, covered, turning once, until the chicken is cooked through, 10–12 minutes.

2. Meanwhile, bring a medium saucepan of water to a boil. Add the asparagus and cook just until crisp-tender, about 3 minutes; drain.

3. Transfer the chicken to a plate. Bring the sauce to a boil over medium-high heat; boil until slightly thickened and reduced to ½ cup, about 2 minutes. Stir in the sesame oil and any accumulated chicken juices. Cut the chicken crosswise into ½-inch-thick slices. Divide the chicken and asparagus among 4 plates. Spoon the sauce over the chicken and asparagus.

PER SERVING (1 chicken breast, ¾ cup asparagus, and 2 tablespoons sauce): 254 Cal, 5 g Total Fat, 1 g Sat Fat, 0 g Trans Fat, 79 mg Chol, 648 mg Sod, 18 g Total Carb, 4 g Fib, 31 g Prot, 65 mg Calc.
PointsPlus value: *6.*

COOK'S TIP

Cooking the chicken in a liquid over gentle heat (poaching) ensures that it will be moist, while slicing it on a diagonal makes it tender eating. Hoisin sauce is found in supermarkets alongside the other Asian products. It is made from soybeans, garlic, chiles, and spices. Once opened, store the hoisin tightly sealed in the refrigerator, where it will keep indefinitely.

Thai Red Curry Chicken

Makes 4 Servings

2 teaspoons canola oil

4 (¼-pound) skinless boneless chicken breast, lightly pounded to even thickness

¼ teaspoon salt

2 scallions, chopped

2 teaspoons grated peeled fresh ginger

2 garlic cloves, minced

¾ cup light (reduced-fat) coconut milk

1 tablespoon Thai red curry paste

1 tablespoon Asian fish sauce

1 tablespoon packed dark brown sugar

2 teaspoons lime juice

2 tablespoons chopped fresh cilantro (optional)

1. Heat the oil in a large nonstick skillet over medium-high heat. Sprinkle the chicken with the salt and add to the skillet. Cook the chicken until browned on the outside and cooked through, 4–5 minutes on each side. Transfer the chicken to a plate and keep warm.

2. Reduce the heat under the skillet to medium; add the scallions, ginger, and garlic; cook, stirring constantly, until fragrant, about 30 seconds. Add the coconut milk, curry paste, fish sauce, sugar, and lime juice; bring to a boil. Reduce the heat and simmer, stirring occasionally, until the mixture begins to thicken, 5–6 minutes. Add the chicken and simmer until heated through, about 1 minute longer. Serve, sprinkled with the cilantro, if using.

PER SERVING (1 piece chicken with 2 tablespoons sauce): 223 Cal, 10 g Total Fat, 3 g Sat Fat, 0 g Trans Fat, 68 mg Chol, 368 mg Sod, 10 g Carb, 2 g Fib, 27 g Prot, 33 mg Calc.
PointsPlus value: *6.*

COOK'S TIP

Thai cooks are fond of combining spicy, pungent, and sweet flavors with meats, poultry, or fish. In this easy skillet dinner, the spicy ginger and red curry paste balance the flavors of the pungent fish sauce and sweet brown sugar. Steamed rice makes a satisfying accompaniment (½ cup cooked white rice per serving will increase the *PointsPlus* value by *3*).

Kung Pao Chicken

Kung Pao Chicken

Makes 8 Servings

½ cup reduced-sodium chicken broth

⅓ cup sake or mirin (rice wine)

3 tablespoons hoisin sauce

2 tablespoons reduced-sodium soy sauce

2 tablespoons cornstarch

2 tablespoons honey

3 teaspoons Asian (dark) sesame oil

1 pound skinless boneless chicken breasts, cut into ½-inch pieces

2 scallions, chopped

1 tablespoon grated peeled fresh ginger

¼ teaspoon red pepper flakes

1 (8-ounce) can sliced water chestnuts, drained

1¼ cups unsalted dry-roasted peanuts

1. Combine the broth, sake, hoisin sauce, soy sauce, cornstarch, and honey in a bowl; mix well.

2. Heat a large nonstick skillet or wok over medium heat until a drop of water sizzles. Pour in 2 teaspoons of the oil and swirl to coat the pan, then add the chicken. Stir-fry until the chicken is cooked through, about 8 minutes. Transfer the chicken to a plate.

3. Add the remaining 1 teaspoon oil to the skillet and swirl to coat the pan. Add the scallions, ginger, and pepper flakes; stir-fry until fragrant, about 30 seconds. Add the water chestnuts and peanuts; stir-fry until heated through, about 1 minute. Add the broth mixture and cook, stirring constantly, until the mixture bubbles and thickens, about 1 minute. Add the chicken and cook until heated through, about 1 minute longer.

PER SERVING (¾ cup): 279 Cal, 15 g Total Fat, 2 g Sat Fat, 0 g Trans Fat, 32 mg Chol, 267 mg Sod, 19 g Carb, 3 g Fib, 18 g Prot, 26 mg Calc.
PointsPlus value: *8.*

COOK'S TIP

This Chinese restaurant take-out favorite gets a burst of enticing flavor from sake (Japanese rice wine), hoisin sauce, ginger, and red pepper flakes. Our version is moderately spicy, though traditionally this dish is quite fiery. Add extra red pepper flakes, if you like. Serve with white rice (½ cup cooked white rice per serving will increase the *PointsPlus* value by *3*).

Chicken Tagine

Makes 4 Servings

1 tablespoon sunflower oil

1 pound skinless boneless chicken breasts, cut into 1-inch pieces

1 (10-ounce) package frozen whole okra

1 onion, chopped

3 garlic cloves, minced

1 tablespoon minced peeled fresh ginger

¼ teaspoon saffron threads, lightly crushed

¾ cup reduced-sodium chicken broth

2 tablespoons lemon juice

12 pimiento-stuffed olives, halved

3 tablespoons chopped fresh cilantro

¼ teaspoon salt

¼ teaspoon black pepper

1. Heat the oil in a large nonstick skillet over medium-high heat. Add the chicken and cook, stirring occasionally, until lightly browned, about 3 minutes. Transfer the chicken to a plate.

2. Add the okra, onion, garlic, ginger, and saffron to the skillet; cook, stirring occasionally, until the onion starts to soften, about 5 minutes. Stir in the broth and lemon juice; bring to a boil. Reduce the heat, stir in the chicken, and simmer, covered, until the chicken is cooked through, about 7 minutes. Uncover and cook until the liquid is slightly reduced, about 3 minutes longer. Remove the skillet from the heat; stir in the olives, cilantro, salt, and pepper.

PER SERVING (1 cup): 207 Cal, 8 g Total Fat, 1 g Sat Fat, 0 g Trans Fat, 63 mg Chol, 568 mg Sod, 10 g Carb, 3 g Fib, 25 g Prot, 85 mg Calc.
PointsPlus value: *5.*

COOK'S TIP

A tagine is a stewlike dish from Morocco that's typically prepared with meat or poultry and vegetables, garlic, and olives. The seasonings vary from ginger to saffron to cilantro. Enjoy it with whole wheat couscous for sopping up all the flavors (½ cup cooked whole wheat couscous per serving will increase the *PointsPlus* value by *3*).

Drumstick Osso Buco

Makes 4 Servings

8 (¼-pound) skinless chicken drumsticks

¾ teaspoon salt

¼ teaspoon black pepper

2 teaspoons extra-virgin olive oil

1 onion, finely chopped

1 carrot, finely chopped

1 celery stalk, finely chopped

3 garlic cloves, minced

½ cup dry red wine

1 (14½-ounce) can diced tomatoes

½ teaspoon dried basil

½ teaspoon dried oregano

2 cups hot cooked white rice

1. Sprinkle the chicken with ½ teaspoon of the salt and ⅛ teaspoon of the pepper. Heat 1 teaspoon of the oil in a large nonstick skillet over medium-high heat. Add the chicken and cook until browned, 3–4 minutes on each side. Transfer the chicken to a plate.

2. Heat the remaining 1 teaspoon oil in the same skillet. Add the onion, carrot, celery, and garlic; cook, stirring frequently, until the vegetables begin to soften, about 5 minutes. Add the wine and simmer 30 seconds. Add the tomatoes, basil, oregano, and the remaining ¼ teaspoon salt and ⅛ teaspoon pepper; bring to a boil. Reduce the heat and simmer, covered, about 10 minutes. Add the chicken and simmer, covered, until the chicken is cooked through, about 25 minutes. Serve with the rice.

PER SERVING (½ cup rice, 2 drumsticks, and ½ cup sauce): 346 Cal, 7 g Total Fat, 2 g Sat Fat, 0 g Trans Fat, 98 mg Chol, 806 mg Sod, 34 g Carb, 3 g Fib, 30 g Prot, 71 mg Calc. *PointsPlus* value: *9.*

COOK'S TIP

Osso buco is a rich stew traditionally made with veal shanks. We've substituted lean skinless chicken drumsticks but retained the flavorful vegetables and garlicky wine broth. Serve this dish with a side of steamed sliced zucchini, green beans, or broccoli.

Chicken and Mixed Mushroom Sauté

Makes 4 Servings

1 tablespoon extra-virgin
   olive oil

4 (¼-pound) skinless boneless
   chicken breasts

½ pound fresh white
   mushrooms, sliced

1 (5-ounce) package fresh
   shiitake mushrooms, stems
   discarded, caps sliced

2 garlic cloves, minced

1 medium shallot, chopped

½ teaspoon dried thyme

1½ cups reduced-sodium
   chicken broth

½ teaspoon salt

¼ teaspoon black pepper

1. Heat the oil in a large nonstick skillet over medium-high heat. Add the chicken and cook until browned, about 3 minutes on each side. Transfer the chicken to a plate.

2. Add the mushrooms, garlic, shallot, and thyme to the skillet. Cook, stirring occasionally, until the mushrooms are golden and softened, about 8 minutes. Add the broth, chicken, salt, and pepper; bring to a boil. Reduce the heat to medium-low and simmer, turning the chicken occasionally, until the chicken is cooked through, about 8 minutes.

3. Transfer the chicken to a serving plate; cover to keep warm. Increase the heat to high and bring the mushroom mixture to a boil. Cook until the liquid has reduced to about 1¼ cups, about 4 minutes. Spoon the mushroom mixture over the chicken.

PER SERVING (1 piece chicken with ⅓ cup mushroom mixture): 186 Cal, 6 g Total Fat, 1 g Sat Fat, 0 g Trans Fat, 63 mg Chol, 581 mg Sod, 6 g Carb, 1 g Fib, 27 g Prot, 21 mg Calc. *PointsPlus* value: *5.*

COOK'S TIP

It used to be that mushroom sauces often included cream or butter to make up for the lack of flavor in white mushrooms. But now that all kinds of earthy-flavored mushrooms, including shiitake, oyster, cremini, and portobello, are readily available, there is no need to rely on cream to deliver great flavor.

Pan-Grilled Jerk Chicken Breasts

Makes 4 Servings

3 scallions, chopped

2 bay leaves, crumbled

1 to 2 jalapeño peppers, seeded and chopped

1 to 2 garlic cloves, chopped

1 tablespoon canola oil

2 teaspoons apple cider vinegar

½ teaspoon ground allspice

½ teaspoon dried thyme, crumbled

¼ teaspoon salt

¼ teaspoon cayenne

4 (¼-pound) skinless boneless chicken breasts

1. Put the scallions, bay leaves, jalapeños, garlic, oil, vinegar, allspice, thyme, salt, and cayenne in a small food processor; pulse until a thick paste forms. Place the paste in a zip-close plastic bag; add the chicken. Squeeze out the air and seal the bag; turn to coat the chicken. Refrigerate, turning the bag occasionally, for at least 2 hours or overnight.

2. Remove the chicken from the marinade; discard the marinade. Spray a ridged grill pan or large nonstick skillet with nonstick spray and set over medium heat. Add the chicken and cook, turning occasionally, until cooked through, 10–12 minutes.

PER SERVING (1 chicken breast half): 160 Cal, 6 g Total Fat, 1 g Sat Fat, 0 g Trans Fat, 63 mg Chol, 202 mg Sod, 2 g Carb, 1 g Fib, 23 g Prot, 26 mg Calc.
PointsPlus value: *4.*

COOK'S TIP

Turn this intensely flavored chicken dish into a meal by serving it with brown rice tossed with finely chopped fresh pineapple and cilantro and a favorite steamed green vegetable (½ cup cooked brown rice for each serving will increase the *PointsPlus* value by *3*).

Sweet-and-Spicy Chicken

Sweet-and-Spicy Chicken

Makes 4 Servings

2 scallions, chopped

3 tablespoons mirin (rice wine)

2 tablespoons rice vinegar

2 tablespoons sugar

2 tablespoons reduced-sodium
soy sauce

2 teaspoons Asian (dark)
sesame oil

½ teaspoon red pepper flakes

4 (¼-pound) skinless boneless
chicken thighs

½ cup reduced-sodium
chicken broth

1. Combine the scallions, mirin, vinegar, sugar, soy sauce, 1 teaspoon of the oil, and the pepper flakes in a zip-close plastic bag; add the chicken. Squeeze out the air and seal the bag; turn to coat the chicken. Refrigerate, turning the bag occasionally, for at least 2 hours or up to overnight.

2. Lift the chicken from the marinade and pat dry with paper towels. Discard the marinade. Heat the remaining 1 teaspoon oil in a large nonstick skillet over medium heat. Add the chicken and cook until lightly browned, about 2 minutes on each side. Add the broth; bring to a boil. Reduce the heat and simmer, covered, turning once, until the chicken is cooked through and the liquid is syrupy, about 10 minutes. Turn the chicken to coat with the liquid. Cut the chicken into slices to serve.

PER SERVING (1 chicken thigh): 236 Cal, 11 g Total Fat, 3 g Sat Fat, 0 g Trans Fat, 74 mg Chol, 346 mg Sod, 10 g Carb, 0 g Fib, 22 g Prot, 19 mg Calc.
PointsPlus value: *6.*

COOK'S TIP

If you like, serve the chicken on a bed of Korean-style coleslaw. Toss together savoy cabbage, matchstick-cut carrots, thinly sliced radishes, and matchstick-cut Gala apple. Sprinkle with lime juice and salt and pepper to taste.

Sunshine Chicken Stir-Fry

Makes 4 Servings

1 pound skinless boneless chicken thighs, cut into ½-inch pieces

1 teaspoon ground cumin

¾ teaspoon salt

3 teaspoons canola oil

3 garlic cloves, minced

1 jalapeño pepper, seeded and finely chopped

1 (12-ounce) bag mixed vegetables for stir-fry (carrots, snow peas, red bell pepper, and broccoli)

⅔ cup orange juice

2 tablespoons lime juice

1. Combine the chicken, cumin, and ½ teaspoon of the salt in a medium bowl; mix well.

2. Heat a large nonstick skillet or wok over medium-high heat until a drop of water sizzles. Pour in 2 teaspoons of the oil and swirl to coat the pan, then add the chicken. Stir-fry until the chicken is browned and cooked through, 4–5 minutes. Transfer the chicken to a plate.

3. Add the remaining 1 teaspoon oil to the same skillet and swirl to coat the pan. Add the garlic and jalapeño; stir-fry until fragrant, about 30 seconds. Add the mixed vegetables and stir-fry until crisp-tender, about 1 minute. Add the orange juice, lime juice, and the remaining ¼ teaspoon salt; cook, stirring occasionally, until the vegetables are tender, about 2 minutes. Add the chicken and cook until heated through, about 1 minute.

PER SERVING (1 cup): 261 Cal, 13 g Total Fat, 3 g Sat Fat, 0 g Trans Fat, 71 mg Chol, 530 mg Sod, 10 g Carb, 3 g Fib, 26 g Prot, 68 mg Calc.
PointsPlus value: *7.*

COOK'S TIP

This recipe is a fusion of Tex-Mex flavors and traditional Chinese stir-fry techniques. You can serve it with warm flour tortillas (a 6- to 7-inch fat-free flour tortilla will up the *PointsPlus* value by *1*) or with brown rice (½ cup cooked brown rice per serving will up the *PointsPlus* value by *3*).

Arroz con Pollo

Makes 4 Servings

- 4 (5-ounce) skinless bone-in chicken thighs
- ½ teaspoon salt
- ¼ teaspoon black pepper
- 2 teaspoons extra-virgin olive oil
- 2 assorted color bell peppers, seeded and chopped
- 1 onion, chopped
- 3 garlic cloves, minced
- 1 cup long-grain white rice
- ½ teaspoon saffron threads, lightly crushed
- 1 (14½-ounce) can diced tomatoes
- 1 cup reduced-sodium chicken broth
- 1 cup frozen peas
- 12 small pimiento-stuffed green olives

1. Sprinkle the chicken with ¼ teaspoon of the salt and ⅛ teaspoon of the black pepper. Heat 1 teaspoon of the oil in a large nonstick skillet over medium-high heat. Add the chicken and cook until browned, 3–4 minutes on each side. Transfer the chicken to a plate.

2. Heat the remaining 1 teaspoon oil in the same skillet. Add the bell peppers, onion, and garlic; cook, stirring frequently, until the vegetables begin to soften, about 7 minutes. Add the rice and saffron; cook, stirring constantly, about 1 minute. Add the tomatoes, broth, and chicken; bring to a boil, stirring occasionally. Reduce the heat and simmer, covered, until the liquid is absorbed and the chicken is cooked through, about 20 minutes. Stir in the peas, olives, and remaining ¼ teaspoon salt and ⅛ teaspoon black pepper. Cook, stirring occasionally, until heated through, about 1 minute. Remove the skillet from the heat and let stand, covered, for about 5 minutes.

PER SERVING (1 chicken thigh with 1⅓ cups rice mixture): 450 Cal, 12 g Total Fat, 3 g Sat Fat, 0 g Trans Fat, 57 mg Chol, 892 mg Sod, 56 g Carb, 5 g Fib, 28 g Prot, 100 mg Calc.
PointsPlus value: *11.*

COOK'S TIP

Arroz con pollo is a traditional dish whose components vary from one region to another throughout Spain, the Caribbean, and Latin America. It is a popular one-pot dinner made with simple, flavorful ingredients. Chicken, rice, onion, garlic, and tomatoes are the base to which a variety of vegetables, such as bell peppers, peas, and olives, are added.

Mu Shu Chicken

Makes 4 Servings

1 teaspoon canola oil

1 pound skinless boneless chicken thighs, cut into thin strips

1 small onion, thinly sliced

1 tablespoon grated peeled fresh ginger

2 garlic cloves, minced

¼ small head napa cabbage, shredded (about 2 cups)

¼ pound white mushrooms, sliced

1 carrot, cut into matchstick-thin sticks

3 tablespoons hoisin sauce

4 (8-inch) fat-free flour tortillas

1. Heat a large nonstick skillet or wok over medium-high heat until a drop of water sizzles. Pour in the oil and swirl to coat the pan. Add the chicken, onion, ginger, and garlic; stir-fry until the chicken is browned and cooked through, 4–5 minutes.

2. Add the cabbage, mushrooms, and carrot; stir-fry until the carrot is crisp-tender, about 5 minutes. Add the hoisin sauce and cook, stirring constantly, until heated through, about 1 minute longer. Remove the skillet from the heat.

3. Heat the tortillas according to package directions. Spoon ½ cup of the chicken mixture onto each tortilla. Roll up the tortillas and serve at once. Serve any extra filling on the side.

PER SERVING (1 filled tortilla)**:** 400 Cal, 11 g Total Fat, 3 g Sat Fat, 0 g Trans Fat, 71 mg Chol, 732 mg Sod, 43 g Carb, 4 g Fib, 31 g Prot, 127 mg Calc.
PointsPlus value: *10.*

COOK'S TIP

Mu shu—meat (usually pork) and vegetables rolled up in a thin pancake—are a favorite in Chinese cuisine. We've substituted lean chicken for the pork and stuffed the filling into flour tortillas for ease of preparation. End the meal with a refreshing salad of mixed berries and diced pineapple.

Mu Shu Chicken

Spiced Chicken-Currant Patties with Yogurt Sauce

Makes 4 Servings

½ cup plain fat-free yogurt

½ garlic clove, minced

1½ teaspoons plus 1 tablespoon extra-virgin olive oil

¾ teaspoon salt

¼ teaspoon black pepper

1 pound ground skinless chicken breast

⅓ cup plain dry bread crumbs

¼ cup dried currants

2 tablespoons tomato paste

1 teaspoon ground coriander

1 teaspoon dried oregano

½ teaspoon ground cinnamon

1. To make the yogurt sauce, combine the yogurt, garlic, the 1½ teaspoons oil, ¼ teaspoon of the salt, and ⅛ teaspoon of the pepper in a small bowl.

2. Combine the chicken, bread crumbs, currants, tomato paste, coriander, oregano, cinnamon, and remaining ½ teaspoon salt and ⅛ teaspoon pepper in a large bowl; mix well. Shape the mixture into 4 (½-inch-thick) patties.

3. Heat the remaining 1 tablespoon oil in a large nonstick skillet over medium heat. Add the patties and cook until browned and an instant-read thermometer inserted in the side of a patty registers 165°F, about 6 minutes on each side. Serve the patties with the yogurt sauce.

PER SERVING (1 patty with 2 tablespoons yogurt sauce): 274 Cal, 9 g Total Fat, 2 g Sat Fat, 0 g Trans Fat, 69 mg Chol, 671 mg Sod, 18 g Carb, 1 g Fib, 28 g Prot, 113 mg Calc. *PointsPlus* value: *7*.

COOK'S TIP

Make this a totally Greek-café experience by serving these aromatic, slightly sweet patties in whole wheat pita breads along with thin slices of red onion and chunks of juicy red tomato (½ fajita-style whole wheat pita bread per serving will increase the *PointsPlus* value by *2*).

Chicken Picadillo with Toasted Tortillas

Makes 4 Servings

1 pound ground skinless
  chicken breast

1 onion, cut into ¼-inch dice

1 red bell pepper, cut into
  ¼-inch pieces

2 garlic cloves, minced

¾ teaspoon ground cumin

½ cup reduced-sodium
  chicken broth

¼ cup golden raisins

1 tablespoon drained capers

2 tomatoes, seeded and
  chopped, about 1 cup

½ teaspoon salt

¼ teaspoon black pepper

4 (6-inch) corn tortillas

1. Spray a large nonstick skillet with nonstick spray and set over medium heat. Add the chicken and cook, breaking up the chicken with a wooden spoon, until browned, about 8 minutes. Add the onion, bell pepper, garlic, and cumin; cook, stirring occasionally, until the vegetables are softened, about 5 minutes. Add the broth, raisins, and capers; bring to a boil. Reduce the heat and simmer, uncovered, until the broth has nearly evaporated, about 2 minutes. Add the tomatoes, salt, and black pepper; cook, stirring occasionally, until the mixture thickens slightly, about 3 minutes.

2. Meanwhile, heat a small nonstick skillet over medium heat. Add the tortillas, one at a time, and cook until lightly toasted, about 2 minutes on each side. Serve the toasted tortillas with the chicken mixture.

PER SERVING (¾ cup chicken mixture with 1 tortilla): 246 Cal, 2 g Total Fat, 1 g Sat Fat, 0 g Trans Fat, 75 mg Chol, 509 mg Sod, 27 g Carb, 3 g Fib, 30 g Prot, 82 mg Calc.
PointsPlus value: *6.*

COOK'S TIP

Picadillo is a winning Mexican dish that is traditionally made with ground pork. We've substituted ground chicken with great results! Start your meal off with a crisp mixed green salad and end with fresh pineapple chunks tossed with chopped fresh cilantro and sprinkled with freshly ground black pepper and ground cinnamon.

Hunan Orange Chicken

Hunan Orange Chicken

Makes 4 Servings

1 cup orange juice

3 tablespoons reduced-sodium
  soy sauce

2 tablespoons cornstarch

2 tablespoons honey

¼ teaspoon red pepper flakes

4 teaspoons Asian (dark)
  sesame oil

1 pound chicken breast cutlets,
  cut into ½-inch pieces

1 red bell pepper, cut into
  ½-inch pieces

1 tablespoon grated peeled
  fresh ginger

¼ pound fresh snow peas,
  trimmed and halved

1. Combine the orange juice, soy sauce, cornstarch, honey, and pepper flakes in a small bowl; stir until smooth.

2. Heat a large nonstick skillet or wok over medium heat until a drop of water sizzles. Pour in 2 teaspoons of the oil and swirl to coat the pan. Add the chicken; stir-fry until browned and cooked through, about 6 minutes. Transfer the chicken to a plate.

3. Heat the remaining 2 teaspoons oil in the same skillet. Add the bell pepper and ginger; stir-fry until fragrant, about 4 minutes. Add the snow peas and stir-fry until the vegetables are crisp-tender, about 1 minute. Add the chicken and the orange juice mixture. Cook, stirring constantly, until the mixture bubbles and thickens, about 1 minute.

PER SERVING (1 cup): 265 Cal, 6 g Total Fat, 1 g Sat Fat, 0 g Trans Fat, 75 mg Chol, 452 mg Sod, 24 g Carb, 2 g Fib, 28 g Prot, 35 mg Calc.
PointsPlus value: *7.*

COOK'S TIP

If you love Chinese orange duck or chicken with its sweet, spicy, and savory flavors, you'll love this dish. Hot cooked rice makes a good carrier for the sauce (½ cup cooked white or brown rice per serving will increase the *PointsPlus* value by *3*).

Mozzarella-Stuffed Meatballs with Penne and Kale

Makes 4 Servings

¼ pound ground skinless chicken breast

½ cup grated Parmesan cheese

¼ cup plain dried bread crumbs

¼ cup chopped fresh flat-leaf parsley

¼ cup fat-free milk

1 large egg white

1 garlic clove, minced

½ teaspoon dried oregano

16 (½-inch) cubes part-skim mozzarella cheese

2 cups fat-free marinara sauce

½ cup water

8 ounces whole wheat penne

2 cups thinly sliced kale

1. Mix together the chicken, ¼ cup of the Parmesan, the bread crumbs, parsley, milk, egg white, garlic, and oregano in a large bowl until combined well. Divide the chicken mixture into 16 equal portions. Shape each portion around a mozzarella cheese cube to form 16 stuffed meatballs.

2. Meanwhile, combine the marinara sauce and water and bring to a simmer in a large skillet. Gently add the meatballs; cover and simmer, turning the meatballs a few times, until cooked through, about 10 minutes.

3. Cook the penne according to the package directions, omitting the salt if desired, and adding the kale during the last 1 minute of cooking; drain.

4. Divide the pasta-kale mixture among 4 plates; top evenly with the meatballs and sauce. Sprinkle with the remaining ¼ cup Parmesan.

PER SERVING (about 1⅓ cups pasta mixture, 4 meatballs, about ½ cup sauce, and 1 tablespoon Parmesan): 415 Cal, 6 g Total Fat, 3 g Sat Fat, 0 g Trans Fat, 30 mg Chol, 774 mg Sod, 61 g Total Carb, 11 g Fib, 30 g Prot, 276 mg Calc.
PointsPlus value: *10.*

COOK'S TIP

Cooking the kale with the pasta is not only easy but a great way to get a serving of this super-nutritious vegetable. Kale, a member of the *Brassica* (cabbage) family, is one of the healthiest greens around, as it contains a high concentration of antioxidants, including vitamins A (beta carotene), C, and K. It is also a great way to add some fiber to your diet.

Saigon Chicken in Lettuce Leaves

Makes 4 Servings

1 ounce cellophane noodles

2 tablespoons lime juice

1 tablespoon Asian fish sauce

1 tablespoon sugar

¾ pound ground skinless
   chicken breast

1 tablespoon grated peeled
   fresh ginger

½ medium cucumber, peeled
   and chopped (about 1 cup)

1 scallion, finely chopped

2 tablespoons chopped fresh
   cilantro or mint

8 Boston lettuce leaves

1. Cook the noodles according to the package directions; drain. Rinse under cold water and chop into small pieces.

2. Combine the lime juice, fish sauce, and sugar in a small bowl; mix well to dissolve the sugar.

3. Spray a large nonstick skillet with nonstick spray and set over medium-high heat. Add the chicken and cook, breaking up the chicken with a wooden spoon, until browned, about 5 minutes. Add the ginger and cook, stirring constantly, until fragrant, about 2 minutes. Transfer the mixture to a medium bowl and let cool about 2 minutes. Add the cucumber, scallion, cilantro, chopped noodles, and the lime juice mixture; mix well.

4. Place 2 lettuce leaves on each of 4 plates. Fill each lettuce leaf with ⅓ cup of the chicken mixture. Serve at once.

PER SERVING (2 lettuce leaves with a total of ⅔ cup chicken mixture): 139 Cal, 1 g Total Fat, 0 g Sat Fat, 0 g Trans Fat, 56 mg Chol, 196 mg Sod, 11 g Carb, 1 g Fib, 21 g Prot, 26 mg Calc. *PointsPlus* value: *3.*

COOK'S TIP

Asian fish sauce is a must-have ingredient in Southeast Asian countries, where it is used like soy sauce is in Japan and China. Don't be put off by the aroma of fish sauce: Its exotic taste makes the sauce authentic and delicious. It is found in the Asian section of large supermarkets and in Asian markets. Once opened, store it in the refrigerator, where it will keep indefinitely.

roasts and bakes

Chicken Baked in a Salt Crust

Makes 8 Servings

6 pounds kosher salt

3 cups water

1 (16-ounce) jar grape leaves, rinsed

3 lemons, cut into quarters

1 (4-pound) chicken, skinned, giblets discarded

1. Preheat the oven to 350°F.

2. Combine the salt and water in a large bowl, stirring until a thick paste forms.

3. Place 3 cups of this salt mixture in the bottom of a large roasting pan, spreading it out to about 6 inches larger than the chicken you will be roasting. Pack the salt dough down, then cover it completely with a double layer of about 18 overlapping grape leaves, leaving a 1-inch border of salt exposed at the edges.

4. Place the lemons inside the chicken cavity, then place the chicken on top of the grape leaves. Fold the grape leaves up to cover parts of the chicken. Use the remaining grape leaves to cover chicken entirely, creating a grape leaf "shell" to protect the meat from the salt.

5. Mound the remaining salt dough onto the grape leaf–covered chicken, shaping the crust to the bird's natural contours. Seal all cracks, but take care not to move the grape leaves underneath.

6. Roast until a meat thermometer inserted in a thigh (through the salt crust) registers 165°F, about 1 hour and 20 minutes. Let the chicken stand for about 10 minutes.

7. Crack the salt crust with a meat mallet or a clean hammer, then remove the crust in chunks, making sure it doesn't crumble onto the meat. Remove the grape leaves. Transfer the chicken to a carving board and carve.

PER SERVING (⅛ of chicken): 168 Cal, 6 g Total Fat, 2 g Sat Fat, 0 g Trans Fat, 78 mg Chol, 369 mg Sod, 0 g Carb, 0 g Fib, 26 g Prot, 13 mg Calc.
PointsPlus value: *4.*

COOK'S TIP

Talk about dramatic: A whole chicken is roasted under a salt dome, which is cracked open with a mallet before serving. Truth is, this ancient way of roasting doesn't add as much salty flavor as you might think. And it's a great way to seal in the chicken's natural juices.

Chicken Baked in a Salt Crust

Herbed Roast Chicken

Makes 8 Servings

¼ cup packed fresh flat-leaf parsley leaves plus 2 parsley stems

¼ cup packed fresh tarragon leaves plus 2 tarragon stems

¼ cup packed fresh sage leaves

2 garlic cloves, minced

1 tablespoon extra-virgin olive oil

½ teaspoon salt

¼ teaspoon black pepper

1 (4-pound) whole chicken, giblets discarded

1. Preheat the oven to 325°F.

2. Place the ¼ cup parsley, the ¼ cup tarragon, the sage, garlic, oil, salt, and pepper in a mini food processor, a spice grinder, or a clean coffee grinder. Pulse until the mixture forms a coarse paste, scraping down the sides of the bowl as necessary.

3. Using a sharp paring knife, make a few small slits in the skin of the chicken thighs and legs. Slip your fingers under these slits to open pockets between the skin and the meat. Also slip your fingers under the skin covering the breast to create large pockets over both breast halves. Rub the spice mixture into the meat under the skin. Place the remaining sprigs of parsley and tarragon inside the body cavity. If desired, tie the legs closed with kitchen string to help hold the shape of the bird during roasting.

4. Place the chicken, breast side up, in a large roasting pan. Roast until an instant-read thermometer inserted in a thigh registers 165°F, about 1 hour and 10 minutes. Transfer the chicken to a carving board and let stand for about 10 minutes before carving. Remove the skin before eating.

PER SERVING (⅛ of chicken): 168 Cal, 8 g Total Fat, 2 g Sat Fat, 0 g Trans Fat, 70 mg Chol, 216 mg Sod, 1 g Carb, 0 g Fib, 23 g Prot, 24 mg Calc.
PointsPlus value: *4.*

COOK'S TIP

Roast chicken is one of life's simplest—and best—pleasures. A fragrant rub that is spread over the meat (under the skin) provides fresh herb flavor. The secret to keeping the chicken moist is to roast it at a fairly low temperature, which also gives the herbs time to infuse the meat with their flavor.

Paprika and Garlic–Rubbed Beer Can Chicken

Makes 6 Servings

1 tablespoon paprika,
    preferably smoked

1 tablespoon sugar

2 teaspoons ground cumin

1 teaspoon garlic powder

1 teaspoon onion powder

1 teaspoon chili powder

¾ teaspoon salt

½ teaspoon black pepper

1 (3½-pound) whole chicken,
    giblets discarded

1 (12-ounce) can beer

1. Preheat the oven to 375°F. Spray a medium roasting pan with nonstick spray.

2. To make the spice paste, stir together the paprika, sugar, cumin, garlic powder, onion powder, chili powder, salt, and pepper in a small bowl. Add just enough water to form a spreadable paste. Rub the spice mixture all over the chicken.

3. Pour off one-fourth of the beer. Hold the chicken upright. Slip the beer can partway into the cavity of the chicken. Set the chicken with the can in the prepared roasting pan, standing it upright with the chicken legs and the beer can forming a secure tripod.

4. Roast the chicken until an instant-read thermometer inserted into a thigh (not touching bone) registers 165°F, 1¼–1½ hours. Transfer the chicken to a carving board. Let stand for 10 minutes, then carefully remove and discard the beer can and beer. Carve the chicken and arrange on a serving platter. Remove the chicken skin before eating.

PER SERVING (⅙ of chicken): 189 Cal, 7 g Total Fat, 2 g Sat Fat, 0 g Trans Fat, 83 mg Chol, 375 mg Sod, 3 g Carb, 0 g Fib, 27 g Prot, 26 mg Calc.
PointsPlus value: *5.*

COOK'S TIP

Cooking the chicken over an open can of beer creates flavorful steam, helping to keep it moist and giving it a subtle beer flavor. Turn this into a meal by serving the chicken with a steamed green vegetable and cooked baby potatoes tossed with fresh parsley and lemon zest (5 ounces of cooked potato for each serving will increase the *PointsPlus* value by *3*).

Rosemary Roast Chicken with Potatoes

Rosemary Roast Chicken with Potatoes

Makes 8 Servings

1 (3½ pound) chicken

4 teaspoons chopped fresh
    rosemary

2 large garlic cloves, minced

½ teaspoon salt

½ teaspoon black pepper

6 medium Yukon Gold potatoes
    (about 2 pounds), cut into
    1-inch chunks

1 cup dry white wine

1. Preheat the oven to 425°F. Spray the bottom of a broiler pan with nonstick spray.

2. To butterfly the chicken, with a large knife or poultry shears, cut the chicken down the backbone. Turn the chicken, breast side up, and push down on the backbone to flatten it slightly.

3. Combine the rosemary, garlic, ¼ teaspoon of the salt, and ¼ teaspoon of the pepper in a small bowl. Gently lift the skin from the chicken breast and legs; spread the herb mixture evenly under the skin. Place the chicken in the pan. Scatter the potatoes around the chicken; sprinkle the potatoes with the remaining ¼ teaspoon salt and ¼ teaspoon pepper.

4. Roast the chicken and potatoes for 20 minutes. Add ½ cup of the wine to the pan. Roast 15 minutes longer, then turn the potatoes and add the remaining ½ cup wine. Roast until an instant-read thermometer inserted in a thigh registers 165°F, and the potatoes are tender, about 10 minutes longer. Cut the chicken into 8 pieces and serve with the potatoes. Remove the skin from the chicken before eating.

PER SERVING (1 piece chicken with ½ cup potatoes): 247 Cal, 3 g Total Fat, 1 g Sat Fat, 0 g Trans Fat, 67 mg Chol, 225 mg Sod, 26 g Carb, 2 g Fib, 23 g Prot, 25 mg Calc.
PointsPlus value: *6.*

COOK'S TIP

Rosemary's assertive flavor goes particularly well with chicken and potatoes. To ensure the chicken cooks evenly, it is butterflied—split through the backbone and flattened. It's easy enough to do yourself, but you can ask your butcher to do it for you.

Chicken with Banana-Curry Sauce

Makes 4 Servings

2 ripe bananas, cut up

¾ cup water

⅓ cup plain low-fat yogurt

1 tablespoon curry powder

2 teaspoons canola oil

½ teaspoon salt

¼ teaspoon black pepper

4 (½-pound) bone-in chicken breast halves, skinned

1. Preheat the oven to 425°F. Spray a roasting pan with nonstick spray.

2. Puree the bananas, ¼ cup of the water, the yogurt, curry powder, oil, salt, and pepper in a food processor or blender.

3. Place the chicken in the roasting pan. Pour the curry mixture over the chicken. Roast until an instant-read thermometer inserted in a breast registers 165°F, 30–35 minutes.

4. Transfer the chicken to a platter; cover loosely with foil and to keep warm. Place the roasting pan directly on top of two burners over medium heat. Whisk in the remaining ½ cup water. Simmer, whisking up the browned bits from the bottom of the pan, until heated through. Strain the sauce through a sieve into a sauce boat; serve with the chicken.

PER SERVING (1 piece chicken with about 3 tablespoons sauce): 293 Cal, 8 g Total Fat, 2 g Sat Fat, 0 g Trans Fat, 100 mg Chol, 400 mg Sod, 16 g Carb, 2 g Fib, 38 g Prot, 67 mg Calc. *PointsPlus* value: *7*.

COOK'S TIP

Bananas lend welcome sweetness to many Caribbean-style curries. You might like to serve this dish with cooked wheat berries and a peppery watercress salad to balance the spicy-sweetness of the dish (½ cup cooked wheat berries per serving will increase the *PointsPlus* value by *3*).

Couscous-Stuffed Chicken Breasts

Makes 6 Servings

⅔ cup reduced-sodium chicken broth

½ cup couscous

3 (¾-pound) bone-in chicken breast halves, skinned and cut in half crosswise

¼ cup golden raisins

1 scallion, thinly sliced

1 teaspoon chopped fresh thyme

¼ teaspoon salt

¼ teaspoon black pepper

6 tablespoons water

2 tablespoons fig jam

½ teaspoon ground ginger

1. Bring the broth to a boil in a small saucepan; remove from the heat. Stir in the couscous; cover and let stand until all of the liquid has been absorbed, about 5 minutes.

2. Meanwhile, make a pocket in each chicken breast by inserting a sharp paring knife into the thickest part, then gently cutting back and forth to make a small pocket in the side. Do not cut through the back or sides of the breasts. Using your fingers, enlarge each pocket until it will hold about ¼ cup stuffing. Set the breasts aside.

3. Preheat the oven to 375°F. Spray a flameproof 9-inch square baking pan with nonstick spray.

4. Fluff the couscous with a fork. Add the raisins, scallion, thyme, salt, and pepper; mix well. Let the mixture cool about 5 minutes. Pack ¼ cup of the mixture into each of the breast pockets. Place the breasts in the baking pan.

5. Combine 3 tablespoons of the water, the fig jam, and ginger in a small bowl; brush half of this mixture over the chicken breasts. Bake 25 minutes. Baste with the remaining fig glaze, then continue baking until the chicken is deeply browned and an instant-read thermometer inserted in a breast registers 165°F, about 10 minutes longer. Transfer the chicken to a serving platter and keep warm. Skim any visible fat from the pan juices.

6. Place the baking pan over medium heat, mix in the remaining 3 tablespoons water, and scrape up any browned bits from the bottom of the pan. Simmer, stirring constantly, until the sauce has reduced by half, about 2 minutes. Serve the chicken with the sauce.

PER SERVING (1 piece chicken with 1 teaspoon sauce): 248 Cal, 4 g Total Fat, 1 g Sat Fat, 0 g Trans Fat, 74 mg Chol, 224 mg Sod, 21 g Carb, 1 g Fib, 30 g Prot, 25 mg Calc.
PointsPlus value: *6.*

COOK'S TIP

Couscous is small grainlike pasta that cooks in minutes and readily absorbs whatever flavors it's paired with.

Lemon-Coriander Chicken

Makes 8 Servings

¾ cup lemon juice

6 scallions, finely chopped

3 large garlic cloves, crushed
through a press

1 tablespoon ground coriander

1 tablespoon grated lemon zest

¾ teaspoon salt

½ teaspoon coarsely ground
black pepper

1 (3¼-pound) chicken,
quartered and skinned,
giblets discarded

1. Combine the lemon juice, scallions, garlic, coriander, lemon zest, salt, and pepper in a small bowl. Measure ½ cup of the juice mixture into another small bowl; cover and refrigerate.

2. Pour the remaining juice mixture into a zip-close plastic bag; add the chicken. Squeeze out the air and seal bag; turn to coat chicken. Refrigerate, turning the bag occasionally, for at least 4 hours or up to overnight.

3. Spray the grill or broiler rack with nonstick spray; prepare the grill or preheat the broiler.

4. Transfer the chicken pieces from the bag to the grill or broiler rack; discard the marinade in the bag. Grill or broil the chicken 5 inches from the heat, turning and basting occasionally with the ½ cup reserved marinade, until an instant-read thermometer inserted in a thigh registers 165°F, 15–20 minutes. Stop basting 5 minutes before the chicken is cooked. Cut each chicken quarter into 2 pieces.

PER SERVING (1 piece chicken): 142 Cal, 5 g Total Fat, 1 g Sat Fat, 0 g Trans Fat, 64 mg Chol, 176 mg Sod, 2 g Carb, 0 g Fib, 21 g Prot, 18 mg Calc.
PointsPlus value: *3.*

COOK'S TIP

Coriander has an aromatic flavor reminiscent of a blend of citrus, sage, and caraway. You can substitute the same amount of ground cumin, if you like, which will give the dish a slightly nutty, peppery taste.

Harissa and Yogurt Chicken

Makes 4 Servings

1 (3½-pound) chicken,
    quartered and skinned,
    giblets discarded

1 (8-ounce) container plain
    low-fat yogurt

⅓ cup chopped fresh mint

2 teaspoons ground cumin

1 teaspoon harissa

½ teaspoon salt

1. Preheat the oven to 400°F. Line a baking sheet with foil; spray the foil with nonstick spray.

2. Using a small, sharp knife, make 3 shallow slashes in each chicken breast, thigh, and drumstick.

3. Combine the yogurt, mint, cumin, harissa sauce, and salt in a large bowl. Add the chicken and toss to coat. Place the chicken on the baking sheet, spooning any excess sauce over the pieces. Roast until an instant-read thermometer inserted in a thigh registers 165°F, about 35 minutes.

PER SERVING (1 chicken quarter): 270 Cal, 7 g Total Fat, 2 g Sat Fat, 0 g Trans Fat, 137 g Chol, 480 mg Sod, 5 mg Carb, 1 mg Fib, 44 g Prot, 143 mg Calc.
PointsPlus value: *6.*

COOK'S TIP

Harissa is a fiery hot sauce from the Middle East made with chiles, garlic, spices, and extra-virgin olive oil. It can be purchased at specialty food stores. In this dish, the addition of yogurt and fresh mint helps tame its heat. Couscous mixed with chopped fresh mint and grated lemon zest makes a fine accompaniment (½ cup cooked couscous per serving will increase the *PointsPlus* value by *2*).

**Sweet-and-Sour
Glazed Chicken**

Sweet-and-Sour Glazed Chicken

Makes 8 Servings

½ cup canned crushed
   pineapple in juice

2 tablespoons reduced-sodium
   soy sauce

2 tablespoons honey

2 tablespoons lemon juice

1 tablespoon grated peeled
   fresh ginger

1 garlic clove, minced

1 small jalapeño pepper, seeded
   and minced

1 (4-pound) chicken, cut into 8
   pieces and skinned, giblets
   discarded

½ teaspoon cornstarch

2 teaspoons water

1. Combine the pineapple, soy sauce, honey, lemon juice, ginger, garlic, and jalapeño pepper in a large zip-close plastic bag; add the chicken. Squeeze out the air and seal the bag; turn to coat the chicken. Refrigerate, turning the bag occasionally, for at least 4 hours or up to overnight.

2. Preheat the oven to 375°F.

3. Place a rack in a roasting pan. Lift the chicken pieces from the marinade and discard the marinade. Place the chicken on the rack and bake until browned and an instant-read thermometer inserted in a thigh registers 165°F, about 35 minutes.

4. Stir the cornstarch and water in a small bowl until smooth. Transfer the chicken to a serving platter; cover and keep warm. Remove the rack from the pan and with a spoon, skim off any fat from the pan juices. Pour the pan juices into a saucepan and simmer over medium heat until the juices are reduced by half, about 2 minutes. Add the cornstarch mixture and cook, stirring constantly, until the mixture bubbles and thickens, about 10 seconds. Serve the chicken with the sauce.

PER SERVING (1 piece chicken with 2 tablespoons sauce): 199 Cal, 6 g Total Fat, 2 g Sat Fat, 0 g Trans Fat, 78 mg Chol, 210 mg Sod, 8 g Carb, 0 g Fib, 26 g Prot, 18 mg Calc. *PointsPlus* value: *5.*

COOK'S TIP

Here's a flavorful chicken dish that makes an easy dinner any night of the week, thanks to a no-fuss Asian-inspired marinade. Accompany the tasty chicken with steamed baby bok choy and cooked white and wild rice blend (½ cup cooked white and wild rice blend per serving will increase the *PointsPlus* value by *3*).

Oven-Fried Buttermilk Chicken with Black Pepper Gravy

Makes 4 Servings

½ cup plus 2 tablespoons all-purpose flour

2 large egg whites, lightly beaten

2 teaspoons dried sage

2 teaspoons dried rosemary

1 ⅓ cups cornflake crumbs

2 (½-pound) bone-in chicken breast halves, skinned

2 (6-ounce) chicken drumsticks, skinned

2 (6-ounce) chicken thighs, skinned

½ teaspoon salt

⅛ teaspoon cayenne

⅓ cup fat-free buttermilk

1 tablespoon butter

1 cup reduced-sodium chicken broth

¼ teaspoon black pepper

1. Preheat the oven to 375°F. Line a large shallow baking pan or roasting pan with foil. Place a wire rack in the pan; spray the rack with nonstick spray.

2. Put ½ cup of the flour on a sheet of wax paper. Mix together the egg whites, sage, and rosemary in a large shallow dish. Place the cornflake crumbs on a separate sheet of wax paper.

3. Put the chicken in a large bowl; sprinkle with the salt and cayenne. Add the buttermilk and turn to coat. Dip the chicken, one piece at a time, into the flour, then into the egg whites, and then into the cornflake crumbs, pressing so they adhere. Place the chicken, skinned side up, on the rack. Lightly spray the chicken with nonstick spray. Bake until golden brown and an instant-read thermometer inserted into a thigh or breast (not touching bone) registers 165°F, about 45 minutes; do not turn.

4. Meanwhile, to make the gravy, melt the butter in a small saucepan over medium heat. Whisk in the remaining 2 tablespoons flour and cook, whisking constantly, 1 minute. Gradually whisk in the chicken broth until smooth. Cook, whisking constantly, until the gravy bubbles and thickens, about 2 minutes. Stir in the black pepper.

PER SERVING (¼ of chicken and ¼ cup gravy): 310 Cal, 11 g Total Fat, 4 g Sat Fat, 0 g Trans Fat, 91 mg Chol, 635 mg Sod, 20 g Carb, 1 g Fib, 32 g Prot, 48 mg Calc. *PointsPlus* value: *8.*

COOK'S TIP

Buttermilk has long been appreciated for its ability to tenderize chicken. If you have the time, cover the buttermilk-covered chicken and refrigerate for up to several hours. Enjoy this Southern dish with some authentic sides, such as baked sweet potatoes and cooked collard or mustard greens (½ large baked sweet potato per serving will increase the *PointsPlus* value by *2*).

Tuscan Baked Chicken Breasts

Makes 6 Servings

3 (¾-pound) bone-in chicken breast halves, skinned and cut in half crosswise

3 garlic cloves, slivered

2 tablespoons chopped fresh rosemary

2 teaspoons grated lemon zest

2 teaspoons extra-virgin olive oil

½ teaspoon red pepper flakes

½ teaspoon salt

1 tablespoon balsamic vinegar

1. Preheat the oven to 400°F.

2. Toss the chicken pieces, garlic, rosemary, lemon zest, oil, pepper flakes, and salt in a zip-close plastic bag until the chicken is coated with the spices.

3. Place the chicken pieces on a rimmed baking sheet. Bake 30 minutes. Increase the oven temperature to 450°F. Sprinkle the vinegar over the chicken. Continue baking until the chicken is browned and an instant-read thermometer inserted in a breast registers 165°F, about 10 minutes longer. Transfer the chicken to a platter and let stand for about 5 minutes. Meanwhile, skim any visible fat from the pan juices. Serve the pan juices with the chicken.

PER SERVING (1 piece chicken with 2 teaspoons juices): 168 Cal, 5 g Total Fat, 1 g Sat Fat, 0 g Trans Fat, 74 mg Chol, 265 mg Sod, 1 g Carb, 0 g Fib, 27 g Prot, 18 mg Calc.
PointsPlus value: *4.*

COOK'S TIP

Lemon zest and lemon rind—what's the difference? The zest is the colored part of the rind where the flavorful lemon oil is located. It doesn't include the under layer of bitter white pith. A Microplane grater is especially good at removing only the flavorful zest.

Green Olive Roast Chicken

Makes 4 Servings

1 (3-pound) chicken, cut into 8 pieces and skinned, giblets discarded

¼ teaspoon salt

¼ teaspoon black pepper

1 pint grape or cherry tomatoes

¼ cup lemon juice

12 green olives, pitted and coarsely chopped

2 large garlic cloves, finely chopped

¼ cup water

1. Preheat the oven to 400°F. Spray a roasting pan with nonstick spray. Place the chicken in the roasting pan. Sprinkle the chicken with the salt and pepper; spray with nonstick spray (preferably extra-virgin olive oil spray).

2. Combine the tomatoes, lemon juice, olives, and garlic in a large bowl; pour over the chicken.

3. Roast the chicken 20 minutes, then spoon the tomato mixture over. Roast until an instant-read thermometer inserted in a thigh registers 165°F, 15–20 minutes longer. Transfer the chicken to a serving platter. Place the roasting pan directly on top of two burners over medium heat. Add the water and bring to a simmer, stirring up the browned bits from the bottom of the pan. Pour the tomato mixture over the chicken.

PER SERVING (2 pieces chicken with about 3 tablespoons tomato mixture): 293 Cal, 12 g Total Fat, 3 g Sat Fat, 0 g Trans Fat, 118 mg Chol, 518 mg Sod, 6 g Carb, 1 g Fib, 39 g Prot, 36 mg Calc. *PointsPlus* value: *7.*

COOK'S TIP

The bold flavor of green olives pairs perfectly with our combo of chicken, lemon, tomatoes, and garlic. This dish is excellent with whole wheat spaghetti (1 cup of cooked whole wheat spaghetti per serving will increase the *PointsPlus* value by *4*).

**Green Olive
Roast Chicken**

Bacon-Wrapped Chicken Breasts

Makes 4 Servings

6 large dried apricots, chopped (about ⅔ cup)

4 large pitted prunes, chopped (about ⅔ cup)

4 teaspoons chopped fresh rosemary

¼ teaspoon black pepper

4 (¼-pound) skinless boneless chicken breasts

4 slices turkey bacon

1. Preheat the oven to 400°F. Spray a 9-inch square baking dish with nonstick spray.

2. Mix the apricots, prunes, rosemary, and pepper in a small bowl.

3. Make a pocket in the side of each chicken breast by inserting a sharp paring knife into the thickest part, then gently cutting back and forth to make a small pocket in the side. Do not cut through to the back or the sides of the breasts. Enlarge the pockets gently with your fingers.

4. Stuff one-fourth of the dried fruit filling into each breast. Wrap a slice of bacon around each breast, to secure the opening. Place the wrapped breasts in the baking dish. Bake until the bacon is brown and crisp and the chicken breasts are cooked through, about 40 minutes. Let the chicken stand for about 5 minutes before serving.

PER SERVING (1 stuffed chicken breast): 285 Cal, 9 g Total Fat, 2 g Sat Fat, 0 g Trans Fat, 84 mg Chol, 451 mg Sod, 22 g Carb, 3 g Fib, 30 g Prot, 34 mg Calc.
PointsPlus value: 7.

COOK'S TIP

This recipe is a very simple way of making boneless chicken breasts truly special. You can use any combination of dried fruits, such as dried cranberries and cherries, and you could substitute fresh basil or oregano for the rosemary. If you like, have your butcher make the pockets in the chicken breasts for you.

Porcini-Stuffed Chicken Breasts

Makes 4 Servings

½ ounce dried porcini
   mushrooms

1 cup boiling water

1 small onion, chopped

1 celery stalk, chopped

1 tablespoon dry vermouth

1½ cups cornflakes

1 tablespoon finely chopped
   fresh sage

1 teaspoon finely chopped
   fresh thyme

¼ teaspoon salt

4 (¼-pound) skinless boneless
   chicken breasts

1. Place the mushrooms in a small bowl; pour the boiling water over them. Set aside to soak until softened, about 10 minutes. Drain, reserving the soaking liquid.

2. Spray a medium nonstick skillet with nonstick spray and set over medium heat. Add the onion and celery; cook, stirring frequently, until slightly softened, about 2 minutes. Add the softened mushrooms and cook, stirring constantly, about 1 minute. Add the vermouth and scrape up any browned bits from the bottom of the skillet. Transfer the mixture to a medium bowl. Add the cornflakes, sage, thyme, salt, and ¼ cup of the reserved mushroom liquid. Set aside until the cornflakes absorb all the liquid, about 3 minutes.

3. Preheat the oven to 350°F. Spray a 9-inch square baking dish with nonstick spray.

4. Make a pocket in the side of each chicken breast by inserting a sharp paring knife into the thickest part, then gently cutting back and forth to open a small pocket in the side. Do not cut through to the back or the sides of the breasts. Enlarge the pockets gently with your fingers.

5. Stuff one-fourth of the stuffing into each breast. Place the breasts in the baking dish. Bake, basting occasionally with the remaining mushroom liquid, until the chicken is browned on the outside and cooked through, about 40 minutes. Let the chicken stand for about 5 minutes before serving.

PER SERVING (1 stuffed chicken breast): 186 Cal, 3 g Total Fat, 1 g Sat Fat, 0 g Trans Fat, 63 mg Chol, 295 mg Sod, 13 g Carb, 1 g Fib, 25 g Prot, 27 mg Calc.
PointsPlus value: *5.*

COOK'S TIP

Porcini mushrooms, also known as cèpes (SEP), have a pungent, woodsy flavor and are highly prized. Traditionally from Italy but now cultivated in the United States, they're more affordable dried than fresh. In this easy baked dish, the dried mushrooms are reconstituted in hot water, then used to make a delicious sauce.

Chicken Rollatini

Makes 6 Servings

6 (¼-pound) skinless boneless chicken breasts

½ teaspoon salt

18 arugula leaves, tough stems removed

1 ounce reduced-fat soft goat cheese

12 marinated sun-dried tomatoes, patted dry and halved

¼ cup apple juice

1½ teaspoons salt-free lemon-pepper seasoning

1. Preheat the oven to 350°F. Spray a 9 × 13-inch baking dish with nonstick spray.

2. Place a sheet of plastic wrap on a work surface, place a chicken breast on top of it, then cover with a second sheet of plastic wrap. Pound the breast to a ¼-inch thickness with a meat mallet or a heavy saucepan. Remove the top layer of plastic wrap, set the chicken breast aside on its bottom layer of plastic wrap, and repeat with the remaining chicken breasts.

3. Top each breast with 3 arugula leaves. Spread 2 teaspoons goat cheese evenly across the leaves on each breast. Place 4 sun-dried tomato halves on the cheese. Roll the chicken breasts up, pulling off plastic wrap as you go. Place the breasts, seam side down, in the baking dish. Sprinkle the apple juice over the chicken, then sprinkle with the lemon-pepper seasoning.

4. Bake, basting occasionally with the pan juices, until the chicken is cooked through, about 45 minutes. Let the chicken stand for about 5 minutes before serving.

PER SERVING (1 stuffed chicken breast): 220 Cal, 8 g Total Fat, 2 g Sat Fat, 0 g Trans Fat, 71 mg Chol, 332 mg Sod, 11 g Carb, 2 g Fib, 28 g Prot, 44 mg Calc.
PointsPlus value: *6.*

COOK'S TIP

Can't find arugula at your market? Shred escarole and use it instead. Or substitute baby spinach leaves and grind some black pepper on top of the cheese for a little flavor boost.

Hoisin Chicken Drumettes

Makes 4 Servings

⅓ cup hoisin sauce

¼ cup dry white wine

2 large garlic cloves, crushed through a press

2 teaspoons grated peeled fresh ginger

2 pounds chicken-wing drumsticks (drumettes), skinned, (about 20)

1. Combine the hoisin sauce, wine, garlic, and ginger in a zip-close plastic bag; add the chicken. Squeeze out the air and seal the bag; turn to coat the chicken. Refrigerate, turning the bag occasionally, for at least 2 hours or up to overnight.

2. Preheat the oven to 425°F. Line the bottom of a baking sheet with foil; spray the foil with nonstick spray. Place the chicken in a single layer on the baking sheet. Roast until the chicken is browned and cooked through, 20–25 minutes.

PER SERVING (5 chicken-wing drumsticks): 218 Cal, 5 g Total Fat, 2 g Sat Fat, 0 g Trans Fat, 3 mg Chol, 367 mg Sod, 6 g Carb, 1 g Fib, 30 g Prot, 28 mg Calc.
PointsPlus value: *5.*

COOK'S TIP

For a little crunch sprinkle the chicken with 2 teaspoons toasted sesame seeds just before serving. To toast the seeds, place them in a small dry skillet over medium-low heat. Cook, shaking the pan, until fragrant, 1 to 2 minutes. Transfer the toasted seeds to a plate to cool.

Moroccan Chicken Skinnies

Makes 6 Servings

1 medium onion, finely chopped

2 garlic cloves, minced

1 pound chicken tenders, chopped

1 teaspoon ground cumin

1 teaspoon ground ginger

1 teaspoon turmeric

½ teaspoon salt

¼ cup reduced-sodium chicken broth

¼ cup chopped fresh flat-leaf parsley

¼ cup sliced almonds

¼ cup currants or raisins

2 large egg whites, lightly beaten

1 tablespoon sugar

1½ teaspoons ground cinnamon

6 (14 × 18-inch) sheets phyllo dough, thawed according to the package directions

1. Spray a large skillet with nonstick spray and set over medium heat. Add the onion and garlic; cook, stirring frequently, until softened, about 3 minutes. Add the chicken and cook, stirring occasionally, until lightly browned, about 5 minutes.

2. Add the cumin, ginger, turmeric, and salt; cook, stirring constantly, until fragrant, about 30 seconds. Add the broth and bring the mixture to a simmer, scraping up any browned bits from the bottom of the skillet. Transfer the mixture to a large bowl; stir in the parsley, almonds, and currants. Set aside to cool, about 10 minutes, then stir in the egg whites.

3. Preheat the oven to 350°F. Line a rimmed baking sheet with parchment paper or a nonstick silicone baking mat. Mix the sugar and cinnamon together in a small bowl.

4. Place 1 sheet of phyllo dough on a work surface with one long side close to you; cut the sheet in half crosswise. Sprinkle both halves with a dash of the cinnamon-sugar. Spread a scant ¼ cup of the filling on each half, placing the filling ½ inch from the edge that is closest to you, spreading it out in a 2-inch-thick line, and leaving a ½-inch border on each side. Fold the short sides of the dough over filling, then roll up the packet, creating a large egg roll. Place, seam side down, on the prepared baking sheet. Repeat with the remaining 5 sheets of phyllo, the cinnamon-sugar, and the filling, making a total of 12 rolls. Lightly spray each roll with nonstick spray. Bake until golden brown, about 45 minutes.

PER SERVING (2 pockets): **241 Cal, 5 g Total Fat, 1 g Sat Fat, 0 g Trans Fat, 46 mg Chol, 364 mg Sod, 26 g Carb, 2 g Fib, 21 g Prot, 45 mg Calc.**
PointsPlus value: *6.*

COOK'S TIP

While these chicken bundles, flavored with sweet spices and wrapped in phyllo, take some time to prepare, they make an elegant choice for a buffet or potluck supper. To save time on serving day, bake the pockets ahead and freeze them in zip-close plastic freezer bags. Don't defrost them—simply reheat in a 350°F oven until hot and crisp, about 15 minutes.

**Moroccan
Chicken Skinnies**

Thai-Style Grilled Chicken

Makes 4 Servings

1 cup light (reduced-fat)
 coconut milk

2 tablespoons chopped fresh
 cilantro

2 tablespoons Asian fish sauce

2 large garlic cloves, crushed
 through a press

½ teaspoon black pepper

4 (½-pound) whole chicken
 legs, skinned

1. Combine the coconut milk, cilantro, fish sauce, garlic, and pepper in a zip-close plastic bag; add the chicken. Squeeze out the air and seal the bag; turn to coat the chicken. Refrigerate, turning the bag occasionally, for at least 4 hours or up to overnight.

2. Spray the grill or broiler rack with nonstick spray. Preheat the grill to medium or preheat the broiler.

3. Transfer the chicken from the bag to the grill rack; discard all but ¼ cup of the marinade. Transfer the reserved marinade to a small saucepan and bring to a rolling boil. Remove from the heat. Grill or broil the chicken 5 inches from the heat, 10 minutes. Baste with the reserved marinade. Turn the chicken and grill or broil until an instant-read thermometer inserted in a thigh registers 165°F, about 5 minutes longer.

PER SERVING (1 leg): 210 Cal, 9 g Total Fat, 4 g Sat Fat, 0 g Trans Fat, 83 mg Chol, 218 mg Sod, 3 g Carb, 0 g Fib, 29 g Prot, 34 mg Calc.
PointsPlus value: *5.*

COOK'S TIP

Be sure not to confuse light coconut milk with sweetened cream of coconut, which is used primarily for beverages and desserts and has a much higher calorie and fat content. In our recipe, it is the coconut milk in the marinade that makes this dish anything but ordinary.

Caribbean Grilled Drumsticks

Makes 4 Servings

¼ cup lemon juice

3 tablespoons packed dark brown sugar

2 large garlic cloves, crushed through a press

1 tablespoon Jamaican jerk seasoning

½ teaspoon salt

8 (¼-pound) skinless chicken drumsticks

1. Combine the lemon juice, sugar, garlic, jerk seasoning, and salt in a zip-close plastic bag; add the chicken. Squeeze out the air and seal the bag; turn to coat the chicken. Refrigerate, turning the bag occasionally, for at least 4 hours or up to overnight.

2. Spray the grill or broiler rack with nonstick spray. Preheat the grill to medium or preheat the broiler.

3. Transfer the chicken from the bag to the grill rack; discard the marinade. Grill or broil the chicken 5 inches from the heat, 10 minutes. Turn the chicken and grill or broil until an instant-read thermometer inserted in a drumstick registers 165°F, about 5 minutes longer.

PER SERVING (2 drumsticks): 159 Cal, 4 g Total Fat, 1 g Sat Fat, 0 g Trans Fat, 102 mg Chol, 74 mg Sod, 3 g Carb, 0 g Fib, 26 g Prot, 28 mg Calc.
PointsPlus value: *4.*

COOK'S TIP

For a taste of the tropics, these chicken drumsticks are slathered with a mix of lemon juice, brown sugar, and a good dose of Jamaican jerk seasoning (a blend of thyme, cayenne, and allspice). The result? Chicken with the perfect balance of sweetness and peppery heat.

Beer-Broiled Chicken Drumsticks

Beer-Broiled Chicken Drumsticks

Makes 4 Servings

1 (12-ounce) bottle dark beer

1 tablespoon seeded and
  minced jalapeño pepper

3 garlic cloves, crushed
  through a press

2 teaspoons five-spice powder

½ teaspoon salt

8 (¼-pound) skinless chicken
  drumsticks

1. Combine 1 cup of the beer, the jalapeño pepper, garlic, five-spice powder, and salt in a zip-close plastic bag; add the chicken. Squeeze out the air and seal the bag; turn to coat the chicken. Refrigerate, turning the bag occasionally, for at least 2 hours or up to overnight.

2. Spray the broiler rack with nonstick spray; preheat the broiler.

3. Transfer the chicken from the bag to the broiler rack; discard the marinade. Broil the chicken 5 inches from the heat, turning occasionally and basting with the remaining ½ cup beer, until an instant-read thermometer inserted in a drumstick registers 165°F, about 15 minutes. Stop basting 5 minutes before the chicken is cooked.

PER SERVING (2 chicken drumsticks): 201 Cal, 5 g Total Fat, 1 g Sat Fat, 0 g Trans Fat, 0 mg Chol, 412 mg Sod, 6 g Carb, 0 g Fib, 27 g Prot, 37 mg Calc.
PointsPlus value: *5.*

COOK'S TIP

If you want to add a bit of smoky flavor to the marinade, substitute 1 teaspoon finely chopped chipotle en adobo for the jalapeño pepper. Also, skinless bone-in chicken thighs can be used instead of the drumsticks.

Spicy Oven-Fried Chicken

Makes 8 Servings

½ cup low-fat buttermilk

2 teaspoons hot pepper sauce

8 (5-ounce) skinless bone-in
   chicken thighs

½ cup seasoned dry bread
   crumbs

½ cup ground almonds

¼ teaspoon salt

½ teaspoon black pepper

1. Preheat the oven to 425°F. Line a roasting pan with foil; spray the rack of the roasting pan with nonstick spray and place it in the pan.

2. Combine the buttermilk and hot pepper sauce in a 9 × 13-inch baking dish. Place the chicken in the buttermilk mixture, turning to coat; set aside.

3. Combine the bread crumbs, almonds, salt, and pepper on a shallow plate. Dip the chicken into the crumb mixture, turning to coat all sides. Discard the excess buttermilk mixture and bread crumb mixture. Place the chicken on the rack; lightly spray the chicken with nonstick spray.

4. Bake 20 minutes, then lightly spray the chicken again with nonstick spray. Bake until the chicken is golden and an instant-read thermometer inserted in a thigh registers 165°F, about 15 minutes longer.

PER SERVING (1 chicken thigh): 222 Cal, 11 g Total Fat, 3 g Sat Fat, 0 g Trans Fat, 58 mg Chol, 207 mg Sod, 7 g Carb, 1 g Fib, 22 g Prot, 69 mg Calc.
PointsPlus value: *6.*

COOK'S TIP

How did we ensure that our oven "fried" chicken is finger-lickin' good? First, the chicken is dipped in buttermilk to keep it juicy and tender, then coated with seasoned bread crumbs and ground almonds for crunch and a delicious nutty flavor.

Spicy Oven–Fried Chicken

**Chicken-Couscous Bake
with Capers and Tomatoes**

Chicken-Couscous Bake with Capers and Tomatoes

Makes 4 Servings

4 (5-ounce) skinless boneless chicken thighs

¼ teaspoon black pepper

⅛ teaspoon salt

1½ cups chicken broth

2 tablespoons chopped, drained capers

1 cup couscous

1 cup cherry tomatoes

1. Preheat the oven to 425°F. Spray a 9-inch square baking dish with nonstick spray; set aside.

2. Sprinkle the chicken with the pepper and salt. Spray a large nonstick skillet with nonstick spray and set over medium-high heat. Add the chicken and cook until browned, about 3 minutes on each side. Transfer the chicken to a plate.

3. Add the broth and capers to the skillet, scraping any browned bits from the bottom of the pan. Bring the mixture to a simmer.

4. Spread the couscous over the bottom of the baking dish; pour the broth mixture over the couscous and stir to combine. Place the chicken on top of the couscous, then add the tomatoes. Cover the dish tightly with foil and bake until the chicken is cooked through and the broth has been absorbed, about 20 minutes.

5. Transfer the chicken and tomatoes to serving plates. Fluff the couscous with a fork and serve with the chicken.

PER SERVING (1 chicken thigh with about ¾ cup couscous mixture): 418 Cal, 12 g Total Fat, 4 g Sat Fat, 0 g Trans Fat, 88 mg Chol, 660 mg Sod, 36 g Carb, 3 g Fib, 38 g Prot, 50 mg Calc. *PointsPlus* value: *10*.

COOK'S TIP

If you're looking for additional fiber, look for whole wheat couscous at your supermarket. Also, check out the variety of seasoned chicken broths now available in markets. We used chicken broth here, but you might like to try this dish with vegetable broth instead.

Drumsticks Roasted with Garlic

Makes 4 Servings

4 celery stalks, cut into ½-inch pieces

1 large onion, chopped

1 large Golden Delicious apple, cored and chopped

2 teaspoons finely chopped fresh tarragon

1 teaspoon finely chopped fresh thyme

2 bay leaves

½ teaspoon salt

¼ teaspoon black pepper

8 (5-ounce) chicken drumsticks, skinned

1 large head garlic, broken into cloves and peeled

1. Preheat the oven to 350°F. Spray a 9 × 13-inch baking pan with nonstick spray.

2. Combine the celery, onion, apple, tarragon, and thyme in a large bowl; turn into the baking pan and spread out, making a bed for the drumsticks. Tuck the bay leaves into the vegetables, then sprinkle the salt and pepper over the mixture. Lay the drumsticks on top, then tuck in the garlic cloves, pushing them down among the vegetables.

3. Cover the baking pan and bake until the vegetables are soft and an instant-read thermometer inserted in a drumstick registers 165°F, about 1 hour and 15 minutes.

4. Discard the bay leaves. Place 2 drumsticks in each of 4 bowls, then spoon the vegetables and roasted garlic around them, like a stew.

PER SERVING (2 drumsticks with 1 cup vegetables and sauce): **207 Cal, 4 g Total Fat, 1 g Sat Fat, 0 g Trans Fat, 98 mg Chol, 402 mg Sod, 16 g Carb, 3 g Fib, 27 g Prot, 67 mg Calc.** *PointsPlus* value: *5.*

COOK'S TIP

Baking the garlic cloves whole mellows their flavor, making them quite delectable. Squeeze out the pulp and eat it with the chicken, or spread it on crisp slices of toasted French baguette (1 ounce thinly sliced baguette for each serving will up the *PointsPlus* value by *2*).

**Drumsticks Roasted
with Garlic**

Apricot Chicken

Makes 6 Servings

1 (15-ounce) can apricot halves in juice, undrained

2 tablespoons orange juice

1½ tablespoons honey

2 teaspoons chopped fresh rosemary

1 teaspoon grated orange zest

6 (½-pound) whole chicken legs, skinned

2 cups hot cooked couscous

1. Preheat the oven to 350°F. Spray a 9 × 13-inch baking pan with nonstick spray.

2. Place the apricot halves and their juice, the orange juice, honey, rosemary, and orange zest in a food processor. Pulse until smooth, scraping down the sides of the bowl as necessary.

3. Place the chicken legs in the pan, arranging them to fit in one layer. Spoon the apricot puree over the chicken; spread it smooth. Bake, uncovered, until an instant-read thermometer inserted in a thigh registers 165°F and the glaze is golden, basting occasionally with the pan juices, about 1 hour and 10 minutes. Serve with the couscous.

PER SERVING (1 leg and ⅓ cup couscous): 298 Cal, 7 g Total Fat, 2 g Sat Fat, 0 g Trans Fat, 81 mg Chol, 214 mg Sod, 28 g Carb, 2 g Fib, 30 g Prot, 43 mg Calc.
PointsPlus value: *7.*

COOK'S TIP

Round out the meal by serving the chicken with steamed fresh asparagus or broccoli.

How to Carve Chicken (or Turkey) Like a Pro

It's easier than you think to carve chicken or turkey. All it takes is a sharp boning knife, a large cutting or carving board, and a bit of patience. You might want to "practice" on a broiler-fryer or roaster before tackling a holiday turkey. Once you get the hang of it, carving poultry will be as easy as pie. Always let a roasted bird rest for about 10 minutes before carving to allow the internal juices to redistribute, keeping the bird juicy.

TO BEGIN

- Place the chicken on a cutting or carving board and remove any string.

REMOVE THE LEGS

- With the tip of a boning knife, cut through the skin between the breast and leg. Continue to cut down until you reach the thigh joint.

- Grab the leg and bend it outward until the joint pops.

- With your knife, cut through the joint, separating the leg from the body. Repeat on the other side.

- Separate the drumsticks from the thighs by cutting through the joint that connects them. Put the drumsticks on a platter.

SLICE THE THIGH MEAT

- Cut along each side of the thighbone to remove the meat in two pieces.

- Cut the thigh meat across the grain into thick slices. Arrange on the platter. Repeat with the second thigh.

REMOVE THE WINGS

- Pull a wing away from the body so you can see where it is attached to the body. Use the tip of your knife to find the joint where the wing meets the body and cut through the joint.

- Put the wing on the cutting board. Cut through the wing joints to separate the wing into 3 parts; discard the wing tip or save it for stock.

- Arrange the remaining wing joints on the platter. Repeat with the second wing.

SLICE THE BREAST MEAT

- Insert a carving fork into the meat on one side of the breast. Cut into the breast on the other side of the breastbone, cutting as close to the bone as possible.

- Continue slicing down following the contour of the bone to separate it from the meat. Help it along with your knife until the breast meat is separated from the breastbone in one piece. Repeat on the other side.

- Cut the breast meat across the grain into thick slices and arrange on the platter.

Red-Cooked Chicken and Chestnuts

Makes 8 Servings

8 (5-ounce) skinless bone-in chicken thighs

1 cup reduced-sodium chicken broth

¼ cup reduced-sodium soy sauce

¼ cup dry sherry or dry vermouth

1 cup jarred steamed peeled chestnuts

⅓ cup slivered peeled fresh ginger

4 scallions, cut into 3-inch pieces

2 garlic cloves, minced

2 teaspoons sugar

2 (4-inch) cinnamon sticks

2 star anise pods

1 large bunch watercress, cleaned and stemmed

1. Adjust the racks to divide the oven into thirds. Preheat the oven to 350°F.

2. Spray a Dutch oven with nonstick spray and set over medium heat. Add the chicken and cook until lightly browned, about 2 minutes on each side.

3. Add the broth, soy sauce, and sherry, scraping up any browned bits from the bottom of the pan. Stir in the chestnuts, ginger, scallions, garlic, sugar, cinnamon sticks, and anise pods; bring to a simmer.

4. Remove the Dutch oven from the heat. Cover and bake in the lower third of the oven for 1 hour and 20 minutes. Add the watercress, laying it on top of the stew. Cover and bake until the chicken is falling off the bone and the watercress has wilted, about 15 minutes longer. Discard the cinnamon sticks and anise pods. Serve the chicken, vegetables, and sauce in bowls.

PER SERVING (1 chicken thigh with about ⅓ cup vegetables and sauce): 229 Cal, 9 g Total Fat, 2 g Sat Fat, 0 g Trans Fat, 72 mg Chol, 357 mg Sod, 13 g Carb, 2 g Fib, 22 g Prot, 59 mg Calc.
PointsPlus value: *6.*

COOK'S TIP

"Red cooking" is a traditional Chinese cooking technique, where the ingredients are slowly braised in a wine and soy sauce broth. In fact, the term "red cooking" is a reference to the color soy sauce sometimes takes on after it has stewed. Serve this dish with wheat berries (½ cup cooked wheat berries per serving will increase the *PointsPlus* value by *3*).

Red-Cooked Chicken and Chestnuts

Jerk Chicken
and Plantains

Jerk Chicken and Plantains

Makes 8 Servings

2 tablespoons salt-free dry jerk
    seasoning

¾ teaspoon salt

8 (5-ounce) skinless bone-in
    chicken thighs

1 large onion, coarsely chopped

1 green bell pepper, chopped

1 large ripe plantain, peeled,
    halved lengthwise, and cut
    into ½-inch pieces

1 (14½-ounce) can diced
    tomatoes, drained

1. Preheat the oven to 350°F. Spray a 9 × 13-inch baking pan with nonstick spray.

2. Combine the jerk seasoning and salt in a cup. Rub into the chicken; set aside about 5 minutes.

3. Toss together the onion, bell pepper, plantain, and tomatoes in a large bowl. Spread this mixture into the baking pan. Place the chicken on top. Cover and bake until the plantains are soft and the chicken is falling off the bone, about 1 hour and 15 minutes.

PER SERVING (1 chicken thigh with scant ½ cup vegetables): 217 Cal, 8 g Total Fat, 2 g Sat Fat, 0 g Trans Fat, 57 mg Chol, 334 mg Sod, 17 g Carb, 2 g Fib, 20 g Prot, 50 mg Calc. *PointsPlus* value: *6.*

COOK'S TIP

If you'd like to make your own jerk seasoning, in a mini food processor or spice grinder, combine 2 teaspoons chili powder, 2 teaspoons dried thyme, 1 teaspoon ground cinnamon, ½ teaspoon ground ginger, ½ teaspoon ground allspice, ¼ teaspoon garlic powder, and at least ⅛ or up to ½ teaspoon cayenne.

Greek Chicken Thighs

Makes 6 Servings

1 (10-ounce) package frozen chopped spinach, thawed and squeezed dry

2 ounces feta cheese, crumbled

3 tablespoons chopped fresh dill

1 teaspoon grated lemon zest

6 (3-ounce) skinless boneless chicken thighs

6 cherry tomatoes, quartered

12 pitted green olives, rinsed and chopped

1 teaspoon lemon juice

1. Adjust the racks to divide the oven into thirds. Preheat the oven to 375°F. Spray a shallow baking dish or au gratin dish with nonstick spray.

2. Mix the spinach, cheese, 1 tablespoon of the dill, and the lemon zest in a medium bowl. Make 6 football-shaped balls of this mixture, using about 2 tablespoons for each ball.

3. Lay the chicken thighs on a work surface and butterfly them: Cut them almost in half, horizontally, then press them open. Place a ball of the stuffing mixture on one side of a thigh; roll up the thigh. Place them, seam side down, in the baking dish. Repeat with the remaining thighs and stuffing balls.

4. Combine the tomatoes, olives, and the remaining 2 tablespoons dill in a small bowl; spoon over the stuffed thighs. Sprinkle lemon juice over the chicken.

5. Cover and bake in the lower third of the oven for 30 minutes. Uncover and bake until the chicken is browned on the outside and cooked through, basting twice with the sauce in the baking dish, about 10 minutes longer.

PER SERVING (1 stuffed thigh): 183 Cal, 10 g Total Fat, 4 g Sat Fat, 0 g Trans Fat, 61 mg Chol, 345 mg Sod, 3 g Carb, 1 g Fib, 20 g Prot, 117 mg Calc.
PointsPlus value: *5.*

COOK'S TIP

The best way to buy feta is from a block that's submerged in water. This keeps it fresh and moist—not dry and crumbly.

Tandoori-Style Chicken with Cucumber-Yogurt Sauce

Makes 4 Servings

1½ cups plain fat-free yogurt

2 tablespoons lemon juice

1 tablespoon paprika

1 tablespoon minced peeled fresh ginger

1 tablespoon pickled jalapeño pepper, minced

2 large garlic cloves, minced

2 teaspoons curry powder

½ teaspoon ground cumin

½ teaspoon ground cinnamon

4 (¼-pound) skinless boneless chicken thighs

½ cucumber, peeled, seeded, and grated

½ teaspoon salt

1. Combine 1 cup of the yogurt, the lemon juice, paprika, ginger, jalapeño, garlic, curry powder, cumin, and cinnamon in a large zip-close plastic bag; add the chicken. Squeeze out the air and seal the bag; turn to coat the chicken. Refrigerate, turning the bag occasionally, for at least 1 hour or up to 8 hours.

2. Meanwhile, to make the sauce, stir together the remaining ½ cup yogurt, the cucumber, and salt in a small bowl. Cover and refrigerate.

3. Preheat the oven to 450°F. Line a large shallow baking pan with foil. Place a wire rack in the pan; spray the rack with nonstick spray.

4. Remove the chicken from the marinade and place on the rack. Discard the marinade. Bake until the chicken is cooked through, 25–30 minutes. Serve with the yogurt sauce.

PER SERVING (1 chicken thigh and about 2 tablespoons sauce): 213 Cal, 9 g Total Fat, 3 g Sat Fat, 0 g Trans Fat, 71 mg Chol, 393 mg Sod, 5 g Carb, 0 g Fib, 26 g Prot, 123 mg Calc. *PointsPlus* value: *5.*

COOK'S TIP

Tandoori chicken is a popular dish in India. The name tandoori comes from the word tandoor, the cylindrical clay oven in which the chicken is traditionally cooked. Tandoori chicken can be mild, medium, or spicy hot. A tomato salad and brown rice would make fine accompaniments (½ cup cooked brown rice per serving will increase the *PointsPlus* value by *3*).

Chicken Meat Loaf

Makes 6 Servings

1 onion, chopped

2 celery stalks, chopped

2 Golden Delicious apples, cored and finely chopped

1½ pounds ground skinless chicken breast

2 large egg whites, lightly beaten

1 cup fresh whole wheat bread crumbs

2 tablespoons chopped fresh dill

1 teaspoon grated lemon zest

½ teaspoon salt

¼ teaspoon freshly grated nutmeg

¼ teaspoon black pepper

2 teaspoons honey mustard

1. Spray a medium nonstick skillet with nonstick spray and set over medium heat. Add the onion and celery; cook, stirring frequently, until slightly softened, about 2 minutes. Add the apples, reduce the heat to low, and cook, stirring occasionally, until the apples are quite soft, the onion is golden, and the mixture is very fragrant, about 8 minutes. Transfer to a large bowl and let cool 15 minutes.

2. Preheat the oven to 350°F. Spray a 5 × 9-inch loaf pan with nonstick spray.

3. Add the chicken, egg whites, bread crumbs, dill, lemon zest, salt, nutmeg, and pepper to the onion mixture; mix until well combined. Spoon into the loaf pan and pack down. Spread the mustard over the top.

4. Bake until an instant-read thermometer inserted into the middle of the meat loaf registers 165°F, about 1 hour and 15 minutes. Let stand for about 5 minutes, then unmold and cut into slices.

PER SERVING (⅙ of meat loaf): 203 Cal, 4 g Total Fat, 1 g Sat Fat, 0 g Trans Fat, 68 mg Chol, 351 mg Sod, 13 g Carb, 2 g Fib, 27 g Prot, 33 mg Calc.
PointsPlus value: *5.*

COOK'S TIP

To make fresh bread crumbs, leave 2 or 3 slices of whole wheat bread overnight on the countertop. Break the bread into large pieces, then grind it in a food processor or mini food processor until crumbs form.

Chicken Meat Loaf

from the grill

Grilled Whole Herbed Chicken

Makes 6 Servings

5 garlic cloves, thinly sliced

1 tablespoon extra-virgin
  olive oil

1 tablespoon grated lemon zest

1 tablespoon chopped fresh
  rosemary

1 teaspoon salt

¼ teaspoon black pepper

1 (3½–4-pound) chicken,
  giblets discarded

½ onion, peeled and halved

½ lemon, halved

1. Spray the grill rack with nonstick spray; prepare the grill for indirect cooking and maintain a medium-hot fire.

2. Combine the garlic, oil, lemon zest, rosemary, salt, and pepper in a small bowl; mix well. Using your fingers loosen the skin over the chicken breasts, legs, and thighs. Rub the garlic mixture into the meat under the skin. Place the onion and lemon inside the body cavity. Tuck the wing tips under the chicken and tie the legs closed with kitchen string to help hold the shape of the bird during grilling.

3. Place the chicken on the indirect heat section of the grill rack (away from the heat source), breast side up. Cover the grill and grill, without turning, until an instant-read thermometer inserted in a thigh registers 165°F, about 1 hour and 50 minutes. Transfer the chicken to a carving board and let stand for about 10 minutes before carving. Remove the skin before eating.

PER SERVING (⅙ of chicken): 198 Cal, 9 g Total Fat, 2 g Sat Fat, 0 g Trans Fat, 81 mg Chol, 473 mg Sod, 1 g Carb, 0 g Fib, 27 g Prot, 20 mg Calc.
PointsPlus value: *5.*

COOK'S TIP

Take advantage of having the grill on and cook up some sides for this tasty chicken. Toss thick slices of portobello mushrooms with salt, pepper, and nonstick cooking spray and grill just until softened. At the same time, put husked and silked ears of corn on the grill and grill, turning, until tender and browned in spots.

Grilled Lemon-Orange Chicken with Gremolata

Makes 8 Servings

2 large lemons

4 large garlic cloves

1½ teaspoons salt

1½ cups orange juice

⅛ teaspoon cayenne

2 (3-pound) chickens, cut into quarters, skinned, and first two wing joints removed, giblets discarded

½ cup loosely packed fresh flat-leaf parsley leaves

1. Grate the zest from 1 lemon and set aside. Using vegetable peeler, remove the zest from the remaining lemon in strips, leaving the bitter white pith behind. Squeeze the juice from the lemons; set aside. Using the side of a large knife, mash 2 of the garlic cloves with ½ teaspoon of the salt until it forms a paste.

2. Combine the orange juice, lemon juice, strips of lemon zest, garlic paste, remaining 1 teaspoon salt, and the cayenne in a jumbo zip-close plastic bag (or divide between 2 large zip-close plastic bags) and add the chicken. Squeeze out the air and seal the bag; turn to coat the chicken. Refrigerate, turning the bag occasionally, for at least 2 hours or up to 6 hours.

3. Meanwhile, spray the grill rack with nonstick spray; prepare a medium-high fire.

4. Remove the chicken from the marinade; discard the marinade. Place the chicken on the grill rack and grill, turning, until an instant-read thermometer inserted in a thigh registers 165°F, about 25 minutes.

5. To make the gremolata, finely chop the remaining 2 garlic cloves with the parsley; stir in the grated lemon zest. Transfer the chicken to a medium serving platter and sprinkle with the gremolata.

PER SERVING (1 chicken quarter): 240 Cal, 9 g Total Fat, 2 g Sat Fat, 0 g Trans Fat, 108 mg Chol, 431 mg Sod, 2 g Carb, 0 g Fib, 35 g Prot, 25 mg Calc.
PointsPlus value: *6.*

COOK'S TIP

Sprinkling gremolata (grehm-oh-LAH-duh) is an easy way to add a bit of bold flavor to lots of dishes, including steamed green beans, boiled baby potatoes, whole wheat spaghetti, and broiled or grilled fish. If you like, substitute orange or lime zest for the lemon or use a combination.

Chicken Under a Brick

Makes 6 Servings

1 (3½–4-pound) chicken, giblets discarded

3 tablespoons balsamic vinegar

3 tablespoons honey

3 garlic cloves, minced

1 tablespoon extra-virgin olive oil

1 teaspoon dried oregano

1 teaspoon salt

¼ teaspoon black pepper

1. Spray the grill rack with nonstick spray; prepare the grill for indirect cooking and maintain a medium-hot fire. Wrap 2 bricks with heavy-duty aluminum foil.

2. To spatchcock the chicken, with a sharp knife or poultry shears, remove the wings from the chicken at the first joint. Then remove the backbone and spread the chicken open, like a book, skin side down. Using a paring knife, cut along each side of the breastbone. Run your thumbs along both sides of the breastbone and pull the white cartilage out, so that the chicken can lie flat. Remove the skin and prick the chicken all over with the tip of a knife.

3. Combine the vinegar, honey, garlic, oil, and oregano in a large zip-close plastic bag; add the chicken. Squeeze out the air and seal the bag; turn to coat the chicken. Refrigerate, turning the bag occasionally, for at least 30 minutes or up to overnight.

4. Lift the chicken from the marinade and sprinkle with the salt and pepper. Discard the marinade. Place the chicken on the indirect heat section of the grill rack (away from the heat source). Place the bricks on top of the chicken and close the grill. Grill 30 minutes. Remove the bricks and turn the chicken over. Grill until an instant-read thermometer inserted in a thigh registers 165°F, about 15 minutes longer. Transfer the chicken to a carving board and let stand for about 10 minutes before carving.

PER SERVING (⅙ of chicken): 210 Cal, 8 g Total Fat, 2 g Sat Fat, 0 g Trans Fat, 92 mg Chol, 482 mg Sod, 2 g Carb, 0 g Fib, 30 g Prot, 18 mg Calc.
PointsPlus value: *5.*

COOK'S TIP

When grilling a whole chicken, we sometimes split it open so it will lie flat on the grill and cook evenly and quickly. The method we use to open chickens is called spatchcocking. It is similar to butterflying except that spatchcocking refers only to poultry, whereas butterflying includes poultry, meat, and fish.

Grilled Citrus-Basil Chicken with Agave Nectar

Makes 6 Servings

2 tablespoons grated lime zest (about 3 large limes)

¼ cup lime juice

¼ cup orange juice

2 tablespoons chopped fresh basil

1 tablespoon medium or dark agave nectar

2 large garlic cloves, minced

2 teaspoons extra-virgin olive oil

1 teaspoon dried oregano

1 teaspoon salt

¼ teaspoon black pepper

1 (3½-pound) chicken, cut into 6 pieces, skinned, giblets discarded

1 lime, cut into 6 wedges

1. To make the marinade, combine the lime zest and juice, orange juice, basil, agave nectar, garlic, oil, oregano, salt, and pepper in a small bowl. Transfer half of the lime mixture to a covered container and refrigerate.

2. Transfer the remaining lime mixture to a large zip-close plastic bag and add the chicken. Squeeze out the air and seal the bag; turn to coat the chicken. Refrigerate, turning the bag occasionally, for at least 2 hours or up to overnight.

3. Meanwhile, spray the grill rack with nonstick spray; prepare the grill for a medium-hot fire.

4. Remove the chicken from the marinade; discard the marinade. Place the chicken on the grill rack and grill, turning occasionally, until an instant-read thermometer inserted in a thigh registers 165°F, 20–30 minutes.

5. Pour the reserved lime mixture into a small saucepan and bring to a simmer. Transfer the chicken to a medium serving platter and spoon the lime sauce over. Serve with the lime wedges.

PER SERVING (1 piece chicken with about 1 tablespoon sauce): 212 Cal, 8 g Total Fat, 2 g Sat Fat, 0 g Trans Fat, 81 mg Chol, 383 mg Sod, 7 g Carb, 1 g Fib, 27 g Prot, 29 mg Calc. *PointPlus* value: *5*.

COOK'S TIP

Turn this citrusy chicken into a complete meal by serving grilled ears of corn and an heirloom tomato salad sprinkled with torn fresh oregano alongside (1 medium ear of corn for each serving will increase the *PointsPlus* value by *2*).

Grilled Chicken Breasts with Tomato-Corn Salsa

Makes 4 Servings

3 fresh ears of corn, husks and
  silk removed

1 pint cherry tomatoes,
  quartered

½ small red onion, chopped,
  about ⅓ cup

1 serrano or habañero pepper,
  seeded and finely chopped

2 tablespoons lime juice

1 tablespoon chopped fresh
  cilantro

¼ teaspoon salt

2 (¾-pound) bone-in chicken
  breast halves, skinned and
  cut in half crosswise

1 tablespoon extra-virgin
  olive oil

2 teaspoons Cajun seasoning

1. Spray the grill rack with nonstick spray; prepare the grill for a medium-hot fire.

2. To make the salsa, place the corn on the grill rack and grill until well marked, about 8 minutes, turning every 2 minutes. Transfer the corn to a cutting board and let cool about 5 minutes. With a sharp knife, cut the kernels from the cobs and transfer to a large bowl. Add the tomatoes, onion, serrano pepper, lime juice, cilantro, and salt; mix well and set aside.

3. Rub the chicken with the oil and sprinkle with Cajun seasoning. Place the chicken on the grill rack and grill until well marked and an instant-read thermometer inserted in a breast registers 165°F, 8–10 minutes on each side. Serve the chicken with the salsa.

PER SERVING (1 piece chicken with 1 cup salsa): 221 Cal, 7 g Total Fat, 1 g Sat Fat, 0 g Trans Fat, 42 mg Chol, 474 mg Sod, 24 g Carb, 3 g Fib, 19 g Prot, 17 mg Calc.
PointsPlus value: *6.*

COOK'S TIP

Hot peppers can irritate skin, so if you are handling serrano or habañero peppers, wear surgical gloves (available in drugstores), and do not touch your eyes or any other tender parts of your body without first washing your hands thoroughly.

**Grilled Chicken Breasts
with Tomato-Corn Salsa**

Coffee BBQ Sauce–Slathered Chicken

Makes 6 Servings

1 cup ketchup

⅔ cup strong brewed coffee

½ cup packed light brown sugar

¼ cup white vinegar

2 garlic cloves, crushed with the side of a large knife

1 teaspoon salt

⅛ –¼ teaspoon cayenne

6 (½-pound) bone-in skinless chicken breast halves

1. To make the BBQ sauce, combine the ketchup, coffee, brown sugar, vinegar, garlic, ½ teaspoon of the salt, and the cayenne in a medium saucepan and set over medium heat. Cook, stirring, until the sugar has dissolved, about 3 minutes. Bring the mixture to a boil, then reduce the heat and simmer 10 minutes. Pour the sauce through a strainer set over a medium bowl; let cool to room temperature.

2. Meanwhile, spray the grill rack with nonstick spray; prepare the grill for indirect cooking and maintain a medium-hot fire.

3. Sprinkle the chicken with the remaining ½ teaspoon salt. Place the chicken, skinned side down, on the cooler portion of the grill rack and grill, covered, turning once or twice, 15 minutes. Uncover the grill and continue to grill the chicken, brushing with the sauce, until an instant-read thermometer inserted in the thickest part of a breast registers 165°F, about 5 minutes longer.

PER SERVING (1 piece chicken): 233 Cal, 4 g Total Fat, 1 g Sat Fat, 0 g Trans Fat, 73 mg Chol, 703 mg Sod, 21 g Carb, 0 g Fib, 27 g Prot, 34 mg Calc.
PointsPlus value: *6.*

COOK'S TIP

To give this chicken some tempting smoky flavor, soak about 1 cup of apple wood, cherry wood, or hickory wood chips in a bowl of water for at least 30 minutes, then drain. If using a charcoal grill, sprinkle the chips directly on top of the ashed-over coals. And, if using a gas grill, put the chips into a small disposable foil pan that has some holes poked in, and place on top of one of the lit burners.

Lemon Chicken with Indian Spices

Makes 4 Servings

4 scallions, cut into 1-inch pieces

½ cup plus 2 tablespoons loosely packed fresh cilantro leaves

3 garlic cloves, peeled

Grated zest and juice of 1 lemon

1 tablespoon water

2 teaspoons extra-virgin olive oil

2 teaspoons ground cumin

1 teaspoon paprika

1 teaspoon turmeric

½ teaspoon salt

¼ teaspoon black pepper

4 (½-pound) bone-in chicken breast halves

1. Combine the scallions, ½ cup of the cilantro, the garlic, lemon zest and juice, water, oil, cumin, paprika, turmeric, salt, and pepper in a food processor; process until it forms a coarse paste.

2. Place the chicken on the work surface. Loosen the skin from the chicken; rub the paste on the meat under the skin, then all over the skin. Cover and refrigerate for at least 2 hours or up to 8 hours.

3. Spray the grill rack with nonstick spray; prepare the grill for a medium-hot fire.

4. Place the chicken on the grill rack and grill, turning occasionally, until an instant-read thermometer inserted into the thickest part of a breast registers 165°F, about 25 minutes. Arrange the chicken on a small serving platter and sprinkle with the remaining 2 tablespoons cilantro. Remove the skin before eating.

PER SERVING (1 piece chicken): 164 Cal, 8 g Total Fat, 2 g Sat Fat, 0 g Trans Fat, 72 mg Chol, 369 mg Sod, 4 g Total Carb, 1 g Fib, 18 g Prot, 49 mg Calc.
PointsPlus value: *4.*

COOK'S TIP

Turning the seasonings into a paste really brings out their flavor and also makes it easier for the chicken to absorb them. Since the grill is already on, why not cook up some thickly sliced zucchini and pieces of red bell pepper to serve alongside.

Grilled Chicken Breast Satay with Peanut Sauce

Makes 4 Servings

1 tablespoon Asian fish sauce

1 tablespoon grated peeled fresh ginger

2 garlic cloves, minced

4 (5-ounce) skinless boneless chicken breasts

½ cup light (reduced-fat) coconut milk

¼ cup reduced-fat peanut butter

1 tablespoon rice vinegar

2 teaspoons packed dark brown sugar

¾ teaspoon Thai green curry paste

1 tablespoon chopped fresh cilantro

1. Combine the fish sauce, ginger, and garlic in a zip-close plastic bag; add the chicken. Squeeze out the air and seal the bag; turn to coat the chicken. Refrigerate, turning the bag occasionally, for at least 1 hour or up to overnight.

2. Spray the grill rack with nonstick spray; prepare the grill for a medium-hot fire.

3. Meanwhile, to make the peanut sauce, combine the coconut milk, peanut butter, vinegar, sugar, and curry paste in a medium saucepan. Cook over medium heat, stirring constantly, until the mixture is smooth and heated through, about 3 minutes. Remove from the heat and stir in the cilantro. Let the sauce cool to room temperature.

4. Lift the chicken from the marinade and place on the grill rack. Discard the marinade. Grill the chicken until well marked and cooked through, 5–6 minutes on each side. Sprinkle the chicken with cilantro and serve.

PER SERVING (1 piece chicken with 3 tablespoons sauce): 277 Cal, 12 g Total Fat, 4 g Sat Fat, 0 g Trans Fat, 68 mg Chol, 194 mg Sod, 13 g Carb, 1 g Fib, 29 g Prot, 29 mg Calc.
PointsPlus value: *7.*

COOK'S TIP

To turn this into an appetizer, cut each chicken breast into ½-inch-wide strips before marinating them, then thread the chicken onto skewers and grill until cooked through, 3 to 4 minutes on each side.

Grilled Stuffed Chicken Breasts

Makes 4 Servings

8 sun-dried tomatoes (not oil-packed)

⅓ cup shredded part-skim mozzarella cheese

2 tablespoons grated Parmesan cheese

8 fresh basil leaves, chopped

3 teaspoons extra-virgin olive oil

4 (5-ounce) skinless boneless chicken breasts

½ teaspoon salt

¼ teaspoon black pepper

1. Spray the grill rack with nonstick spray; prepare the grill for a medium-hot fire.

2. Combine the sun-dried tomatoes with enough boiling water to cover in a small bowl; let stand until softened, about 15 minutes. Drain the tomatoes then finely chop. Transfer the tomatoes to a medium bowl. Add the mozzarella cheese, Parmesan cheese, basil, and 1 teaspoon of the oil; mix well.

3. Make a pocket in the side of each chicken breast by inserting a sharp paring knife into the thickest part, then gently cutting back and forth to make a small pocket in the side. Do not cut through to the back or the sides of the breasts. Enlarge the pockets gently with your fingers. Fill each pocket evenly with the filling (about 3 tablespoons in each). Secure the opening with wooden picks.

4. Brush the chicken with the remaining 2 teaspoons oil, then sprinkle with the salt and pepper. Place on the grill rack and grill until well marked and the chicken is cooked through, 8–10 minutes on each side.

PER SERVING (1 stuffed chicken breast): 232 Cal, 10 g Total Fat, 3 g Sat Fat, 0 g Trans Fat, 76 mg Chol, 472 mg Sod, 5 g Carb, 1 g Fib, 30 g Prot, 130 mg Calc.
PointsPlus value: *6.*

COOK'S TIP

Elegant enough for entertaining, these chicken breasts are stuffed with sun-dried tomatoes, a mixture of cheeses, and fresh basil. You can stuff the chicken breasts and keep them refrigerated for up to 24 hours so they are ready to grill when your guests arrive.

**Grilled Buffalo
Chicken Tenders**

Grilled Buffalo Chicken Tenders

Makes 8 Servings

¼ cup Louisiana-style hot
    sauce, such as Frank's

½ teaspoon hot pepper sauce

1½ tablespoons unsalted butter

1 pound chicken tenders

8 baby carrots

2 celery stalks, cut into
    2 × ¼-inch sticks

¼ cup fat-free blue cheese
    dressing

1. Spray the grill rack with nonstick spray; prepare the grill for a medium-hot fire. Or spray the broiler rack with nonstick spray and preheat the broiler.

2. Combine the hot sauce and pepper sauce in a small saucepan over medium heat. Bring to a simmer and cook 1 minute. Remove from the heat and swirl in 1 tablespoon of the butter.

3. Melt the remaining ½ tablespoon butter and toss with chicken tenders in a medium bowl. Place the chicken on the grill or broiler rack; grill or broil 4 inches from the heat until cooked through, 4–5 minutes on each side. Transfer the chicken to a clean bowl and toss with the hot sauce mixture. Serve with the carrots, celery sticks, and blue cheese dressing.

PER SERVING (about 2 chicken tenders, a few vegetable sticks, and ½ tablespoon dressing): 224 Cal, 8 g Total Fat, 4 g Sat Fat, 0 g Trans Fat, 80 mg Chol, 456 mg Sod, 12 g Carb, 1 g Fib, 26 g Prot, 29 mg Calc.
PointsPlus value: *6.*

COOK'S TIP

To make this dish ahead, toss the cooled cooked chicken with the hot sauce in a casserole dish, then cover and refrigerate overnight to allow the chicken to absorb all the flavors from the sauce. Reheat the chicken in the covered casserole dish in a 350°F oven until heated through, about 10 minutes.

Moroccan Chicken Legs

Makes 4 Servings

2 garlic cloves, minced

1 scallion, finely chopped

1 tablespoon extra-virgin
    olive oil

2 teaspoons grated orange zest

1 teaspoon dried mint

1 teaspoon ground cumin

¾ teaspoon hot paprika

¼ teaspoon ground ginger

¼ teaspoon ground cinnamon

4 (½-pound) whole chicken
    legs, skinned

¾ teaspoon salt

1. Combine the garlic, scallion, oil, orange zest, mint, cumin, paprika, ginger, and cinnamon in a zip-close plastic bag; add the chicken. Squeeze out the air and seal the bag; turn to coat the chicken. Refrigerate, turning the bag occasionally, for at least 4 hours or up to overnight.

2. Spray the grill rack with nonstick spray; prepare the grill for a medium-hot fire.

3. Lift the chicken from the marinade and sprinkle with the salt. Discard the marinade. Place the chicken on the grill rack and grill until well marked and an instant-read thermometer inserted in a thigh registers 165°F, 8–10 minutes on each side.

PER SERVING (1 chicken leg): 192 Cal, 8 g Total Fat, 2 g Sat Fat, 0 g Trans Fat, 83 mg Chol, 520 mg Sod, 0 g Carb, 0 g Fib, 28 g Prot, 35 mg Calc.
PointsPlus value: *5.*

COOK'S TIP

Orange zest and garlic team up deliciously with North African spices to give this chicken exotic Moroccan flavor. Serve it with a shepherd's salad of chopped tomatoes, cucumbers, parsley, scallions, and red-wine vinegar.

Thai Chicken Legs

Makes 4 Servings

1 garlic clove, minced

1 tablespoon grated peeled
    fresh ginger

2 tablespoons rice vinegar

1 tablespoon Asian fish sauce

1 tablespoon sugar

1 tablespoon chopped fresh
    cilantro

1 tablespoon chopped
    fresh mint

2 teaspoons grated lime zest

1 teaspoon red chili paste

½ teaspoon salt

4 (½-pound) whole chicken
    legs, skinned

1. Combine the garlic, ginger, vinegar, fish sauce, sugar, cilantro, mint, lime zest, chili paste, and salt in a zip-close plastic bag; add the chicken. Squeeze out the air and seal the bag; turn to coat the chicken. Refrigerate, turning the bag occasionally, for at least 4 hours or up to overnight.

2. Spray the grill rack with nonstick spray; prepare the grill for a medium-hot fire.

3. Lift the chicken from the marinade and place on the grill rack. Discard the marinade. Grill the chicken until well marked and an instant-read thermometer inserted in a thigh registers 165°F, 8–10 minutes on each side.

PER SERVING (1 chicken leg): 188 Cal, 7 g Total Fat, 2 g Sat Fat, 0 g Trans Fat, 83 mg Chol, 183 mg Sod, 1 g Carb, 0 g Fib, 28 g Prot, 33 mg Calc.
PointsPlus value: *4*.

COOK'S TIP

Thai roasted red chili paste is a condiment made from crushed roasted red Thai chiles, sugar, tamarind, dried shrimp, and spices. It lends a delicious smoky, spicy flavor to many dishes. You can find it in the international aisle of most supermarkets and in Asian markets.

Grilling and Transporting Tips

Americans love to grill—and for good reason. It imparts a unique flavor to just about any food. Whether you use a gas grill, a charcoal grill, or a tabletop hibachi, all grills function pretty much the same way. The food is placed on parallel metal bars with the heat coming from underneath by gas or charcoal.

- When barbecuing chicken outdoors, keep the chicken refrigerated until you are ready to grill. Do not place the cooked chicken on the same plate that was used to transport it to the grill.

- Marinate chicken in the refrigerator— never on the countertop. The marinade in which raw chicken has been soaking should never be used on the cooked chicken. When brushing chicken with a fresh marinade, stop brushing it 5 minutes before the end of the cooking time. Then, either discard the remaining marinade or bring it to a rolling boil and boil for 2 minutes before serving it.

- When storing uncooked poultry or other foods in a cooler, place the cooler in a shady spot and avoid opening the lid too often. Use ice packs to keep the food as cool as possible.

- To cut the fat and prevent charring and flare-ups, remove all visible fat from poultry before grilling it.

- When grilling away from home, bring enough water for any food preparation and cleaning. Also pack wet wipes and paper towels for cleaning hands and surfaces.

- Cook chicken to a safe internal temperature to destroy any harmful bacteria. Use an instant-read thermometer to ensure the chicken has reached the proper temperature. The safe internal temperature for all cooked cuts of poultry, including ground meat, is 165°F.

- To test for doneness, insert the thermometer into the thickest part of the meat (not touching any bone). For burgers, insert the thermometer into its side.

- Let poultry stand for at least 5 minutes before serving. During this time, the internal temperature will rise about 5°F, and the poultry juices will redistribute themselves, ensuring the chicken will be juicy.

- If the outside temperature goes above 80°F, don't let cooked food sit out longer than 1 hour.

- When transporting cooked chicken, put it in an insulated container or cooler until you are ready to eat. Keep cold food below 40°F and hot food above 140°F to keep it safe to eat. Look for standard-size casserole dishes that come with insulated carrying bags with a pack that you can either freeze or heat to maintain the food at a safe temperature.

Smoky Glazed Chicken Thighs

Makes 6 Servings

¼ cup ketchup

3 tablespoons packed
   brown sugar

2 tablespoons red-wine vinegar

¾ teaspoon dried oregano

1 tablespoon smoked paprika

2 teaspoons ground cumin

2 teaspoons onion powder

2 teaspoons chili powder

¾ teaspoon salt

½ teaspoon black pepper

6 skinless bone-in chicken
   thighs (about 1½ pounds)

1. Spray the grill rack with nonstick spray; prepare the grill for a medium-hot fire.

2. To make the glaze, mix together the ketchup, 2 tablespoons of the brown sugar, the vinegar, and oregano in a small bowl.

3. To make the spice rub, mix together the paprika, cumin, onion powder, chili powder, salt, pepper, and the remaining 1 tablespoon brown sugar in another small bowl. Rub the spice mixture all over the chicken thighs.

4. Place the chicken on the grill rack and grill 8 minutes. Turn the chicken and grill 8 minutes longer. Turn the chicken and brush with half of the glaze; grill 3 minutes. Turn the chicken and brush with remaining glaze; grill until an instant-read thermometer inserted in thickest part of a thigh registers 165°F, about 3 minutes longer.

PER SERVING (1 chicken thigh)**:** 194 Cal, 8 g Total Fat, 2 g Sat Fat, 0 g Trans Fat, 67 mg Chol, 483 mg Sod, 11 g Carb, 1 g Fib, 19 g Prot, 27 mg Calc.
PointsPlus value: *5.*

COOK'S TIP

Mix up a double, triple, or even larger batch of the spice rub to have on hand for other times when you grill. Transfer it to a glass jar and store in your pantry for up to several months. Rub it on salmon, shrimp, filet mignons, round steak, pork chops, or pork tenderloin.

Chicken Thighs with Grilled Stone Fruit Salsa

Makes 4 Servings

3 firm-ripe peaches, about ¾ pound, halved and pitted

3 firm-ripe nectarines, about ¾ pound, halved and pitted

3 firm-ripe plums, about ½ pound, halved and pitted

1 small red onion, cut into ¼-inch-thick slices

2 tablespoons chopped fresh cilantro

1 tablespoon apple cider vinegar

1 tablespoon sugar

¾ teaspoon salt

¼ teaspoon black pepper

4 (5-ounce) skinless bone-in chicken thighs

1. Spray the grill rack with nonstick spray; prepare the grill for a medium-hot fire.

2. To make the salsa, place the peaches, nectarines, and plums on the grill rack and grill until well marked and slightly softened, 4–5 minutes on each side; transfer to a bowl and let cool. Place the onion slices on the grill rack and grill until well marked and tender, 5–6 minutes on each side; transfer to a cutting board and let cool 5 minutes. Coarsely chop the onion, peaches, nectarines, and plums; transfer to a bowl. Add the cilantro, vinegar, sugar, ¼ teaspoon of the salt, and ⅛ teaspoon of the pepper; mix well and set aside.

3. Sprinkle the chicken with the remaining ½ teaspoon salt and ⅛ teaspoon pepper; place on the grill rack. Grill until an instant-read thermometer inserted in a thigh registers 165°F, about 8 minutes on each side. Serve the chicken with the salsa.

PER SERVING (1 chicken thigh with ¾ cup salsa): 278 Cal, 8 g Total Fat, 2 g Sat Fat, 0 g Trans Fat, 57 mg Chol, 494 mg Sod, 32 g Carb, 4 g Fib, 22 g Prot, 37 mg Calc. *PointsPlus* value: *7*.

COOK'S TIP

This recipe takes advantage of summer's bounty of juicy and flavorful stone fruit. Starting in mid-June and throughout the summer, you should be able to find freestone fruit (where the pits are easily removed). Serve with whole wheat couscous (½ cup cooked whole wheat couscous per serving will up the *PointPlus* value by *3*).

Chicken Thighs with Grilled Stone Fruit Salsa

Curried Drumsticks

Makes 4 Servings

½ cup plain fat-free yogurt

2 tablespoons lemon juice

1 tablespoon Madras curry
    powder

1 tablespoon grated peeled
    fresh ginger

1 garlic clove, minced

1 teaspoon ground coriander

⅛ teaspoon cayenne

8 (5-ounce) chicken
    drumsticks, skinned

¾ teaspoon salt

1. Combine the yogurt, lemon juice, curry powder, ginger, garlic, coriander, and cayenne in a zip-close plastic bag; add the drumsticks. Squeeze out the air and seal the bag; turn to coat the chicken. Refrigerate, turning the bag occasionally, for at least 30 minutes or up to overnight.

2. Spray the grill rack with nonstick spray; prepare the grill for a medium-hot fire.

3. Lift the chicken from the marinade and sprinkle with the salt. Discard the marinade. Place the chicken on the grill rack and grill, turning occasionally, until well marked and an instant-read thermometer inserted in a drumstick registers 165°F, about 15 minutes.

PER SERVING (2 drumsticks): 158 Cal, 4 g Total Fat, 1 g Sat Fat, 0 g Trans Fat, 99 mg Chol, 525 mg Sod, 2 g Carb, 0 g Fib, 26 g Prot, 61 mg Calc.
PointsPlus value: *4.*

COOK'S TIP

You can also broil these drumsticks: Spray the broiler rack with nonstick spray and preheat the broiler. Place the chicken on the broiler rack and broil 4 inches from the heat, turning occasionally, until an instant-read thermometer inserted in a drumstick registers 165°F, about 15 minutes.

Miso-Marinated Chicken Thighs

Makes 4 Servings

⅓ cup miso paste

¼ cup mirin (rice wine)

¼ cup orange juice

1 tablespoon grated peeled
    fresh ginger

1 teaspoon Asian (dark)
    sesame oil

4 (6-ounce) skinless bone-in
    chicken thighs

1. Combine the miso paste, mirin, orange juice, ginger, and oil in a zip-close plastic bag; add the chicken. Squeeze out the air and seal the bag; turn to coat the chicken. Refrigerate, turning the bag occasionally, for at least 30 minutes or up to overnight.

2. Spray the grill rack with nonstick spray; prepare the grill for a medium-hot fire.

3. Lift the chicken from the marinade. Wipe the excess marinade from the chicken and place the chicken on the grill rack. Discard the marinade. Grill the chicken until well marked and an instant-read thermometer inserted in a thigh registers 165°F, about 8 minutes on each side.

PER SERVING (1 chicken thigh): 281 Cal, 11 g Total Fat, 3 g Sat Fat, 0 g Trans Fat, 86 mg Chol, 800 mg Sod, 15 g Carb, 4 g Fib, 28 g Prot, 14 mg Calc.
PointsPlus value: *7.*

COOK'S TIP

Miso is a key element in Japanese cuisine. It is made from fermented soybeans and can be found in Japanese markets, health-food stores, and the Asian section of large supermarkets. Using it in a marinade allows it to impart a mild but distinctive flavor to the chicken.

Tequila-Citrus Chicken

Tequila-Citrus Chicken

Makes 4 Servings

2 garlic cloves, minced

½ cup orange juice

3 tablespoons tequila

2 tablespoons lime juice

1 tablespoon extra-virgin olive oil

1 teaspoon ground cumin

4 (¼-pound) skinless boneless chicken thighs

½ teaspoon salt

¼ teaspoon black pepper

1. Combine the garlic, orange juice, tequila, lime juice, oil, and cumin in a zip-close plastic bag; add the chicken. Squeeze out the air and seal the bag; turn to coat the chicken. Refrigerate, turning the bag occasionally, for at least 8 hours or up to overnight.

2. Spray the grill rack with nonstick spray; prepare the grill for a medium-hot fire.

3. Lift the chicken from the marinade, shake off the excess marinade, then sprinkle the chicken with the salt and pepper. Discard the marinade. Place the chicken on the grill rack and grill until well marked and cooked through, 6–7 minutes on each side.

PER SERVING (1 chicken thigh): 238 Cal, 12 g Total Fat, 3 g Sat Fat, 0 g Trans Fat, 74 mg Chol, 361 mg Sod, 5 g Carb, 0 g Fib, 21 g Prot, 21 mg Calc.
PointsPlus value: *6*.

COOK'S TIP

Serve these slightly tangy, sweet thighs with fresh lime wedges and grilled corn tortillas for South-of-the-border flair. You can grill the tortillas directly on a grill rack for about 1 minute on each side. A 6-inch corn tortilla for each serving will increase the *PointsPlus* value by *1*.

Chile Chicken Patties with Chipotle Sauce on Sourdough

Makes 4 Servings

6 tablespoons low-fat
  mayonnaise

2 tablespoons sweet pickle
  relish

1 tablespoon drained capers,
  chopped

2 teaspoons chopped fresh dill

1 chipotle en adobo, minced

1 pound ground skinless
  chicken breast

1 tablespoon chili powder

1 teaspoon dried oregano

4 slices (about 3 × 4 inches
  each) sourdough bread

1. Spray the grill rack with nonstick spray; prepare the grill for a medium-hot fire.

2. To make the chipotle sauce, combine the mayonnaise, pickle relish, capers, dill, and chipotle in a small bowl; mix well and set aside.

3. Combine the chicken, chili powder, and oregano in a medium bowl; mix well. Shape the mixture into 4 patties, about 3½ inches in diameter. Place the patties on the grill rack and grill until an instant-read thermometer inserted in the side of a patty registers 165°F, 4–5 minutes on each side. Transfer the patties to a plate.

4. Place the bread slices on the grill rack and grill until lightly toasted, 1–2 minutes on each side. Place the chicken patties on the bread slices and top each evenly with the sauce.

PER SERVING (1 open-faced sandwich with 2 tablespoons sauce): 371 Cal, 8 g Total Fat, 2 g Sat Fat, 1 g Trans Fat, 68 mg Chol, 904 mg Sod, 43 g Carb, 3 g Fib, 31 g Prot, 74 mg Calc. *PointsPlus* value: *9.*

COOK'S TIP

Chipotle chiles add intriguing taste to many Mexican dishes. Just one chile adds flavor, heat, and a tempting touch of smokiness to these juicy patties. Look for small cans of chipotles en adobo in the same aisle as other Mexican and Tex-Mex products.

**Chile Chicken Patties with
Chipotle Sauce on Sourdough**

**Grilled Sausage and Peppers
with Parmesan Polenta**

Grilled Sausage and Peppers with Parmesan Polenta

Makes 4 Servings

¾ pound sweet Italian chicken sausage (4 sausages)

3 teaspoons extra-virgin olive oil

1 teaspoon balsamic vinegar

1 large red onion, cut into ¼-inch-thick slices

2 assorted color bell peppers, cut into eighths

¼ teaspoon salt

⅛ teaspoon black pepper

1 (8-ounce) tube refrigerated fat-free plain polenta, cut into 4 rounds

4 teaspoons grated Parmesan cheese

1. Spray the grill rack with nonstick spray; prepare the grill for a medium-hot fire.

2. Place the sausages on the grill rack and grill, turning occasionally, until browned and cooked through, 12–15 minutes. Transfer to a plate and keep warm.

3. Meanwhile, combine 2 teaspoons of the oil with the vinegar in a small bowl; mix well. Brush the onion slices and bell peppers with the oil mixture and sprinkle with the salt and black pepper. Grill the onions and bell peppers until well marked and tender, 6–7 minutes on each side; transfer to a cutting board and roughly chop.

4. Brush both sides of the polenta slices with the remaining 1 teaspoon oil. Place on the grill rack and grill 4 minutes; turn and sprinkle each slice with 1 teaspoon of the cheese. Grill 4 minutes longer. Transfer the polenta slices to 4 plates. Top each slice with one-fourth of the vegetables and 1 sausage.

PER SERVING (1 slice polenta, ½ cup vegetables, and 1 sausage): 260 Cal, 14 g Total Fat, 4 g Sat Fat, 0 g Trans Fat, 51 mg Chol, 797 mg Sod, 16 g Carb, 2 g Fib, 17 g Prot, 55 mg Calc. *PointsPlus* value: 7.

COOK'S TIP

Store-bought prepared polenta is a great time-saver. It comes in tubes and can be found in the dairy section of most supermarkets in a variety of flavors, including plain, Italian herb, and wild mushroom.

slow-cooker dinners

Spice-Rubbed Chicken with Carrots and Onion

Makes 8 Servings

8 carrots, sliced

1 red onion, quartered and
    thinly sliced

2 teaspoons paprika

1 teaspoon chili powder

1 teaspoon dried thyme

1 teaspoon garlic powder

1 teaspoon salt

½ teaspoon black pepper

¼ teaspoon cayenne

1 (4-pound) chicken, skinned,
    giblets discarded

1. Combine the carrots and onion in a 5- or 6-quart slow cooker. Mix together the paprika, chili powder, thyme, garlic powder, salt, black pepper, and cayenne in a cup. Rub the spice mixture all over the chicken, sprinkling any remaining rub in the cavity of the chicken.

2. Place the chicken on top of the vegetables. Cover and cook until a thigh and the vegetables are fork-tender, 4–6 hours on high.

3. Transfer the chicken to a cutting board and cut into 8 pieces. Serve with the vegetables and any accumulated broth.

PER SERVING (1 piece chicken and about ½ cup vegetables with 3 tablespoons broth): 193 Cal, 7 g Total Fat, 2 g Sat Fat, 0 g Trans Fat, 81 mg Chol, 300 mg Sod, 5 g Carb, 1 g Fib, 27 g Prot, 32 mg Calc. *PointsPlus* value: *5.*

COOK'S TIP

You can tailor the spice rub to your own taste by substituting other herbs for the thyme, including rosemary, oregano, or sage and using onion powder instead of, or in addition to, the garlic powder. If you like a touch of smoke, use smoked paprika instead of the regular.

Chorizo Chicken with Tomatoes, Bell Peppers, and Peas

Makes 4 Servings

1 (14½-ounce) can fire-roasted
    diced tomatoes

3 tablespoons balsamic
    vinegar

2 tablespoons tomato paste

1 tablespoon smoked paprika

¼ teaspoon salt

1 red onion, chopped

3 celery stalks, sliced

¼ cup chopped chorizo
    sausage

4 (¼-pound) skinless boneless
    chicken breasts

1 small red bell pepper, coarsely
    chopped

1 small yellow bell pepper,
    coarsely chopped

1 tablespoon cornmeal

1 cup frozen peas, thawed

2 tablespoons chopped fresh
    flat-leaf parsley

1. Mix together the tomatoes, vinegar, tomato paste, paprika, and salt in a 5- or 6-quart slow cooker. Stir in the onion, celery, and chorizo. Top with the chicken and bell peppers. Cover and cook until chicken and vegetables are fork-tender, 3–4 hours on high or 6–8 hours on low.

2. About 20 minutes before the cooking time is up, slowly stir in the cornmeal until blended. Stir in the peas. Cover and cook on high until the mixture simmers and thickens and the peas are just tender, about 15 minutes. Sprinkle with parsley and serve.

PER SERVING (1 piece chicken with ¾ cup vegetables and sauce): **272 Cal, 6 g Total Fat, 2 g Sat Fat, 0 g Trans Fat, 75 mg Chol, 533 mg Sod, 22 g Carb, 5 g Fib, 31 g Prot, 83 mg Calc.** *PointsPlus* value: *6.*

COOK'S TIP

Spooning the vegetables and sauce over cooked quinoa is a great way to enjoy this good-for-you grain and to make this tasty dish even more satisfying (½ cup cooked quinoa for each serving will increase the *PointsPlus* value by *3*).

Chicken Breast in Wine
Sauce with Asparagus

Chicken Breast in Wine Sauce with Asparagus

Makes 4 Servings

2 teaspoons canola oil

4 carrots, diced

½ fennel bulb or 2 celery stalks, diced

2 garlic cloves, minced

2 tablespoons all-purpose flour

1½ cups reduced-sodium chicken broth

½ cup dry white wine or chicken broth

2 all-purpose potatoes (about ¾ pound), peeled and cut into 1-inch cubes

1 cup frozen small whole onions

½ teaspoon salt

¼ teaspoon black pepper

1 (1¼-pound) bone-in chicken breast, skinned

1 bunch (about 1 pound) fresh asparagus, trimmed and cut into 1-inch pieces

1½ tablespoons chopped fresh tarragon or 1½ teaspoons dried

1. Heat the oil in a large nonstick saucepan over medium heat. Add the carrots, fennel, and garlic; cook, stirring occasionally, until softened, about 8 minutes. Add the flour and cook, stirring constantly, about 1 minute. Stir in the broth, wine, potatoes, onions, salt, and pepper; bring to a simmer, stirring constantly.

2. Put the chicken in a 5- or 6-quart slow cooker; pour the vegetable mixture over the chicken. Cover the slow cooker and cook until the chicken and vegetables are fork-tender, 3–4 hours on high or 6–8 hours on low. Lift the chicken from the slow cooker and set aside until cool enough to handle. Pull the chicken from the bones, then tear or cut the meat into bite-size pieces.

3. Meanwhile, add the asparagus and tarragon to the slow cooker; cover and cook on high until the asparagus is just tender, about 20 minutes. Return the chicken to the slow cooker; cover and cook on high until heated through, about 10 minutes.

PER SERVING (scant 2 cups): 337 Cal, 6 g Total Fat, 1 g Sat Fat, 0 g Trans Fat, 63 mg Chol, 441 mg Sod, 36 g Carb, 7 g Fib, 30 g Prot, 91 mg Calc.
PointsPlus value: *8.*

COOK'S TIP

Browning the vegetables in a saucepan before cooking them in the slow cooker adds rich flavor to the finished dish. To add a spark of bright color and crisp-tender texture, we've added fresh asparagus and tarragon to the stew during the last 20 minutes of cooking.

Orange-Mustard Chicken with Sweet Potato and Apple

Makes 4 Servings

4 carrots, halved lengthwise and sliced

2 sweet potatoes, peeled and cut into 1-inch chunks

1 onion, thinly sliced

¾ cup orange juice

2 tablespoons Dijon mustard

2 garlic cloves, thinly sliced

1 teaspoon dried thyme

¾ teaspoon salt

½ teaspoon black pepper

2 (¾-pound) bone-in chicken breasts, skinned

2 tablespoons cold water

1 tablespoon cornstarch

1 Gala apple, peeled and thinly sliced

¼ cup fat-free sour cream

1. Mix together the carrots, sweet potatoes, and onion in a 5- or 6-quart slow cooker.

2. Stir together the orange juice, mustard, garlic, thyme, salt, and pepper in a glass measure; pour over the vegetables. Place the chicken on top. Cover and cook until the chicken and vegetables are fork-tender, 3–4 hours on high or 6–8 hours on low.

3. About 25 minutes before the cooking time is up, mix together the water and cornstarch in a small bowl until smooth. Stir the cornstarch mixture and apple into the slow cooker. Cover and cook on high until the mixture simmers and thickens and the apple is just tender, about 20 minutes.

4. Transfer the chicken to a cutting board; cut each breast crosswise in half. Transfer the chicken to a medium serving platter; spoon the vegetables around the chicken and the sauce over the chicken. Place a dollop of sour cream on top of each serving of chicken.

PER SERVING (1 piece chicken, 1 cup vegetables with sauce, and 1 tablespoon sour cream)**: 611 Cal, 5 g Total Fat, 1 g Sat Fat, 0 g Trans Fat, 77 mg Chol, 651 mg Sod, 45 g Carb, 7 g Fib, 31 g Prot, 102 mg Calc.**
PointsPlus value: *8.*

COOK'S TIP

This simple dish is just what you want on a cold winter's day. Round out the meal by serving it with steamed broccoli and enjoy a sweet ending of unsweetened applesauce topped with fresh raspberries.

Slow-Cooker Know-How

The slow cooker has been a favorite way to cook one-pot meals for over 30 years. At the high setting food is ready in 3 to 6 hours, while at the low setting it is ready in 8 to 10 hours. Put the fixings for a soup, stew, or braise in the cooker, turn it on, and return at the end of the day to a tasty home-cooked meal! Here are the varsious sizes, shapes, and types.

SIZES AND SHAPES

Slow cookers range in size from 1½ quarts to 7 quarts, with the most useful from 4 to 6 quarts. Depending on its size, from 2 or to 12 people can be served. It's important not to use a cooker that is smaller or larger than what is called for. This is because a slow cooker works most efficiently when half to two-thirds full, as the heat comes from the side—not the bottom—of the pot. Here are the types:

Manual Slow Cookers
These cookers have two or three heat settings (warm, low, high), a removable dishwasher-safe ceramic insert, and a glass lid.

Programmable Slow Cookers
They offer one-touch control with several time and temperature settings, a ceramic insert, and a glass lid. These cookers automatically shift to the warm setting when the cooking is finished and can be programmed to cook for 30 minutes or up to 20 hours.

Cook and Carry Slow Cookers
These cookers are ideal for taking food on the road. They have two or three heat settings, can be programmed to cook for 30 minutes or up to 20 hours, and have a ceramic insert. They also have a secure-fitting lid and locking system, which ensures that your food will reach its final destination without any spillage.

High-End Slow Cookers
They allow you to brown meat or cook vegetables in the cooker's ceramic insert on the stove, while two handles make it easy to transfer the insert to and from the slow cooker and to use it as a serving dish.

ADAPTING STANDARD RECIPES TO A SLOW COOKER

Choose a cut of meat that benefits from long, slow cooking. Trim the meat and brown first in a skillet to boost the flavor and seal in the juices, if you like. Place any cut-up vegetables in the bottom of the cooker (sauté them first, if desired). Place the meat on top of the vegetables. Reduce the liquids in the recipe by about half (since they won't cook down as they do in a regular recipe). And, if adding sour cream, cream, or cheese, do so at the end of the cooking time.

Slow-Cooker Tangerine-Honey Chicken Thighs

Makes 4 Servings

⅓ cup frozen tangerine juice concentrate, thawed

3 tablespoons honey

Grated zest of 1 lemon

1 tablespoon chili powder

1½ teaspoons ground cumin

1 teaspoon dried oregano

¾ teaspoon salt

½ teaspoon ground coriander

1 red onion, quartered and thinly sliced

4 (¼-pound) bone-in chicken thighs, skinned

4 small zucchini, cut into ¾-inch slices

¼ cup chopped fresh flat-leaf parsley

1. Whisk together the tangerine juice concentrate, honey, lemon zest, chili powder, cumin, oregano, salt, and coriander in a 5- or 6-quart slow cooker. Stir in the onion; top with the chicken and zucchini. Cover and cook until the chicken and vegetables are fork-tender, 3–4 hours on high or 6–8 hours on low.

2. Transfer the chicken to a small serving platter. Stir the parsley into the vegetables in the slow cooker. Pour the vegetables and sauce over the chicken.

PER SERVING (1 piece chicken with ¾ cup vegetables and sauce): 312 Cal, 10 g Total Fat, 3 g Sat Fat, 0 g Trans Fat, 70 mg Chol, 518 mg Sod, 32 g Carb, 3 g Fib, 27 g Prot, 81 mg Calc. *PointsPlus* value: *8.*

COOK'S TIP

If you like, substitute agave nectar for the honey. It is 1½ times sweeter than honey or sugar, so only 2 tablespoons are needed. Agave nectar comes light, medium, and dark. The light is best used in delicate dishes, while the medium is pretty much for all purposes. The dark, on the other hand, is ideal for drizzling over pancakes and French toast.

Slow-Cooked Chicken in Spicy Peanut Sauce

Makes 8 Servings

1 (14½-ounce) can crushed tomatoes

6 carrots, halved lengthwise and sliced

3 tablespoons reduced-fat creamy peanut butter

2 tablespoons minced peeled fresh ginger

3 large garlic cloves, minced

2 teaspoons ground cumin

1 teaspoon ground coriander

1 teaspoon salt

½–1 teaspoon cayenne

4 (¼-pound) bone-in skinless chicken thighs

4 ¼-pound) chicken drumsticks, skinned

2 tablespoons cold water

1 tablespoon cornstarch

¼ cup chopped fresh cilantro

1. Combine the tomatoes, carrots, peanut butter, ginger, garlic, cumin, coriander, salt, and cayenne in a 5- or 6-quart slow cooker. Top with the chicken. Cover and cook until the chicken and vegetables are fork-tender, 3–4 hours on high or 6–8 hours on low.

2. About 20 minutes before the cooking time is up, mix together the water and cornstarch in a small bowl until smooth. Stir the cornstarch mixture into the slow cooker. Cover and cook on high until the sauce simmers and thickens, about 15 minutes. Stir in the cilantro.

PER SERVING (1 piece chicken with ½ cup vegetables and sauce): 172 Cal, 6 g Total Fat, 2 g Sat Fat, 0 g Trans Fat, 42 mg Chol, 601 mg Sod, 13 g Carb, 3 g Fib, 17 g Prot, 58 mg Calc. *PointsPlus* value: *4.*

COOK'S TIP

Sweet potatoes or yams are often included in this spicy stew, a welcome counterpoint to the stew's enticing heat. Serving cooked chunks of sweet potatoes alongside is also an easy way to get some of your daily dose of vitamins and fiber into your diet (½ of a cooked large sweet potato for each serving will increase the *PointsPlus* value by *2*).

Sage Chicken and Red Potatoes

Makes 6 Servings

2 teaspoons extra-virgin olive oil

1 large onion, chopped

3 celery stalks, diced

2 garlic cloves, minced

1 tablespoon all-purpose flour

1 cup reduced-sodium chicken broth

6 (¼-pound) skinless chicken drumsticks

1 pound small red potatoes, cut into quarters

1 (1-pound) bag baby carrots

1 bay leaf

½ teaspoon salt

¼ teaspoon black pepper

½ cup chopped fresh flat-leaf parsley

1 tablespoon chopped fresh sage, or 1 teaspoon dried

1 (2-inch) strip lemon zest

2 teaspoons lemon juice

1. Heat the oil in a large nonstick saucepan over medium heat. Add the onion, celery, and garlic; cook, stirring occasionally, until softened, about 8 minutes. Add the flour and cook, stirring constantly, about 1 minute. Add the broth and bring to a simmer, stirring constantly.

2. Put the chicken, potatoes, carrots, bay leaf, salt, and pepper in a 5- or 6-quart slow cooker; pour the broth mixture over the chicken and vegetables. Cover the slow cooker and cook until the chicken and vegetables are fork-tender, 4–5 hours on high or 8–10 hours on low.

3. Discard the bay leaf. Add the parsley, sage, lemon zest, and lemon juice to the slow cooker; cover and cook on high until the flavors blend, about 10 minutes.

PER SERVING (1 drumstick with 1 cup vegetables and sauce): 212 Cal, 4 g Total Fat, 1 g Sat Fat, 0 g Trans Fat, 51 mg Chol, 366 mg Sod, 28 g Carb, 5 g Fib, 17 g Prot, 64 mg Calc. *PointsPlus* value: *5.*

COOK'S TIP

This comforting, hearty stew is similar to the classic French dish Poulet Bonne Femme, which means "Good Wife's Chicken." You can substitute tarragon, rosemary, or thyme for the sage, if you like.

Sage Chicken and
Red Potatoes

Vietnamese Chicken Noodle Soup, Slow-Cooker Style

Makes 4 Servings

2 (½-pound) bone-in chicken breasts, skinned

6 fresh cilantro sprigs plus leaves for garnish

3 scallions, white and green parts separated

1 lemongrass stalk, trimmed and finely chopped

2 garlic cloves, crushed with the side of a large knife

1 (3-inch) cinnamon stick

2 star anise (optional)

½ teaspoon salt

⅛ teaspoon black pepper

2 (32-ounce) cartons reduced-sodium chicken broth

2 ounces thin rice noodles (vermicelli)

½ small red onion, very thinly sliced

Fresh mint leaves

Fresh basil leaves, torn if large

4 lime wedges

1. Combine the chicken, cilantro sprigs, white parts of the scallions, lemongrass, garlic, cinnamon stick, star anise if using, salt, and pepper in a 5- or 6-quart slow cooker. Pour the broth over the chicken and vegetables. Cover and cook until the chicken is fork-tender, 4–5 hours on high or 8–10 hours on low.

2. At the end of the cooking time, using a slotted spoon, transfer the chicken to a plate; let stand until cool enough to handle.

3. Meanwhile, cook the noodles according to the package directions. Drain and rinse under cold running water.

4. Remove and discard the bones from the chicken; cut the chicken meat into bite-size pieces. Pour the broth through a large sieve set over a large bowl. Discard the vegetables and spices.

5. Stir the chicken and noodles into the slow cooker. Cover and cook on high until chicken and noodles are heated through, about 10 minutes.

6. Finely slice the green parts of the scallions. Ladle the soup into 4 large bowls; sprinkle evenly with the scallions. Garnish each serving with cilantro leaves, red onion, mint leaves, basil leaves, and a lime wedge.

PER SERVING (2½ cups): 293 Cal, 6 g Total Fat, 2 g Sat Fat, 0 g Trans Fat, 70 mg Chol, 562 mg Sod, 27 g Carb, 1 g Fib, 31 g Prot, 63 mg Calc.
PointsPlus value: *7.*

COOK'S TIP

Pho (FUH), a staple in Vietnamese cuisine, is often eaten for breakfast. Add more flavor and crunch to our pho by topping each serving with mung bean sprouts, thinly sliced jalapeño or serrano pepper, and a bit of hoisin sauce.

Mexican Chicken Soup

Makes 6 Servings

3 (8-ounce) whole chicken legs, skinned

7 cups reduced-sodium chicken broth

4 carrots, thinly sliced on the diagonal

1 cup peeled and diced jicama

3 fresh cilantro sprigs

2 garlic cloves, minced

1 jalapeño pepper, seeded and minced

3 cups corn kernels, thawed if frozen

1 tomato, chopped

¼ cup chopped fresh cilantro

4 scallions, thinly sliced

1½ cups baked tortilla chips, broken up

6 lime wedges

1. Put the chicken, broth, carrots, jicama, cilantro sprigs, garlic, and jalapeño pepper in a 5- or 6-quart slow cooker; cover and cook until the chicken and vegetables are fork-tender, 4–5 hours on high or 8–10 hours on low.

2. Lift the chicken from the soup and set aside until cool enough to handle. Discard the cilantro sprigs. Pull the chicken meat from the bones, then tear or cut the meat into bite-size pieces.

3. Meanwhile, add the corn and tomato to the slow cooker; cover and cook on high until heated through, about 20 minutes. Return the chicken to the slow cooker and add the chopped cilantro; cook on high until heated through, about 10 minutes. Serve each bowl of soup sprinkled with a few sliced scallions and a few tortilla chips, with a lime wedge on the side.

PER SERVING (generous 2 cups soup with ¼ cup chips)**: 253 Cal, 6 g Total Fat, 2 g Sat Fat, 0 g Trans Fat, 42 mg Chol, 662 mg Sod, 29 g Carb, 5 g Fib, 23 g Prot, 57 mg Calc.**
PointsPlus value: *6.*

COOK'S TIP

We recommend using paper towels to help you get a good grip on the raw chicken skin when pulling it off.

Chicken and Ham Cassoulet

Makes 6 Servings

3 garlic cloves, minced

¼ teaspoon salt

1 teaspoon extra-virgin olive oil

6 (¼-pound) skinless bone-in
   chicken thighs

1 large onion, chopped

2 carrots, chopped

1 (1-ounce) piece cooked ham
   steak, diced

1 (14½-ounce) can diced
   tomatoes

½ cup dry white wine

2 (15½-ounce) cans cannellini
   (white kidney) beans, rinsed
   and drained

1 tablespoon chopped fresh
   thyme, or 1 teaspoon dried

3 slices firm white bread, made
   into crumbs

3 tablespoons finely chopped
   fresh flat-leaf parsley

1 teaspoon melted butter or
   extra-virgin olive oil

1. Combine the garlic and salt in a small bowl; rub the mixture onto the chicken thighs.

2. Heat the oil in a large nonstick skillet over medium-high heat. Add the chicken and cook until lightly browned, about 3 minutes on each side.

3. Place the onion and carrots in a 5- or 6-quart slow cooker. Place the browned chicken and ham on top of the vegetables. Pour the tomatoes and wine around the chicken; cover and cook until the chicken and vegetables are fork-tender, 4–5 hours on high or 8–10 hours on low.

4. Stir in the beans and thyme; cover and cook on high until heated through, about 30 minutes.

5. Meanwhile, combine the bread crumbs, parsley, and butter in a small bowl. Spoon the cassoulet into 6 shallow bowls and serve sprinkled with the crumb topping.

PER SERVING (1 chicken thigh, 1 cup vegetables and beans, and 3 tablespoons crumb topping): 355 Cal, 9 g Total Fat, 3 g Sat Fat, 0 g Trans Fat, 61 mg Chol, 852 mg Sod, 37 g Carb, 9 g Fib, 28 g Prot, 124 mg Calc.
PointsPlus value: *9.*

COOK'S TIP

Foods tend to lose their vibrant colors and some of their fresh flavor when slow-cooked, so here chopped fresh thyme is stirred into the stew 30 minutes before serving to brighten up the color and flavor.

Chicken with Rice and Peas

Makes 4 Servings

1 pound skinless boneless chicken breasts, cut into ¾-inch pieces

1 large onion, finely chopped

2 carrots, finely chopped

2 garlic cloves, minced

1 (14½-ounce) can diced tomatoes

¾ cup reduced-sodium chicken broth

⅔ cup long-grain white rice

½ teaspoon turmeric

¼ teaspoon salt

¼ teaspoon black pepper

⅛ teaspoon cayenne

1 cup frozen green peas, thawed

½ cup finely diced green bell pepper

¼ cup sliced pimiento-stuffed green olives

1. Put the chicken, onion, carrots, garlic, tomatoes, broth, rice, turmeric, salt, black pepper, and cayenne in a 5- or 6-quart slow cooker; cover and cook until the chicken and rice are tender, 4–5 hours on high or 8–10 hours on low.

2. Stir in the peas and bell pepper. Cover and cook on high until heated through, about 20 minutes. Serve sprinkled with the olives.

PER SERVING (1¼ cups stew with 1 tablespoon olives): 361 Cal, 6 g Total Fat, 1 g Sat Fat, 0 g Trans Fat, 68 mg Chol, 736 mg Sod, 44 g Carb, 5 g Fib, 32 g Prot, 90 mg Calc.
PointsPlus value: *9.*

COOK'S TIP

Similar to the popular Spanish dish arroz con pollo, this one-pot dinner is perfect for a slow cooker. Just before serving, toss the rice mixture with a fork to separate the grains. If you like your food spicy, double the amount of cayenne.

Chicken with Rice and Peas

Lemony Chicken and Lentil Soup

Makes 4 Servings

1¼ pounds skinless bone-in
chicken thighs

5 cups reduced-sodium
chicken broth

1 cup dried lentils, picked over
and rinsed

1 onion, chopped

1 green bell pepper, chopped

2 garlic cloves, minced

1 teaspoon ground coriander

1 (10-ounce) package frozen
chopped spinach, thawed
and squeezed dry

1 teaspoon grated lemon zest

1 tablespoon lemon juice

2 tablespoons chopped fresh
dill or flat-leaf parsley

1. Put the chicken, broth, lentils, onion, bell pepper, garlic, and coriander in a 5- or 6-quart slow cooker; cover and cook until the chicken and lentils are tender, 4–5 hours on high or 8–10 hours on low.

2. Lift the chicken from the soup and set aside until cool enough to handle. Pull the chicken meat from the bones, then tear or cut the meat into bite-size pieces.

3. Meanwhile, add the spinach, lemon zest, lemon juice, and dill to the slow cooker. Return the chicken to the pot; cover and cook on high until heated through, about 20 minutes.

PER SERVING (2 cups): 386 Cal, 10 g Total Fat, 3 g Sat Fat, 0 g Trans Fat, 57 mg Chol, 700 mg Sod, 36 g Carb, 13 g Fib, 40 g Prot, 143 mg Calc.
PointsPlus value: *9.*

COOK'S TIP

To quickly thaw the spinach before adding it to the soup, remove the spinach from its package, put it into a microwavable bowl, and microwave on high until thawed, about 3 minutes.

Creamy Garlic, Chicken, and Potato Soup

Makes 6 Servings

1 tablespoon unsalted butter

1 large leek, cleaned and sliced (about 4 cups)

10 garlic cloves, minced

4 cups reduced-sodium chicken broth

4 large Yukon Gold potatoes (about 2 pounds), scrubbed and cut into ½-inch pieces (about 5 cups)

1 bay leaf

½ teaspoon salt

¼ teaspoon black pepper

2 cups shredded cooked chicken breast

2 ounces goat cheese, crumbled

1 tablespoon chopped fresh tarragon, or 1 teaspoon dried

3 tablespoons chopped fresh flat-leaf parsley

1. Melt the butter in a large nonstick saucepan over medium heat. Add the leek and garlic; cook, stirring frequently, until golden, about 10 minutes. Stir in the broth; bring to a boil.

2. Put the potatoes, bay leaf, salt, and pepper in a 5- or 6-quart slow cooker; pour the broth mixture over the potatoes. Cover the slow cooker and cook until the potatoes are fork-tender, 3–4 hours on high or 6–8 hours on low.

3. Discard the bay leaf. Transfer the mixture to a blender or food processor in batches and puree. Return the mixture to the slow cooker. Add the chicken, cheese, and tarragon; cover and cook on high until the chicken is heated through and the cheese melts, about 30 minutes. Serve the soup sprinkled with the parsley.

PER SERVING (1⅓ cups): 290 Cal, 7 g Total Fat, 3 g Sat Fat, 0 g Trans Fat, 48 mg Chol, 615 mg Sod, 34 g Carb, 4 g Fib, 22 g Prot, 66 mg Calc.
PointsPlus value: *7.*

COOK'S TIP

The combination of potatoes and garlic is a match made in heaven. We've combined these two favorites to make a delicious, fragrant soup and then tempered the garlic flavor with the addition of creamy goat cheese.

Meatballs in
Cinnamon-Tomato Sauce

Meatballs in Cinnamon-Tomato Sauce

Makes 4 Servings

2 teaspoons extra-virgin
   olive oil

1 large onion, chopped

3 garlic cloves, minced

1 (14½-ounce) can Italian plum
   tomatoes, broken up

1 (4-inch) cinnamon stick

1 teaspoon dried oregano

¼ teaspoon sugar

¼ teaspoon black pepper

1 pound ground skinless turkey
   breast

⅓ cup seasoned dry bread
   crumbs

1 large egg, lightly beaten

½ teaspoon salt

2 cups hot cooked orzo

1. Heat the oil in a large nonstick skillet over medium-high heat. Add the onion and garlic; cook, stirring frequently, until golden, about 7 minutes. Transfer half of the onion mixture to a medium bowl; set aside.

2. Transfer the remaining onion mixture to a 5- or 6-quart slow cooker. Add the tomatoes, cinnamon, oregano, sugar, and pepper; stir well.

3. Add the turkey, bread crumbs, egg, and salt to the onion mixture in the bowl; mix well. Shape into 24 meatballs; place on top of the tomato mixture in the slow cooker. Carefully spoon some of the tomato mixture over the meatballs. Cover the slow cooker and cook until the meatballs are cooked through, 3–4 hours on high or 6–8 hours on low. Discard the cinnamon stick. Serve the meatballs and sauce with the orzo.

PER SERVING (6 meatballs, about ¼ cup sauce, and ½ cup orzo): 335 Cal, 6 g Total Fat, 1 g Sat Fat, 0 g Trans Fat, 128 mg Chol, 689 mg Sod, 35 g Carb, 3 g Fib, 34 g Prot, 92 mg Calc. *PointsPlus* value: 8.

COOK'S TIP

Save *3 PointsPlus* value by serving the meatballs and sauce over spaghetti squash instead of the orzo. A 1- to 1½-cup serving of cooked spaghetti squash per serving should be just about the right amount.

Sausage, Kale, and Shrimp with Black-Eyed Peas

Makes 6 Servings

1 teaspoon extra-virgin olive oil

½ pound Italian turkey sausage, casings removed

1 Vidalia onion, chopped

3 garlic cloves, minced

1 (14½-ounce) can crushed tomatoes

1 tablespoon paprika

¼ teaspoon red pepper flakes

1 pound kale, trimmed and coarsely chopped

2 (15-ounce) cans black-eyed peas, rinsed and drained

1 pound large shrimp, peeled and deveined

½ cup sliced drained roasted red peppers

1 tablespoon chopped fresh oregano, or 1 teaspoon dried

1. Heat the oil in a large nonstick skillet over medium-high heat. Add the sausage, onion, and garlic; cook, breaking up the sausage with a wooden spoon, until browned, about 10 minutes. Add the tomatoes, paprika, and red pepper flakes; bring to a boil, stirring to scrape up the browned bits from the skillet.

2. Put the sausage mixture in a 5- or 6-quart slow cooker. Add the kale and black-eyed peas; mix well. Cover and cook until the kale is tender, 3–4 hours on high or 6–8 hours on low.

3. Add the shrimp, roasted red peppers, and oregano; mix well. Cover and cook on high until the shrimp are just opaque in the center, about 30 minutes.

PER SERVING (generous 1 cup): 272 Cal, 7 g Total Fat, 2 g Sat Fat, 0 g Trans Fat, 93 mg Chol, 660 mg Sod, 31 g Carb, 9 g Fib, 24 g Prot, 146 mg Calc.
PointsPlus value: *7.*

COOK'S TIP

Kale, a member of the cabbage family—and very nutritious—stands up well to long, slow cooking. To prepare kale, trim the stems and remove the tough center ribs, then rinse the leaves well to remove any grit. A dollop of light sour cream makes a tasty topping for this dish (2 tablespoons light sour cream per serving will up the *PointsPlus* value by *1*).

Sausage, Kale, and Shrimp
with Black-Eyed Peas

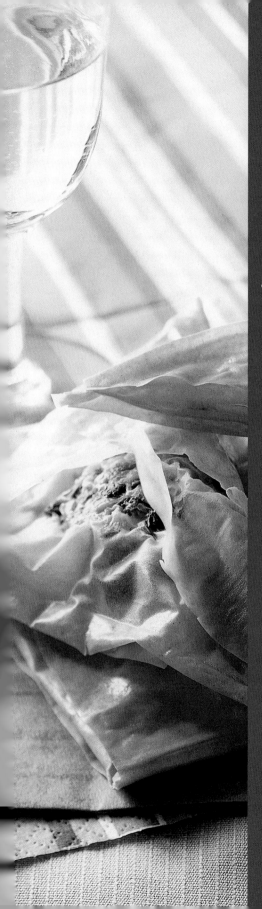

just a bite

Pretzel-Coated Chicken Bites with Mustard-Chipotle Sauce

Makes 8 Servings

2 ounces (1 cup) low-fat unsalted mini pretzels

⅓ cup fat-free mayonnaise

2 tablespoons whole-grain Dijon mustard

2 teaspoons chipotle pepper sauce

1 teaspoon red-wine vinegar

¼ teaspoon black pepper

¾ pound skinless boneless chicken breasts, cut into 24 chunks

1. Preheat the oven to 400°F. Spray a shallow baking pan with nonstick spray.

2. Pulse the pretzels in a food processor just until finely chopped, not ground (or crush with a meat mallet or rolling pin). Transfer to a zip-close plastic bag.

3. To make the mustard sauce, combine the mayonnaise, mustard, pepper sauce, vinegar, and black pepper in a small bowl.

4. Put the chicken in a medium bowl and toss with 2 tablespoons of the mustard sauce until evenly coated. Add the chicken to the pretzels and seal the bag. Shake the bag until the chicken is evenly coated with pretzels.

5. Place the chicken in the baking pan in one layer. Spray the chicken lightly with nonstick spray. Bake until golden on the outside and cooked through, about 15 minutes. Pile the chicken on a plate and serve with the remaining mustard sauce.

PER SERVING (3 chicken bites with 2 teaspoons sauce): 95 Cal, 2 g Total Fat, 1 g Sat Fat, 0 g Trans Fat, 26 mg Chol, 219 mg Sod, 7 g Carb, 0 g Fib, 10 g Prot, 8 mg Calc.
PointsPlus value: *2*.

COOK'S TIP

Crunchy, tasty pretzels make a super coating for chicken. When chopping pretzels in a food processor, watch carefully to avoid overprocessing: You want the pretzels to be in little pieces—not crumbs. Chipotle pepper sauce, readily available in supermarkets, has a deliciously smoky, not overly hot flavor.

Chicken Skewers with Spicy Peanut Dipping Sauce

Makes 8 Servings

3 (¼-pound) skinless boneless chicken breasts

½ cup plain fat-free yogurt

1½ teaspoons curry powder, preferably Madras

½ teaspoon salt

⅛ teaspoon black pepper

¼ cup smooth peanut butter

¼ cup hot water

1½ teaspoons red-wine vinegar

1 tablespoon reduced-sodium soy sauce

1 teaspoon Asian (dark) sesame oil

1 small garlic clove, minced

¼ teaspoon hot pepper sauce, or more to taste

1. Place the chicken between pieces of plastic wrap and pound to an even thickness. Cut the breasts lengthwise, on the diagonal, into 16 (1-inch-wide) strips. Combine the chicken, yogurt, curry powder, salt, and pepper in a large bowl; toss to coat. Cover and refrigerate for at least 30 minutes or up to several hours.

2. Meanwhile, soak 16 (6–8-inch) wooden skewers in water for at least 30 minutes.

3. To make the dipping sauce, whisk together the peanut butter, hot water, vinegar, soy sauce, oil, garlic, and hot pepper sauce in a small bowl until blended and smooth. Taste the sauce and season with additional pepper sauce, if desired. Transfer the sauce to a serving dish; cover and set aside.

4. Spray the broiler rack with nonstick spray; preheat the broiler.

5. Thread 1 chicken strip onto each skewer in a snakelike fashion. Cover the ends of the skewers with aluminum foil to prevent them from charring. Arrange the skewers on the broiler rack. Broil 5 inches from the heat, turning once, until the chicken is browned on the outside and cooked through, about 6 minutes. Pile the skewers onto a plate and serve the sauce alongside.

PER SERVING (2 skewers with 1 tablespoon sauce): 117 Cal, 6 g Total Fat, 1 g Sat Fat, 0 g Trans Fat, 26 mg Chol, 288 mg Sod, 3 g Carb, 1 g Fib, 12 g Prot, 41 mg Calc. *PointsPlus* value: *3.*

COOK'S TIP

When the weather permits, grill these kebabs. For extra flavor, sprinkle 1 cup of soaked hickory wood or apple wood chips over the charcoal just before adding the chicken. If using a gas grill, put the chips in a disposable foil tray with some holes poked in, and place on top of a lit burner.

Chicken Cakes with Tomato Jam

Chicken Cakes with Tomato Jam

Makes 16 Servings

1 pound skinless boneless chicken breasts, cooked and coarsely shredded

2 large egg whites, lightly beaten

2 tablespoons fat-free mayonnaise

2 teaspoons Dijon mustard

¼ teaspoon black pepper

6 tablespoons panko bread crumbs

2 teaspoons extra-virgin olive oil

¼ cup finely chopped onion

1 tablespoon finely chopped peeled fresh ginger

1 (14½-ounce) can diced tomatoes, drained

1 teaspoon sugar

Pinch of cayenne

1. Lightly spray a jelly-roll pan with nonstick spray.

2. Put the chicken into a food processor and pulse until finely chopped. Transfer to a medium bowl. Add the egg whites, mayonnaise, mustard, and black pepper; mix until well blended.

3. Put the bread crumbs on a plate. Shape level measuring tablespoons of the chicken mixture into 1½-inch cakes, coat with the bread crumbs, and place in the jelly-roll pan. Refrigerate for at least 30 minutes or up to several hours.

4. Preheat the oven to 425°F.

5. To make the tomato jam, heat the oil in a medium saucepan over medium heat. Add the onion and ginger; cook, stirring, until softened, about 5 minutes. Stir in the tomatoes, sugar, and cayenne; bring to a boil. Reduce the heat and simmer, stirring occasionally, until the tomato mixture thickens, about 15 minutes. Transfer to a serving bowl.

6. Meanwhile, lightly spray the chicken cakes with nonstick spray. Bake for 10 minutes. Turn the cakes over and spray with nonstick spray. Bake until golden and heated through, about 10 minutes longer. Arrange the chicken cakes on a platter. Serve the tomato jam alongside.

PER SERVING (2 chicken cakes with 2 teaspoons jam): 60 Cal, 2 g Total Fat, 0 g Sat Fat, 0 g Trans Fat, 17 mg Chol, 93 mg Sod, 3 g Carb, 0 g Fib, 7 g Prot, 13 mg Calc.
PointsPlus value: *1.*

COOK'S TIP

Panko, Japanese bread crumbs that are slowly dried and flaked, makes these chicken cakes super-crisp on the outside and moist on the inside. They are found in the bread aisle alongside other types of bread crumbs or in the Asian aisle of supermarkets.

Grilled Chicken Strips with Turkish Yogurt Sauce

Makes 8 Servings

1 cup plain fat-free Greek yogurt

3 scallions, finely chopped

2 tablespoons lemon juice

1 small garlic clove, minced

½–1 jalapeño pepper, seeded and minced

⅛ plus ¼ teaspoon salt

¼ teaspoon black pepper

1 pound skinless boneless chicken breasts, cut crosswise into 16 strips

½ teaspoon extra-virgin olive oil

1. Combine the yogurt, scallions, 1 tablespoon of the lemon juice, the garlic, jalapeño pepper, the ⅛ teaspoon salt, and ⅛ teaspoon of the black pepper in a medium bowl. Stir to mix well. Transfer to a serving bowl and refrigerate until ready to serve.

2. Meanwhile, soak 16 (6–8-inch) wooden skewers in water for at least 30 minutes.

3. Spray the grill or broiler rack with nonstick spray; prepare the grill or preheat the broiler.

4. Put the chicken strips into a medium bowl; sprinkle with the remaining 1 tablespoon lemon juice, ¼ teaspoon salt, and ⅛ teaspoon pepper; toss to mix well. Thread 1 chicken strip onto each skewer in a snakelike fashion. Cover the ends of the skewers with foil to prevent them from charring.

5. Place the skewers on the grill or broiler rack and grill or broil about 4 inches from the heat until cooked through, about 3 minutes on each side. Pile the skewered chicken onto a small platter; drizzle the oil over the yogurt sauce. Serve the sauce with the chicken.

PER SERVING (2 skewers with 2–3 tablespoons sauce): 110 Cal, 2 g Total Fat, 1 g Sat Fat, 0 g Trans Fat, 35 mg Chol, 190 mg Sod, 6 g Carb, 0 g Fib, 16 g Prot, 134 mg Calc.
PointsPlus value: *3.*

COOK'S TIP

This very flavorful, thick yogurt sauce also makes a great dipping sauce for raw vegetables. If you like, you can thicken regular yogurt if you have it on hand to use here: Line a sieve with a double thickness of damp paper towels and set over a medium bowl. Add 2 cups plain fat-free yogurt and refrigerate for at least 2 hours or up to 6 hours; discard the drained liquid. Use as directed.

Buffalo-Style Chicken Skewers

Makes 4 Servings

2 (5-ounce) skinless boneless
    chicken breasts

2 teaspoons canola oil

1 tablespoon plus 1 teaspoon
    hot sauce, such as Frank's

¼ teaspoon salt

4 celery stalks

¼ cup fat-free sour cream

¼ cup plain fat-free yogurt

2 tablespoons crumbled
    reduced-fat blue cheese

1. Remove the tender from the chicken breasts and cut lengthwise in half. Cut each chicken breast on a long diagonal into 6 thin strips. Toss together the chicken, oil, hot sauce, and salt in a medium bowl until coated evenly.

2. Cut the celery stalks lengthwise in half, then crosswise into thirds. To make the dressing, stir together the sour cream, yogurt, and blue cheese in a serving bowl.

3. Thread the chicken strips on 16 (8- to 10-inch) metal skewers (if using wooden skewers, soak in water 30 minutes).

4. Spray a nonstick ridged grill pan with nonstick spray and set over medium heat. Place the skewers in the pan, in batches if needed, and cook until the chicken is just cooked through, about 2 minutes on each side. Arrange the blue cheese dressing, celery sticks, and chicken skewers on a large serving platter.

PER SERVING (4 skewers, 2½ tablespoons dressing, and 6 celery sticks): 143 Cal, 5 g Total Fat, 1 g Sat Fat, 0 g Trans Fat, 47 mg Chol, 292 mg Sod, 4 g Carb, 1 g Fib, 19 g Prot, 104 mg Calc. *PointsPlus* value: *3*.

COOK'S TIP

Here's how to turn this recipe into a tasty chicken salad for two. Prepare and cook the chicken as directed but remove it from the skewers and cut into bite-size chunks. Dice the celery and add to the chicken along with the dressing and toss until mixed well. Place a Boston lettuce leaf or two on each of 2 plates and top with the salad. This will increase the per-serving *PointsPlus* value by *3*.

Chicken Yakitori with Bell Pepper and Scallions

Makes 12 Servings

1 (4-inch) piece fresh ginger

¼ cup mirin (rice wine) or dry sherry

2 tablespoons reduced-sodium soy sauce

2 tablespoons white or yellow miso

2 tablespoons packed brown sugar

1 pound skinless boneless chicken thighs, cut into 24 chunks

1 large red or green bell pepper, cut into 24 pieces

5 scallions (white and light green portion only), cut into 24 pieces

1. To make the marinade, peel and finely grate the ginger. Put the ginger into a piece of cheesecloth and squeeze it to extract as much ginger juice as possible into a medium bowl. Add the mirin, soy sauce, miso, and sugar to the ginger juice; stir until well mixed. Add the chicken and toss to coat. Cover and refrigerate for at least 30 minutes or up to several hours.

2. Meanwhile, soak 24 (6–8-inch) wooden skewers in water for at least 30 minutes.

3. Spray the broiler rack with nonstick spray; preheat the broiler.

4. Thread 1 piece of chicken, bell pepper, and scallion onto each skewer. Place the skewers on the broiler rack. Broil about 4 inches from the heat, turning the skewers once or twice, until the chicken is browned on the outside and cooked through, about 10 minutes.

PER SERVING (2 skewers): 87 Cal, 3 g Total Fat, 1 g Sat Fat, 0 g Trans Fat, 25 mg Chol, 237 mg Sod, 6 g Carb, 1 g Fib, 8 g Prot, 11 mg Calc.
PointsPlus value: *2.*

COOK'S TIP

In Japanese, yakitori means "chicken seared with heat." Often the chicken is not seasoned before being cooked. Instead, it is presented with a variety of highly seasoned sauces that are set out in small decorative bowls. Our yakitori is glaze-grilled: Coated with a slightly sweet soy sauce and miso mixture, which gives it a lavish sheen.

Cooking Poultry Perfectly Every Time

Whether cooking a whole bird or parts, the key is cooking it just enough so it's still succulent and juicy. Use an instant-read thermometer and the chart below to cook poultry to exactly the correct internal temperature. Keep in mind that whether you're cooking a whole bird, parts, or ground poultry, according to the USDA, poultry is safely cooked when the internal temperature reaches 165°F.

Here's how to check: Remove the poultry from the oven. Insert an instant-read thermometer into the thickest part of the meat, not touching any bone. For a whole bird, check the thickest part of a thigh. Whole birds should rest at least 10 minutes or up to 15 minutes before being carved, during which time the internal temperature will rise about 5°F.

WHOLE BIRDS	Roasting Time at 350°F	Grilling Time
Chicken (3 to 4 pounds)	1¼ to 1½ hours	60 to 75 minutes
Roaster (5 to 7 pounds)	2 to 2¼ hours	20 minutes per pound
Cornish Hens (18 to 24 ounces)	50 to 60 minutes	45 to 55 minutes
Poussin (14 to 20 ounces)	50 to 60 minutes	45 to 55 minutes
Guinea Hen (2 to 3 pounds)	1 to 1½ hours	not recommended
Squab (12 to 16 ounces)	about 45 minutes	about 30 minutes
Quail (3 to 7 ounces)	30 to 45 minutes	30 to 45 minutes

CHICKEN PARTS	Roasting Time at 350°F	Grilling Time
Bone-in Breast Halves (6 to 8 ounces)	30 to 40 minutes	20 to 30 minutes
Boneless Breast Halves (4 ounces)	20 to 30 minutes	12 to 16 minutes
Bone-in Leg or Thigh (4 to 8 ounces)	40 to 50 minutes	20 to 30 minutes
Boneless Thighs (3 ounces)	20 to 30 minutes	12 to 16 minutes
Drumsticks (4 ounces)	35 to 45 minutes	16 to 24 minutes
Chicken burger (6 ounces)	—	10 to 15 minutes

For turkey roasting times, see page 358.

Spinach and Chicken Triangles

Makes 14 Servings

2 teaspoons extra-virgin olive oil

1 large onion, chopped

1 (10-ounce) package frozen chopped spinach, thawed and squeezed dry

1 cup finely chopped cooked chicken breast

⅓ cup finely crumbled reduced-fat feta cheese

¼ cup chopped fresh dill

1 large egg white

¼ teaspoon salt

⅛ teaspoon black pepper

14 (14 × 18-inch) sheets phyllo dough, thawed according to the package directions if frozen

1. Heat the oil in a large nonstick skillet over medium heat. Add the onion and cook, stirring frequently, until golden, about 7 minutes.

2. Combine the onion, spinach, chicken, cheese, dill, egg white, salt, and pepper in a medium bowl until well mixed.

3. Preheat the oven to 375°F. Spray 2 jelly-roll pans or baking sheets with nonstick spray.

4. Place 1 phyllo sheet on a work surface. Cover the remaining sheets of phyllo with plastic wrap to keep them from drying out as you work. Lightly spray the phyllo sheet with nonstick spray. Cut it lengthwise into 4 strips. Put a rounded teaspoon of the spinach mixture in one corner of each phyllo strip and fold the phyllo diagonally over the filling to form a triangle. Continue to fold the phyllo (as if folding a flag) to the end of the strip. Place the phyllo triangles, seam side down, on a jelly-roll pan. Cover with a damp paper towel to prevent the phyllo from drying out. Repeat with the remaining phyllo and filling to make a total of 56 triangles.

5. Bake the triangles until the phyllo is puffed and golden, about 15 minutes. Serve hot, warm, or at room temperature.

PER SERVING (4 pieces): 117 Cal, 2 g Total Fat, 1 g Sat Fat, 0 g Trans Fat, 10 mg Chol, 189 mg Sod, 17 g Carb, 1 g Fib, 6 g Prot, 44 mg Calc.
PointsPlus value: *3*.

COOK'S TIP

Our Americanized version of the Greek spinach pastry spanakopita is extra satisfying due to the addition of chicken. In the Mediterranean, it is popular street food that is sold in various shapes and sizes. To ensure that the filling is just the right texture, be sure to squeeze all of the moisture out of the spinach.

Spinach and
Chicken Triangles

Herbed Chicken Salad on Warm Corn Cakes

Makes 14 Servings

2 cups chopped cooked
  chicken breast

¼ cup chopped fresh cilantro

3 tablespoons fat-free
  mayonnaise or sour cream

1 scallion, finely chopped

½–1 jalapeño pepper, seeded
  and minced

1 tablespoon lime juice

½ teaspoon salt

⅛ teaspoon black pepper

½ cup all-purpose flour

½ cup yellow cornmeal,
  preferably stone-ground

1 teaspoon baking powder

⅔ cup fat-free milk

2 large egg whites

1 tablespoon canola oil

Fresh cilantro leaves

1. To make the chicken salad, combine the chicken, cilantro, mayonnaise, scallion, jalapeño pepper, lime juice, ¼ teaspoon of the salt, and the black pepper in a medium bowl until well mixed. Cover and refrigerate for at least 1 hour or up to overnight.

2. To make the corn cakes, combine the flour, cornmeal, baking powder, and the remaining ¼ teaspoon salt in a medium bowl. Combine the milk, egg whites, and oil in a small bowl. Add the milk mixture to the flour mixture; stir just until blended.

3. Spray a large nonstick skillet or griddle with nonstick spray and set over medium-high heat. Drop the cornmeal batter, by scant measuring tablespoons, into the skillet, about 2 inches apart. Cook just until bubbles begin to appear around the edges, about 1½ minutes. Flip the corn cakes and cook until golden on bottom, about 1 minute longer. Transfer to a shallow baking pan and cover loosely with foil. Repeat with the remaining batter, to make a total of 28 corn cakes.

4. Spoon about 1 tablespoon of the chicken salad onto each warm cake, garnish each with a cilantro leaf, and arrange on a platter.

PER SERVING (2 pieces): 86 Cal, 2 g Total Fat, 0 g Sat Fat, 0 g Trans Fat, 17 mg Chol, 174 mg Sod, 8 g Carb, 1 g Fib, 8 g Prot, 39 mg Calc.
PointsPlus value: *2*.

COOK'S TIP

We like to use stone-ground cornmeal for these corn cakes because you get a slight crunch from the germ and hull, and it is also more nutritious than regular cornmeal. Stone-ground cornmeal is available in many supermarkets and organic supermarkets. It is best stored in the refrigerator. If you like, you can also use exotic-looking blue cornmeal, which is made from blue corn.

Roasted Tomato and Chicken–Topped Parmesan Crisps

Makes 16 Servings

8 plum tomatoes, halved lengthwise

2 teaspoons extra-virgin olive oil

½ teaspoon salt

⅛ teaspoon black pepper

1 cup (4 ounces) grated Parmesan cheese

1 tablespoon all-purpose flour

¼ pound thin-sliced deli roast chicken breast, cut into 16 pieces

4 fresh basil leaves, thinly sliced

1. Preheat the oven to 375°F. Spray a shallow baking pan with nonstick spray and line a baking sheet with parchment paper or foil.

2. Arrange the tomatoes, cut-side up, in the baking pan. Brush with the oil and sprinkle with the salt and pepper. Roast until the tomatoes are tender and the skins wrinkle, about 1 hour. Remove from the oven and let cool.

3. Meanwhile, stir together the cheese and flour in a small bowl. Drop the cheese mixture by tablespoons onto the lined baking sheet about 2 inches apart, making a total of 16 mounds. Spread each mound of cheese to form 2-inch rounds. Bake until golden, 8–10 minutes. Let the crisps cool about 2 minutes. Using a wide spatula, transfer the cheese crisps to a rack to cool completely.

4. When cool, transfer the Parmesan crisps to a platter. Place a piece of chicken on each crisp, top with a tomato half, then sprinkle with the basil.

PER SERVING (1 piece): 52 Cal, 3 g Total Fat, 1 g Sat Fat, 0 g Trans Fat, 11 mg Chol, 207 mg Sod, 2 g Carb, 0 g Fib, 5 g Prot, 87 mg Calc.
PointsPlus value: *1.*

COOK'S TIP

Roasting tomatoes intensifies their flavor, whether using fresh tomatoes from a local farmers' market during the height of summer or tomatoes from the supermarket in the dead of winter. These roasted tomatoes are also great tossed with pasta, served over grilled fish, or mixed with grilled zucchini or eggplant.

Chicken Tea Sandwiches

Chicken Tea Sandwiches

Makes 12 Servings

2 cups finely chopped cooked chicken breast

3 tablespoons fat-free mayonnaise

2 scallions, finely chopped

1 tablespoon chopped fresh tarragon

Grated zest of 1 lemon

1 tablespoon lemon juice

½ teaspoon salt

⅛ teaspoon black pepper

6 (3½-inch-square) thin slices dark bread, crusts removed

12 (3½-inch-long) very thin slices seedless cucumber

6 (3½-inch-square) thin slices white bread, crusts removed

1. Combine the chicken, mayonnaise, scallions, tarragon, lemon zest, lemon juice, salt, and pepper in a medium bowl until well mixed. Refrigerate for at least 20 minutes or up to several hours to allow flavors to blend.

2. Place the slices of dark bread on a work surface. Top each slice with 2 cucumber slices. Spread ¼ cup of the chicken salad over the cucumber on each slice of bread, spreading it all the way to the edge. Top each with a slice of the white bread. Cut each sandwich on the diagonal to form 4 sandwich triangles, making a total of 24 triangles.

PER SERVING (2 sandwich triangles): 85 Cal, 2 g Total Fat, 0 g Sat Fat, 0 g Trans Fat, 19 mg Chol, 242 mg Sod, 9 g Carb, 1 g Fib, 8 g Prot, 22 mg Calc.
PointsPlus value: *2.*

COOK'S TIP

Fresh tarragon and lemon add bright flavor to these little tea sandwiches. You can prepare the sandwiches early in the day and store them, covered with lightly dampened paper towels and overwrapped with plastic wrap, in the refrigerator for up to 8 hours. Let the sandwiches stand at room temperature for about 30 minutes before serving for the best flavor.

Chicken and Cheddar Quesadillas

Makes 12 Servings

6 (8-inch) fat-free flour tortillas

1 cup (4 ounces) shredded reduced-fat Cheddar cheese

¼ pound thinly sliced cooked chicken breast

½ cup roasted red peppers, drained and chopped

½ cup loosely packed fresh cilantro leaves

2 scallions, thinly sliced

Hot pepper sauce

1. Place the tortillas on a work surface; sprinkle the cheese evenly over half of each tortilla. Arrange the chicken, roasted peppers, cilantro, and scallions evenly over the cheese. Sprinkle each with a few drops of hot pepper sauce. Fold the unfilled half of each tortilla over the filling, lightly pressing down on the tortillas.

2. Heat a large nonstick skillet over medium heat. Spray the top of each quesadilla with extra-virgin olive oil nonstick spray. Place 3 of the tortillas, sprayed side down, in the skillet. Cook until crisp on the bottom, 1–2 minutes. Spray the tops of the tortillas with nonstick spray and turn them over. Cook until crisp on the second side, 1–2 minutes. Transfer the quesadillas to a cutting board and cover loosely with foil. Cook the remaining 3 quesadillas. Cut each quesadilla into 4 wedges, making a total of 24 wedges. Stack the wedges on a serving plate and serve hot or warm.

PER SERVING (2 wedges): 115 Cal, 2 g Total Fat, 1 g Sat Fat, 0 g Trans Fat, 10 mg Chol, 362 mg Sod, 16 g Carb, 1 g Fib, 7 g Prot, 97 mg Calc.
PointsPlus value: *3.*

COOK'S TIP

These quesadillas are prepared the classic way—half of each tortilla is covered with the filling ingredients, and then the unfilled half is folded over the filling, forming a half-moon shape. Quesadillas are often fried. In this lighter—but equally flavorful version—they are lightly sprayed with nonstick spray and cooked in a skillet until the cheese melts and the tortillas are temptingly crisp.

Chopped Chicken Liver Spread

Makes 12 Servings

1 tablespoon extra-virgin
  olive oil

1 large onion, chopped

½ pound chicken livers, rinsed
  and patted dry

1 cup frozen peas, thawed

¾ teaspoon salt

½ teaspoon dried sage

¼ teaspoon black pepper

Whites of 2 hard-cooked large
  eggs

1. Heat the oil in a large nonstick skillet over medium heat. Add the onion and cook, stirring frequently, until translucent, about 5 minutes. Add the livers, peas, salt, sage, and pepper; cook, stirring occasionally, until the livers are cooked through, about 10 minutes. Remove the skillet from the heat and let the mixture cool slightly.

2. Transfer the liver mixture to a food processor and pulse to form a rough puree. Add the hard-cooked egg whites and pulse until almost smooth. Transfer the mixture to a serving bowl.

PER SERVING (generous 2 tablespoons): 44 Cal, 2 g Total Fat, 0 g Sat Fat, 0 g Trans Fat, 74 mg Chol, 172 mg Sod, 3 g Carb, 1 g Fib, 4 g Prot, 8 mg Calc.
PointsPlus value: *1*.

COOK'S TIP

Serve the spread in a bowl surrounded by carrot and celery sticks, red and yellow bell pepper strips, and English cucumber slices. Melba toast, a traditional accompaniment, makes a good addition to the mix (3 rye, wheat, garlic, or plain melba toasts per serving will increase the *PointsPlus* value by *2*).

Skewered Sesame Meatballs with Sweet-Sour Sauce

Makes 12 Servings

1 pound ground skinless
 chicken breast

1 (7-ounce) can whole water
 chestnuts, drained and
 finely chopped

¼ cup plain dry bread crumbs

2 large egg whites

2 tablespoons reduced-sodium
 soy sauce

1 large shallot, finely chopped

1 tablespoon minced peeled
 fresh ginger

1 tablespoon sesame seeds

36 snow peas (about 3 ounces),
 trimmed

¾ cup bottled sweet-and-sour
 dipping sauce

1. Preheat the oven to 375°F. Spray a jelly-roll pan with nonstick spray.

2. To make the meatballs, combine the chicken, water chestnuts, bread crumbs, egg whites, soy sauce, shallot, and ginger in a medium bowl until well blended. Shape the mixture into 36 meatballs and place in the pan. Sprinkle the meatballs with the sesame seeds, then lightly spray with nonstick spray. Bake until the meatballs are cooked through, about 20 minutes.

3. Meanwhile, bring a large saucepan of water to a boil. Add the snow peas and boil for 1 minute. Drain and rinse under cold running water to stop the cooking. Drain again.

4. Skewer a snow pea and meatball onto each wooden pick. Repeat with the remaining 35 snow peas and 35 meatballs. Pile the skewers onto a platter and serve the dipping sauce alongside.

PER SERVING (3 skewers with 1 tablespoon sauce): 96 Cal, 2 g Total Fat, 0 g Sat Fat, 0 g Trans Fat, 25 mg Chol, 195 mg Sod, 9 g Carb, 1 g Fib, 10 g Prot, 23 mg Calc.
PointsPlus value: *2.*

COOK'S TIP

It's nice to have fresh ginger on hand so you can add it to dishes whenever you want. To store pieces of ginger, place it in a container, cover with cold water and refrigerate, changing the water every few days. It will keep for at least 3 weeks. To store sliced ginger, peel the ginger and cut it into thin rounds. Put it into a glass jar, cover with dry sherry, and refrigerate for up to several weeks.

**Skewered Sesame Meatballs
with Sweet-Sour Sauce**

Slow-Cooker Herbed Tomato–Italian Sausage Dip

Makes 12 Servings

1 pound sweet or hot Italian chicken sausage links, casings removed

1 onion, finely chopped

1 carrot, finely chopped

1 green bell pepper, finely chopped

3 large garlic cloves, minced

1 (28-ounce) can crushed tomatoes

1 (6-ounce) can tomato paste

1 teaspoon dried oregano

1 teaspoon fennel seeds, crushed

¼ teaspoon black pepper

1. Spray a large nonstick skillet with olive oil nonstick spray and set over medium heat. Add the sausage meat, onion, carrot, and bell pepper; cook, breaking the sausage apart with a wooden spoon, until browned, 7–8 minutes. Add the garlic and cook, stirring, until fragrant, about 1 minute.

2. Transfer the sausage mixture to a 5- or 6-quart slow cooker. Stir in the tomatoes, tomato paste, oregano, fennel seeds, and black pepper. Cover and cook until the mixture simmers and thickens, 2–3 hours on high or 4–6 hours on low. Serve hot or warm.

PER SERVING (⅓ cup): 91 Cal, 2 g Total Fat, 1 g Sat Fat, 0 g Trans Fat, 23 mg Chol, 445 mg Sod, 10 g Carb, 1 g Fib, 8 g Prot, 8 mg Calc.
PointsPlus value: *2*.

COOK'S TIP

Big chunks of red bell pepper, whole endive spears, and whole wheat pita breads, cut into wedges and toasted, make great dippers for this dip (½ of a whole wheat pita bread for each serving will increase the *PointsPlus* value by *2*).

Greek-Style Pita Pizza

Makes 4 Servings

4 (7-inch) pocketless whole wheat pita breads

2 (14½-ounce) cans no-salt-added diced tomatoes, well drained

2 cups chopped cooked chicken breast

¼ cup finely chopped red onion

4 Kalamata olives, pitted and chopped

¼ teaspoon black pepper

Large pinch of dried oregano

½ cup crumbled reduced-fat feta cheese

2 tablespoons chopped fresh flat-leaf parsley

1. Preheat the oven to 450°F. Place the pita breads on a large baking sheet.

2. Combine the tomatoes, chicken, onion, olives, pepper, and oregano in a bowl.

3. Spoon the chicken mixture evenly onto the pita breads, then sprinkle evenly with the cheese. Bake until the pizzas are heated through and the cheese is slightly melted, about 7 minutes. Sprinkle with the parsley, cut each pizza into 4 wedges, and serve at once.

PER SERVING (1 pizza): 400 Cal, 8 g Total Fat, 2 g Sat Fat, 0 g Trans Fat, 70 mg Chol, 752 mg Sod, 52 g Carb, 8 g Fib, 33 g Prot, 184 mg Calc.
PointsPlus value: *10.*

COOK'S TIP

Pocketless pita breads make tasty pizza crusts with almost infinite ways to top them. This chicken, tomato, feta, and olive combination is one of our favorites. Kalamata olives are full flavored, so just a few go a long way. To save time, buy them pitted.

Tex-Mex Pizza

Tex-Mex Pizza

Makes 4 Servings

1 tablespoon canola oil

¾ pound skinless boneless chicken breasts, cut into ½-inch pieces

½ small yellow bell pepper, cut into ½-inch pieces

¼ teaspoon salt

4 (8-inch) jalapeño or whole wheat flour tortillas

½ cup hot, medium, or mild salsa

⅔ cup shredded reduced-fat Monterey Jack cheese

1 tablespoon chopped fresh cilantro

1. Preheat the oven to 450°F.

2. Heat the oil in a large nonstick skillet over medium heat. Add the chicken, bell pepper, and salt; cook, stirring frequently, until the chicken is cooked through, about 7 minutes. Transfer to a plate to cool.

3. Toast the tortillas in a dry large nonstick skillet over medium heat, about 1 minute on each side. Place the tortillas on a large baking sheet and spread evenly with the salsa; top with the chicken mixture and sprinkle with the cheese.

4. Bake until the cheese melts, about 6 minutes. Sprinkle with the cilantro, cut each pizza into 4 wedges, and serve at once.

PER SERVING (1 pizza): 286 Cal, 11 g Total Fat, 4 g Sat Fat, 0 g Trans Fat, 64 mg Chol, 671 mg Sod, 19 g Carb, 3 g Fib, 27 g Prot, 162 mg Calc.
PointsPlus value: 7.

COOK'S TIP

Tex Mex–flavored toppings, scattered across the top of toasted flour tortillas, make an unconventional—and delectable—pizza. Consider other creative topping combinations: Substitute Cheddar cheese for the Monterey Jack, use skinless boneless turkey instead of the chicken, and serve with fat-free tomatillo salsa for no additional *PointsPlus* value.

done in
20 minutes

Spiced Chicken with Orange-Chipotle Glaze

Makes 4 Servings

¼ cup orange juice

2 tablespoons orange marmalade

1 teaspoon chopped chipotle en adobo

1½ teaspoons ground cumin

½ teaspoon ground coriander

½ teaspoon salt

4 (¼-pound) skinless boneless chicken breasts

1. Combine the orange juice, marmalade, and chipotle in a small bowl. Combine the cumin, coriander, and salt in a large bowl; add the chicken tossing to coat with the spices.

2. Spray a nonstick ridged grill pan with nonstick spray and set over medium-high heat. Add the chicken and cook, turning and brushing with the glaze every 4 minutes, until browned on the outside and cooked through, about 12 minutes. Stop glazing 5 minutes before the chicken is done.

PER SERVING (1 piece chicken): 177 Cal, 4 g Total Fat, 1 g Sat Fat, 0 g Trans Fat, 68 mg Chol, 369 mg Sod, 9 g Carb, 0 g Fib, 25 g Prot, 24 mg Calc.
PointsPlus value: *4.*

COOK'S TIP

For a double dose of flavor, these skinless boneless chicken breasts are rubbed with cumin and coriander, then basted with a smoky chile–orange marmalade glaze while being grilled. Fantastic! The glaze is also excellent with pork tenderloin, salmon steaks, and shrimp.

Sautéed Chicken with Artichokes, Olives, and Oregano

Makes 4 Servings

4 (4-ounce) thin-sliced chicken breast cutlets

1 teaspoon dried oregano

⅛ teaspoon salt

¼ teaspoon black pepper

2 teaspoons extra-virgin olive oil

¾ cup reduced-sodium chicken broth

1 (14-ounce) can artichoke hearts, drained and halved

¼ cup pitted Kalamata olives, halved

2 tablespoons lemon juice

2 tablespoons chopped fresh flat-leaf parsley

1. Sprinkle the chicken with the oregano, salt, and pepper. Heat the oil in a large nonstick skillet over medium-high heat. Add the chicken and cook until browned on the outside and cooked through, about 3 minutes on each side. Transfer the chicken to a serving plate; cover and keep warm.

2. Add the broth, artichoke hearts, olives, and lemon juice to the skillet; bring to a boil, scraping any browned bits from the bottom of the pan. Reduce the heat and simmer, uncovered, until the liquid has reduced slightly, about 2 minutes. Stir in the parsley, then spoon the sauce over the chicken.

PER SERVING (1 piece chicken with ¼ cup sauce): 217 Cal, 7 g Total Fat, 2 g Sat Fat, 0 g Trans Fat, 68 mg Chol, 524 mg Sod, 10 g Carb, 4 g Fib, 28 g Prot, 63 mg Calc.
PointsPlus value: *5.*

COOK'S TIP

This skillet dinner features the simple and delectable sun-drenched flavors of the Mediterranean. Try it over whole wheat strand pasta, such as linguine or thin spaghetti, and serve it with a salad of very thinly sliced fennel, orange segments, and flat-leaf parsley leaves. One cup cooked whole wheat pasta per serving will increase the *PointsPlus* value by *4.*

Chile-Rubbed Chicken with Fresh Pineapple Salsa

Chile-Rubbed Chicken with Fresh Pineapple Salsa

Makes 4 Servings

4 (4–5-ounce) thin-sliced chicken breast cutlets

2 teaspoons ancho chile powder

¼ plus ⅛ teaspoon salt

2 teaspoons canola oil

1 (8-ounce) package peeled and diced fresh pineapple

½ red bell pepper, diced

3 tablespoons mango chutney

2 tablespoons chopped fresh cilantro

Pinch of black pepper

4 lime wedges

1. Rub the chicken with the chile powder and the ¼ teaspoon salt. Heat the oil in a large nonstick skillet over medium-high heat. Add the chicken and cook until browned on the outside and cooked through, about 3 minutes on each side. Transfer the chicken to a serving plate; cover and keep warm.

2. Meanwhile, combine the pineapple, bell pepper, chutney, cilantro, the remaining ⅛ teaspoon salt, and the black pepper in a small bowl. Serve the chicken with the salsa and the lime wedges.

PER SERVING (1 piece chicken with ½ cup salsa): 214 Cal, 6 g Total Fat, 1 g Sat Fat, 0 g Trans Fat, 68 mg Chol, 304 mg Sod, 14 g Carb, 2 g Fib, 26 g Prot, 25 mg Calc.
PointsPlus value: *5*.

COOK'S TIP

For fiery flavor in a flash, thin-sliced chicken breasts are rubbed with chile powder and topped with fruit salsa to tame the heat. Convenient precut fresh pineapple lets you assemble the salsa in seconds. Add ½ cup cooked rice to each serving and you'll increase your *PointsPlus* value by *3*).

Creamy Chicken and Corn Avgolemono Soup

Makes 4 Servings

4 cups reduced-sodium chicken broth

½ pound skinless boneless chicken breast, cut into 2 x ¼-inch strips

2 cups fresh or frozen corn kernels

2 large eggs

3 tablespoons lemon juice

3 tablespoons chopped fresh flat-leaf parsley

⅛ teaspoon black pepper

2 scallions (white and light green portion only), thinly sliced

1. Bring the broth to a boil in a large saucepan. Add the chicken and corn; return to a boil. Reduce the heat and simmer, uncovered, until the chicken is just cooked through, about 5 minutes.

2. Meanwhile, lightly beat the eggs, lemon juice, parsley, and pepper in a small bowl. Stir about 2 tablespoons of the hot broth into the egg mixture. Gradually pour the egg mixture into the simmering soup and cook, stirring constantly, until the egg forms shreds, about 1 minute. Serve the soup sprinkled with the scallions.

PER SERVING (scant 1½ cups): 211 Cal, 6 g Total Fat, 2 g Sat Fat, 0 g Trans Fat, 140 mg Chol, 553 mg Sod, 17 g Carb, 2 g Fib, 23 g Prot, 42 mg Calc.
PointsPlus value: *5.*

COOK'S TIP

This substantial soup, inspired by the Greek classic, can be ready in minutes. Eggs, quickly whisked in, make it creamy, while lemon juice adds zing. If fresh corn is not available, use frozen petite white corn, which is especially sweet and good. Enjoy this soup with tasty pumpernickel bread (1 slice of pumpernickel bread per serving will increase the *PointsPlus* value by *2*).

Chicken Cheese Steaks

Makes 4 Servings

1 teaspoon extra-virgin olive oil

½ medium onion, thinly sliced

½ small poblano pepper, seeded and thinly sliced

1 garlic clove, crushed through a press

1 pound chicken tenders

¼ teaspoon salt

2 (1-ounce) slices provolone cheese

2 (3–4-ounce) hero or hoagie rolls, split and toasted

1. Heat the oil in a large nonstick skillet over medium heat. Add the onion, poblano chile, and garlic; cook, partially covered, stirring occasionally, until golden and softened, 3–4 minutes.

2. Add the chicken and salt; cook, uncovered, turning occasionally, until the chicken is browned and cooked through, about 4 minutes. Remove the skillet from the heat. Top the chicken with the cheese; cover the skillet and let stand until the cheese melts, about 1 minute.

3. Fill each roll with half of the chicken filling. Cut each sandwich in half.

PER SERVING (½ **sandwich**): 326 Cal, 10 g Total Fat, 4 g Sat Fat, 0 g Trans Fat, 78 mg Chol, 593 mg Sod, 25 g Carb, 2 g Fib, 32 g Prot, 157 mg Calc.
PointsPlus value: *8.*

COOK'S TIP

If you are a fan of the Philly cheese steak but want to skip the beef and trim the fat, check out our healthier interpretation that is just as tasty. Here, poblanos stand in for the usual bell peppers to lend the sandwich a touch of heat. This dark green chile pepper is about 5 inches long and 2½ inches wide with a mild to medium amount of heat.

Chicken and Edamame Stir-Fry

Makes 4 Servings

½ cup reduced-sodium chicken broth

2 teaspoons rice wine vinegar

2 teaspoons reduced-sodium soy sauce

1 teaspoon cornstarch

2 teaspoons canola oil

1 (10-ounce) package frozen edamame (green soybeans), thawed (2 cups)

1 teaspoon grated peeled fresh ginger

1 garlic clove, crushed through a press

¼ teaspoon red pepper flakes

1 pound chicken tenders, cut into 1-inch chunks

1. Combine the broth, vinegar, soy sauce, and cornstarch in a small bowl until smooth; set aside.

2. Heat a nonstick wok or a large skillet over high heat until a drop of water sizzles. Add 1 teaspoon of the oil, swirl to coat the pan, then add the edamame. Stir-fry until lightly browned, 2–3 minutes. Transfer the edamame to a plate.

3. Add the remaining 1 teaspoon oil to the wok, swirl to coat the pan, then add the ginger, garlic, and pepper flakes. Stir-fry until fragrant, about 15 seconds. Add the chicken; stir-fry until lightly browned, 3–4 minutes. Stir in the broth mixture and cook, stirring constantly, until the mixture bubbles and thickens and the chicken is just cooked through, 1–2 minutes. Stir in the edamame and heat through, about 1 minute.

PER SERVING (1 cup): 271 Cal, 11 g Total Fat, 2 g Sat Fat, 0 g Trans Fat, 68 mg Chol, 222 mg Sod, 10 g Carb, 3 g Fib, 34 g Prot, 118 mg Calc.
PointsPlus value: *7.*

COOK'S TIP

Edamame, the Japanese name for fresh green soybeans, have become so popular in the U.S. that they're available shelled and frozen—good news for speedy stir-fries like this one. To quickly thaw them, put the edamame in a colander and rinse under warm water.

Thai Chicken Salad

Makes 4 Servings

3 tablespoons lime juice

2 teaspoons canola oil

2 teaspoons Asian fish sauce

1½ teaspoons reduced-sodium soy sauce

½ teaspoon sugar

2 cups shredded cooked chicken breast

1 (5-ounce) package baby Asian salad mix

1 cup loosely packed fresh mint leaves

1 cup shredded carrots

1 small red onion, thinly sliced

Whisk together the lime juice, oil, fish sauce, soy sauce, and sugar in a large bowl. Add the chicken, salad mix, mint, carrots, and onion to the dressing; toss well to coat. Serve at once.

PER SERVING (2 cups): 171 Cal, 6 g Total Fat, 1 g Sat Fat, 0 g Trans Fat, 57 mg Chol, 229 mg Sod, 7 g Carb, 2 g Fib, 22 g Prot, 57 mg Calc.
PointsPlus value: *4.*

COOK'S TIP

To reduce your kitchen time, we've used short-cut ingredients, including precooked chicken, packaged baby greens, and shredded carrots. You only need to allow enough time to squeeze lime juice.

Citrus Chicken and Napa Slaw

Makes 4 Servings

3 tablespoons mirin (rice wine)

2 tablespoons lime juice

2 teaspoons canola oil

½ teaspoon salt

¼ teaspoon black pepper

5 cups thinly sliced napa cabbage

2 cups shredded cooked chicken breast

1 cup shredded carrots

3 scallions, thinly sliced

¼ cup chopped fresh cilantro

Whisk together the mirin, lime juice, oil, salt, and pepper in a large bowl. Add the cabbage, chicken, carrots, scallions, and cilantro; toss well to coat. Serve at once, or cover and refrigerate until ready to serve, up to 2 hours.

PER SERVING (1½ cups): 197 Cal, 5 g Total Fat, 1 g Sat Fat, 0 g Trans Fat, 60 mg Chol, 376 mg Sod, 10 g Carb, 2 g Fib, 24 g Prot, 80 mg Calc.
PointsPlus value: *5.*

COOK'S TIP

If you have the time, cook the chicken yourself. Place ¾ pound skinless boneless chicken breast on a baking sheet lightly sprayed with nonstick spray and lightly spray the chicken. Cover tightly with foil and bake in a 400°F oven until the chicken is cooked through, about 30 minutes. Let the chicken cool, then shred.

Chicken Stir-Fry with Almonds and Snap Peas

Chicken Stir-Fry with Almonds and Snap Peas

Makes 4 Servings

2 teaspoons canola oil

¼ cup sliced almonds

3 tablespoons dry sherry

3 tablespoons reduced-sodium soy sauce

2 tablespoons water

2 teaspoons cornstarch

½ teaspoon five-spice powder

1 pound chicken tenders, cut into 1-inch chunks

¼ pound fresh sugar snap peas, trimmed

3 scallions, cut into 1-inch pieces

2 garlic cloves, crushed through a press

1. Heat a nonstick wok or a large skillet over high heat until a drop of water sizzles. Add 1 teaspoon of the oil, swirl to coat the pan, then add the almonds. Stir-fry until lightly browned, about 2 minutes. Transfer the almonds to a plate.

2. Combine the sherry, soy sauce, water, cornstarch, and five-spice powder in a small bowl until smooth; set aside.

3. Add the remaining 1 teaspoon oil to the wok, swirl to coat the pan, then add the chicken. Stir-fry until lightly browned, 3–4 minutes. Add the snap peas, scallions, and garlic; stir-fry about 1 minute. Stir in the sherry mixture and cook, stirring constantly, until the mixture bubbles and thickens, and the chicken is just cooked through, 1–2 minutes. Stir in the almonds.

PER SERVING (scant 1 cup): 222 Cal, 8 g Total Fat, 1 g Sat Fat, 0 g Trans Fat, 63 mg Chol, 459 mg Sod, 9 g Carb, 2 g Fib, 26 g Prot, 55 mg Calc.
PointsPlus value: *6.*

COOK'S TIP

Sweet sugar snap peas are a cook's best friend. They're entirely edible—pod and all, so there's practically no prep. Plus, they taste best when only briefly cooked—or not at all—so they retain their crisp texture. Available during the spring and fall, select sugar snaps with plump, bright green pods and no wrinkling at the ends.

Chicken Picadillo Wraps

Makes 4 Servings

1 teaspoon extra-virgin olive oil

1 pound ground skinless
　　chicken breast

2 teaspoons ground cumin

1 teaspoon dried oregano

1 (14½-ounce) can diced
　　tomatoes with jalapeños

1 cup rinsed and drained
　　canned black beans

⅓ cup golden raisins

2 (10-inch) fat-free flour
　　tortillas

1. Heat the oil in a large nonstick skillet over medium-high heat. Add the chicken and cook, breaking it up with a wooden spoon, until browned and cooked through, about 5 minutes. Stir in the cumin and oregano; cook about 1 minute. Stir in the tomatoes, beans, and raisins; bring to a boil. Reduce the heat and simmer, uncovered, about 2 minutes.

2. Meanwhile, stack the tortillas on a microwavable plate. Cover with a damp paper towel and microwave on High, about 30 seconds. Divide the chicken filling evenly onto each warm tortilla. Fold the sides over and roll up to enclose the filling. Cut each wrap in half.

PER SERVING (½ wrap): 399 Cal, 6 g Total Fat, 1 g Sat Fat, 0 g Trans Fat, 68 mg Chol, 873 mg Sod, 54 g Carb, 5 g Fib, 33 g Prot, 127 mg Calc.
PointsPlus value: *10.*

COOK'S TIP

Picadillo—usually a mix of ground pork and beef, onions, and tomatoes—is a favorite in many Spanish-speaking countries. To keep it lean, we've substituted chicken for the pork and beef and, as in Mexico, we've added raisins, which is a fruity counterpoint to the heat of the jalapeños.

Chicken Caesar Pitas

Makes 4 Servings

¼ cup plain low-fat yogurt

2 tablespoons low-fat mayonnaise

2 tablespoons grated Parmesan cheese

1 small garlic clove, crushed through a press

2 teaspoons lemon juice

½ teaspoon Dijon mustard

¼ teaspoon anchovy paste

¼ teaspoon black pepper

2 cups chopped cooked chicken breast

4 (6-inch) whole wheat pita breads

8 small romaine lettuce leaves

1. Combine the yogurt, mayonnaise, cheese, garlic, lemon juice, mustard, anchovy paste, and pepper in a medium bowl. Add the chicken and toss to coat with the dressing.

2. Cut a pocket in each pita. Fill each pita with one-fourth of the chicken mixture and 2 lettuce leaves.

PER SERVING (1 sandwich): 304 Cal, 6 g Total Fat, 2 g Sat Fat, 0 g Trans Fat, 61 mg Chol, 522 mg Sod, 34 g Carb, 4 g Fib, 29 g Prot, 100 mg Calc.
PointsPlus value: *8.*

COOK'S TIP

Peppery watercress makes a very flavorful substitute for the romaine. To store watercress at home, cut off the bottom inch of the stems, place the cress in a glass filled with enough water to come about 1 inch up its side, and cover loosely with a plastic bag. Refrigerated, the watercress will keep for at least 4 days.

Cumin-Spiced Chicken with Pears

Makes 4 Servings

8 (5-ounce) skinless boneless
    chicken thighs

2 teaspoons ground cumin

¼ teaspoon salt

¼ teaspoon black pepper

1 teaspoon extra-virgin olive oil

1 large ripe pear

¾ cup apple cider

2 tablespoons apple cider
    vinegar

1. Sprinkle the chicken with the cumin, salt, and pepper. Heat the oil in a large nonstick skillet over medium-high heat. Add the chicken and cook until browned on the outside and cooked through, about 4 minutes on each side. Transfer to a serving platter; cover and keep warm.

2. Meanwhile, to cut the pear, set it upright on its base. Cut in ½-inch slices down the length of the pear towards the base; remove any seeds. (You should have eight ½-inch-thick slices.)

3. Add the pear slices to the skillet; reduce the heat to medium and cook until lightly browned, about 1 minute on each side. Transfer the pears to the serving platter.

4. Add the cider and cider vinegar to the skillet; bring to a boil, scraping any browned bits from the bottom of the pan. Boil 1 minute. Spoon the sauce over the chicken and pears.

PER SERVING (2 chicken thighs, 2 pear slices, and about 1 tablespoon sauce): 297 Cal, 13 g Total Fat, 4 g Sat Fat, 0 g Trans Fat, 88 mg Chol, 229 mg Sod, 14 g Carb, 1 g Fib, 30 g Prot, 52 mg Calc. *PointsPlus* value: *8.*

COOK'S TIP

Pears are best bought still firm, which prevents them from getting damaged on the way home from the market. Leave them out at room temperature until ripened, which will take a day or two, then refrigerate the pears so they don't overripen.

**Cumin-Spiced
Chicken with Pears**

Asian Chicken Lettuce Wraps

Makes 4 Servings

1 teaspoon canola oil

3 scallions, thinly sliced

1 yellow or red bell pepper,
    diced

½ teaspoon grated peeled
    fresh ginger

1 pound ground skinless
    chicken breast

½ teaspoon chili powder

3 tablespoons reduced-sodium
    soy sauce

8 large iceberg lettuce leaves

1. Heat the oil in a large nonstick skillet over medium-high heat. Add the scallions, bell pepper, and ginger; cook, stirring constantly, about 1 minute.

2. Add the chicken and chili powder; cook, breaking it up with a wooden spoon, until browned and cooked through, about 5 minutes. Stir in the soy sauce.

3. Divide the chicken mixture evenly among the lettuce leaves; roll up tightly and serve at once.

PER SERVING (2 wraps): 155 Cal, 2 g Total Fat, 1 g Sat Fat, 0 g Trans Fat, 75 mg Chol, 456 mg Sod, 5 g Carb, 1 g Fib, 28 g Prot, 33 mg Calc.
PointsPlus value: *4.*

COOK'S TIP

Lettuce leaves make an instant no-*PointsPlus* value wrapper—perfect for the time-pressed cook. They also offer a cooling contrast to the spicy chicken filling with its crunchy bell peppers and fragrant ginger.

Tzatziki Chicken Salad

Makes 6 Servings

¾ cup plain fat-free yogurt

2 tablespoons chopped
fresh mint

2 teaspoons grated lemon zest

1 tablespoon lemon juice

1 garlic clove, minced

1 teaspoon extra-virgin olive oil

3 cups chopped cooked
chicken breast

2 cups torn romaine lettuce
leaves

1 tomato, chopped

1 red onion, finely chopped

½ cucumber, peeled, seeded,
and diced

6 Kalamata olives, pitted and
chopped

1. To make the dressing, whisk together the yogurt, mint, lemon zest, lemon juice, garlic, and oil in a small bowl until blended; set aside.

2. Place the chicken, lettuce, tomato, onion, cucumber, and olives in a large bowl. Drizzle with the dressing and toss well to coat. Serve at once.

PER SERVING (1⅓ **cups**)**: 162 Cal, 4 g Total Fat, 1 g Sat Fat, 0 g Trans Fat, 58 mg Chol, 114 mg Sod, 6 g Carb, 1 g Fib, 21 g Prot, 87 mg Calc.**
PointsPlus value: *4.*

COOK'S TIP

You can make the flavorful Greek dressing up to 1 day ahead and store in the refrigerator. Serve this salad with warmed or grilled—use a grill pan—whole wheat pita breads for a satisfying lunch (1 small pita bread per serving will up the *PointsPlus* value by *2*).

Chicken with
Couscous, Tomatoes,
and Mint

Chicken with Couscous, Tomatoes, and Mint

Makes 4 Servings

2 teaspoons extra-virgin
  olive oil

2 large garlic cloves, crushed
  through a press

1¼ cups reduced-sodium
  chicken broth

1 cup couscous

2 cups chopped cooked
  chicken breast

2 plum tomatoes, diced

¼ cup finely chopped red onion

¼ cup fresh mint leaves,
  coarsely chopped

⅓ cup crumbled feta cheese

1 tablespoon sherry vinegar

¼ teaspoon black pepper

1. Heat the oil in a medium saucepan over medium heat. Add the garlic and cook, stirring constantly, until fragrant, about 15 seconds. Stir in the broth; cover and bring to a boil. Stir in the couscous; remove from the heat. Cover and let stand for 5 minutes.

2. Fluff the couscous with a fork. Add the chicken, tomatoes, onion, mint, cheese, vinegar, and pepper; toss lightly until combined. Serve at once while still warm.

PER SERVING (1¼ cups): **357 Cal, 9 g Total Fat, 3 g Sat Fat, 0 g Trans Fat, 68 mg Chol, 348 mg Sod, 37 g Carb, 3 g Fib, 30 g Prot, 95 mg Calc.**
PointsPlus value: *9.*

COOK'S TIP

This Aegean-inspired dish is terrific with other fresh herbs. You can replace the mint with an equal amount of chopped fresh basil or 1 to 2 tablespoons of chopped fresh dill.

Chicken and Slaw with Creamy Dressing

Makes 4 Servings

6 tablespoons fat-free mayonnaise

1 tablespoon Dijon mustard

1 tablespoon apple cider vinegar

¾ teaspoon celery seed

2 teaspoons sugar

1 (1-pound) bag coleslaw mix (about 4 cups)

2 cups chopped cooked chicken breast

1 tomato, cut into ½-inch pieces

4 slices bacon, crisp-cooked, drained, and crumbled

1. To make the dressing, whisk together the mayonnaise, mustard, vinegar, celery seed, and sugar in a small bowl until blended; set aside.

2. Combine the coleslaw mix, chicken, and tomato in a large bowl. Drizzle with the dressing and toss well to coat. Divide the mixture evenly among 4 plates and sprinkle with the bacon just before serving.

PER SERVING (1½ cups slaw with 1 slice crumbled bacon): 214 Cal, 7 g Total Fat, 2 g Sat Fat, 0 g Trans Fat, 63 mg Chol, 448 mg Sod, 14 g Carb, 3 g Fib, 25 g Prot, 77 mg Calc.
PointsPlus value: *5*.

COOK'S TIP

This quick and easy main-dish salad can be put together in under 15 minutes—especially if you use prepared coleslaw mix. You can prepare this slaw several hours ahead and keep it covered in the refrigerator. Sprinkle it with the bacon just before serving.

Almost Pizza Margherita

Makes 4 Servings

2 (7-inch) individual prebaked pizza crusts

1 (14½-ounce) can no-salt-added diced tomatoes, well drained

2 cups chopped cooked chicken breast

¼ teaspoon salt

Pinch of black pepper

⅔ cup shredded part-skim mozzarella cheese

8 fresh basil leaves, torn

1. Preheat the oven to 450°F. Split each pizza crust horizontally to make a total of 4 rounds. Place on 2 large baking sheets.

2. Combine the tomatoes, chicken, salt, and pepper in a bowl. Top the crusts with the tomato mixture and sprinkle with the cheese. Bake until the pizzas are heated through and the cheese melts, about 5 minutes. Sprinkle with the basil leaves, cut each pizza into 4 wedges, and serve at once.

PER SERVING (1 pizza): 349 Cal, 10 g Total Fat, 3 g Sat Fat, 0 g Trans Fat, 68 mg Chol, 576 mg Sod, 33 g Carb, 2 g Fib, 31 g Prot, 188 mg Calc.
PointsPlus value: *9.*

COOK'S TIP

According to history, the first pizza Margherita was created in 1889 in honor of Queen Margherita, who was visiting Naples and expressed an interest in pizza, a dish she had never tasted. The owner of a local pizzeria showed his respect for the Queen by creating a pizza that contained the colors of the Italian flag—red, white, and green.

Endive Spears with Chicken Salad and Red Grapefruit

Makes 8 Servings

2 large heads Belgian endive

1 red grapefruit

1 cup finely chopped roasted chicken breast

3 tablespoons chopped fresh chives

2 teaspoons basil-flavored olive oil

2 teaspoons champagne vinegar or white wine vinegar

½ teaspoon salt

⅛ teaspoon black pepper

1. Cut off the base of each endive; separate the endive into spears. Set aside the 16 largest spears. Finely chop enough of the remaining endive to equal ⅓ cup. Peel and section the grapefruit. Cut 8 of the grapefruit sections crosswise in half. Reserve any remaining grapefruit sections for another use.

2. Combine the chopped endive, the chicken, 2 tablespoons of the chives, the oil, vinegar, salt, and pepper in a medium bowl.

3. Place a grapefruit section at the wide end of each endive spear. Place a 1-tablespoon mound of the chicken mixture on top of each grapefruit section. Sprinkle with the remaining 1 tablespoon chives. Arrange the stuffed endive spears on a platter.

PER SERVING (2 stuffed endive spears): 54 Cal, 2 g Total Fat, 0 g Sat Fat, 0 g Trans Fat, 14 mg Chol, 167 mg Sod, 4 g Carb, 1 g Fib, 6 g Prot, 22 mg Calc.
PointsPlus value: *1*.

COOK'S TIP

It's best to prepare this dish when tasty ruby red—or another variety of red grapefruit—is in season. When buying grapefruit, pick it up and notice how heavy it feels. Choose grapefruit that is relatively heavy for its size, which indicates lots of flavorful juice. Also, take a good look and make sure that the skin is firm all over, without any wrinkling at the stem end, which would indicate fruit past its prime.

Endive Spears with Chicken Salad and Red Grapefruit

Cajun-Style Chicken Dip

Makes 8 Servings

⅓ cup fat-free sour cream

2 tablespoons fat-free cream
  cheese

1 tablespoon lemon juice

¼ teaspoon ground cumin

¼ teaspoon salt

¼ teaspoon black pepper

¼ teaspoon hot pepper sauce

⅛ teaspoon cayenne

1 cup finely chopped cooked
  chicken breast

2 tablespoons minced onion

1 tablespoon chopped fresh dill

Combine the sour cream, cream cheese, lemon juice, cumin, salt, black pepper, hot pepper sauce, and cayenne in a medium bowl until well blended. Add the chicken, onion, and dill; stir until blended. Transfer the dip to a serving bowl. Serve at once or cover and refrigerate for up to several hours.

PER SERVING (2 tablespoons): 41 Cal, 1 g Total Fat, 0 g Sat Fat, 0 g Trans Fat, 15 mg Chol, 119 mg Sod, 2 g Carb, 0 g Fib, 6 g Prot, 33 mg Calc.
PointsPlus value: *1*.

COOK'S TIP

Here's a great way to serve this dip as finger food: Cut off the tops of large cherry tomatoes and scoop out the insides with a melon baller. Dip the melon baller into the dip and fill each tomato—it does a super-neat job. Line a platter with dried black beans—to form a decorative bed—and arrange the tomatoes on top.

Useful Equivalents

Here's a list of some often-used ingredients and their basic equivalents.

Apples	1 pound = 3–4 medium = 3 cups sliced
Banana	1 pound = 3 medium = 2 cups sliced or 1–1½ cups mashed
Beans, Dried	1 pound = 2 cups uncooked = 6–7 cups cooked
Beans, Canned	15½-ounce can = 1¾ cups drained beans
Bell Pepper	1 medium = about 1 cup chopped
Bread	1 slice = ½ cup fresh crumbs = ⅓ cup dried crumbs
Bulgur	1 cup dry = 2–3 cups cooked
Carrots	1 pound medium = 6–8 = about 2 cups diced
Celery	1 stalk = ½ cup sliced or about ⅓ cup diced
Cheddar	4 ounces = 1 cup coarsely shredded
Corn	1 medium ear = ½ cup kernels
Cranberries	12-ounce bag = 3 cups berries
Eggplant	1-pound eggplant = about 4 cups diced or about 15 slices
Eggs	1 large egg = ¼ cup; 1 yolk = 1½ tablespoons; 1 white = 2½ tablespoons
Green Beans	1 pound = 3 cups raw or 2½ cups cooked
Herbs	1 tablespoon chopped fresh = 1 teaspoon dried
Macaroni	1 cup dried = 1¾ cups cooked
Mushrooms	1 pound fresh = about 5 cups sliced or 2 cups cooked
Noodles	8 ounces dried = about 6 cups dried = 4 cups cooked
Onion	1 large = 2 cups chopped; 1 medium = 1 cup chopped; 1 small = ½ cup chopped
Strand Pasta	1 ounce (1-inch bundle) dried spaghetti or fettuccine = 1 cup cooked
Peaches	1 pound = 4–6 = 2½ cups sliced or 1 cup puree
Pears	1 pound = 3 medium = 2 cups chopped
Potatoes, Baking	1 pound = 3 medium = about 4 cups sliced or 2¼ cups diced or 1¾ cups mashed
Rice	16 ounces = 1½ cups raw; 1 cup raw = about 3 cups cooked
Spinach	1 pound fresh = 12 cups stemmed or 1½ cups cooked
Summer Squash	1 pound = about 3 cups sliced or diced or 2 cups shredded
Sweet Potatoes	1 pound = 2 medium = 2 cups mashed
Tomatoes	1 pound = 4 small = 16 slices or 1½ cups peeled and seeded

**Sausage and Penne with
Vodka-Tomato Sauce**

Sausage and Penne with Vodka-Tomato Sauce

Makes 6 Servings

6 ounces penne pasta

3 teaspoons extra-virgin olive oil

1 (9-ounce) package fully cooked Mediterranean-style chicken sausage, cut into ½-inch pieces

1 onion, chopped

2 garlic cloves, minced

1 (14½-ounce) can Italian-seasoned diced tomatoes

1 tablespoon vodka

3 tablespoons fat-free milk

3 tablespoons grated Pecorino Romano cheese

1. Cook the pasta according to the package directions, omitting the salt, if desired.

2. Meanwhile, heat 1 teaspoon of the oil in a large nonstick skillet over medium-high heat. Add the sausage and cook, turning occasionally, until browned, about 4 minutes. Transfer the sausage to a plate.

3. Meanwhile, heat the remaining 2 teaspoons oil in the same skillet. Add the onion and garlic; cook, stirring frequently, until softened, about 3 minutes. Add the tomatoes and vodka; bring to a boil. Reduce the heat and simmer, uncovered, about 2 minutes. Add the sausage and milk; simmer until heated through, about 2 minutes. Remove the skillet from the heat and stir in the cheese. Serve with the pasta.

PER SERVING (1 cup pasta with scant ½ cup sauce): 244 Cal, 7 g Total Fat, 2 g Sat Fat, 0 g Trans Fat, 39 mg Chol, 442 mg Sod, 29 g Carb, 2 g Fib, 14 g Prot, 74 mg Calc.
PointsPlus value: *6.*

COOK'S TIP

Vodka sauce is traditionally made with high-fat heavy cream. We've lightened the dish by making it with a little milk and bold-flavored Pecorino Romano cheese. If you can't find Mediterranean-style chicken sausage, use artichoke-and-garlic chicken sausage instead.

Chicken Sausage with Polenta and Greens

Makes 4 Servings

1 (10-ounce) package frozen
    chopped mustard greens

2 (3½-ounce) hot Italian
    chicken sausages, casings
    removed

3 cups hot water

⅔ cup instant polenta

½ teaspoon salt

2 tablespoons grated
    Parmesan cheese

1. Thaw the mustard greens in the microwave according to the package directions.

2. Meanwhile, spray a large nonstick skillet with nonstick spray and set over medium-high heat. Add the sausages and cook, breaking them up with a wooden spoon, until browned and cooked through, about 6 minutes. Add the mustard greens and cook, stirring frequently, until thoroughly heated through, about 2 minutes.

3. Bring the water to a boil in a medium saucepan. Whisking constantly, gradually add the polenta in a slow, steady stream; reduce the heat and cook, stirring constantly, until thick, but not stiff, about 5 minutes. Whisk in the salt.

4. Divide the polenta among 4 serving bowls; top with sausage and greens, then sprinkle evenly with the cheese.

PER SERVING (⅔ **cup polenta,** ½ **cup sausage and greens, and** ½ **tablespoon cheese): 204 Cal, 7 g Total Fat, 2 g Sat Fat, 0 g Trans Fat, 31 mg Chol, 685 mg Sod, 22 g Carb, 4 g Fib, 12 g Prot, 140 mg Calc.** *PointsPlus* value: *5.*

COOK'S TIP

This robust meal-in-a-bowl is the perfect warming solution for a chilly winter day. Instead of mustard greens, you can substitute whatever chopped greens are available in the freezer case, including kale or spinach.

Roasted Chicken Panini

Makes 4 Servings

2 ounces reduced-fat herbed goat cheese, at room temperature

2 tablespoons finely chopped roasted red pepper

1 teaspoon capers, drained and finely chopped

Pinch of black pepper

4 whole grain sandwich rolls

1½ cups shredded roasted chicken breast

16 arugula leaves

1. Combine the cheese, roasted pepper, capers, and black pepper in a small bowl.

2. Slice the rolls horizontally almost all the way through; spread open. Pull out some of the bread from the center, if desired. Spread the cheese mixture evenly on both sides of each of the rolls. Arrange the chicken and arugula evenly on the bottom halves of the rolls. Close the rolls. Serve at once or wrap in plastic wrap and refrigerate for up to 4 hours.

PER SERVING (1 sandwich): 211 Cal, 6 g Total Fat, 2 g Sat Fat, 0 g Trans Fat, 50 mg Chol, 414 mg Sod, 18 g Carb, 3 g Fib, 22 g Prot, 67 mg Calc.
PointsPlus value: *5.*

COOK'S TIP

Made famous in Milan, one of the few places in Italy where people are ever in a hurry, the panini is their quick lunch, occasionally even eaten on the run. Sometimes served hot and at other times cold, sometimes pressed and sometimes not, panini are always welcome.

company
favorites

Hunter-Style Chicken

Hunter-Style Chicken

Makes 8 Servings

1 (2½–3-pound) chicken, cut into 8 pieces and skinned

½ teaspoon salt

¼ teaspoon black pepper

3 teaspoons extra-virgin olive oil

1 onion, chopped

3 garlic cloves, minced

2 assorted color bell peppers, cut into ½-inch pieces

¼ pound white mushrooms, sliced

1 celery stalk, chopped

1 (1-pint) container refrigerated fresh marinara sauce

1. Sprinkle the chicken with the salt and black pepper. Heat 2 teaspoons of the oil in a large nonstick skillet over medium-high heat. Add the chicken and cook until browned, 3–4 minutes on each side. Transfer the chicken to a plate and set aside.

2. Add the remaining 1 teaspoon oil to the same skillet and heat over medium-high heat. Add the onion and garlic; cook, stirring occasionally, until softened, about 3 minutes. Add the bell peppers, mushrooms, and celery; cook, stirring occasionally, until softened, 5–6 minutes. Return the chicken to the skillet; add the pasta sauce and stir to coat. Bring the mixture to a boil. Reduce the heat and simmer, covered, until the chicken is cooked through and the vegetables are tender, about 20 minutes.

PER SERVING (1 piece chicken with scant ½ cup vegetables and sauce): 203 Cal, 8 g Total Fat, 2 g Sat Fat, 0 g Trans Fat, 48 mg Chol, 510 mg Sod, 16 g Carb, 2 g Fib, 18 g Prot, 33 mg Calc. *PointsPlus* value: *5.*

COOK'S TIP

"Hunter-style" refers to a dish cooked with onions, peppers, mushrooms, and tomatoes. You might be more familiar with its Italian name—*cacciatore*. No matter what you call it, however, this dish is delicious over whole wheat pasta (1 cup cooked whole wheat pasta per serving will increase the *PointsPlus* value by *4*).

Braised Chicken Breasts with Dried Figs and Apricots

Makes 4 Servings

1½ tablespoons all-purpose flour

1 teaspoon salt

¼ teaspoon black pepper

1 tablespoon extra-virgin olive oil

2 (¾-pound) bone-in chicken breast halves, skinned and cut in half crosswise

1 large shallot, chopped

2 garlic cloves, minced

¾ cup dry white wine

½ cup reduced-sodium chicken broth

8 dried Calimyrna figs, halved

½ cup dried apricots

1 tablespoon sugar

2 teaspoons dried tarragon

1. Combine the flour, ½ teaspoon of the salt, and ⅛ teaspoon of the pepper in a zip-close plastic bag. Add the chicken and shake to coat.

2. Heat the oil in a large nonstick skillet over medium-high heat. Add the chicken and cook until browned, 3–4 minutes on each side. Add the shallot and garlic; cook, stirring constantly, until fragrant, about 1 minute. Add the wine, stirring to scrape the brown bits from the skillet. Add the broth, figs, apricots, sugar, tarragon, and the remaining ½ teaspoon salt and ⅛ teaspoon pepper; bring to a boil. Reduce the heat and simmer, covered, until the chicken is cooked through, 20–25 minutes.

3. Transfer the chicken to a serving plate. Increase the heat to high and bring the sauce to a boil. Cook until slightly thickened, about 5 minutes. Serve the sauce over the chicken.

PER SERVING (1 piece chicken with ⅓ cup sauce): 288 Cal, 7 g Total Fat, 2 g Sat Fat, 0 g Trans Fat, 76 mg Chol, 660 mg Sod, 18 g Carb, 2 g Fib, 30 g Prot, 52 mg Calc.
PointsPlus value: *8.*

COOK'S TIP

You can make the chicken and sauce 1 or 2 days before serving. Transfer the dish to a covered container and keep it refrigerated—the flavors of the fruits will blend and permeate the chicken, making for an even tastier dish.

Chicken with Forty Cloves of Garlic

Makes 8 Servings

3 medium garlic bulbs (about 40 cloves), separated and unpeeled

1 (3½–4-pound) chicken, cut into 8 pieces and skinned

¼ teaspoon salt

¼ teaspoon black pepper

2 teaspoons extra-virgin olive oil

1 cup dry white wine

1 cup reduced-sodium chicken broth

1. Preheat the oven to 425°F.

2. Place the garlic in a single layer in a small baking dish; spray with extra-virgin olive oil nonstick spray. Cover tightly with aluminum foil and roast 15 minutes. Stir, then cover and roast until the garlic just begins to brown, about 15 minutes. Uncover, then stir and spray with nonstick spray and roast until browned and tender, about 10 minutes longer.

3. Meanwhile, sprinkle the chicken with the salt and pepper. Heat the oil in a large cast-iron or other ovenproof skillet over medium-high heat. Add the chicken and cook until browned, about 5 minutes on each side. Transfer the chicken to a large plate. Add the wine and broth to the skillet; bring to a boil, scraping any browned bits from the bottom of the skillet. Add the garlic to the skillet, then add the chicken, nestling the pieces among the garlic cloves.

4. Place the skillet in the oven and roast the chicken until an instant-read thermometer inserted in a thigh registers 165°F, 10 to 15 minutes. Lift the chicken from the broth mixture in the skillet and transfer to a serving dish; cover with aluminum foil and keep warm. Transfer 12 of the garlic cloves to a fine-mesh sieve. Arrange the remaining garlic around chicken. With a rubber spatula, press the reserved garlic through the sieve into a bowl; discard the skins. Whisk the pressed garlic paste into the broth mixture in the skillet; bring to a simmer. Serve the chicken with the remaining roasted garlic and the sauce.

PER SERVING (1 piece chicken, about 3 cloves roasted garlic, and 2 tablespoons sauce): 215 Cal, 5 g Total Fat, 1 g Sat Fat, 0 g Trans Fat, 79 mg Chol, 153 mg Sod, 6 g Carb, 0 g Fib, 30 g Prot, 43 mg Calc. *PointsPlus* value: *5.*

COOK'S TIP

If you have any roasted garlic cloves left, by all means save them. Squeeze the flesh from the cloves, wrap in plastic wrap, and refrigerate up to 1 week. Use the roasted garlic to add rich flavor to soups, stews, pastas, marinades, and sauces.

Wild Mushroom and Goat Cheese—Stuffed Chicken Breasts

Makes 4 Servings

3 teaspoons extra-virgin olive oil

2 garlic cloves, minced

½ pound shiitake mushrooms, stems discarded, caps finely chopped

¾ teaspoon herbes de Provence

¾ teaspoon salt

¼ teaspoon black pepper

2 ounces reduced-fat goat cheese, softened

4 (¼-pound) skinless boneless chicken breasts

1 shallot, chopped

¾ cup reduced-sodium chicken broth

6 tablespoons dry sherry

1 teaspoon cornstarch

2 teaspoons cold water

1. Heat 2 teaspoons of the oil in a large nonstick skillet over medium-high heat. Add the garlic; cook until fragrant, about 30 seconds. Add the mushrooms, herbes de Provence, ¼ teaspoon of the salt, and ⅛ teaspoon of the pepper; cook, stirring occasionally, until the mushrooms are golden, 5–6 minutes. Transfer the mixture to a bowl; add the cheese and stir until combined. Let the mixture cool completely.

2. Make a pocket in the side of each chicken breast by inserting a sharp paring knife into the thickest part, then gently cutting back and forth to make a small pocket in the side. Do not cut through to the back or the sides of the breasts. Enlarge the pockets gently with your fingers. Fill each pocket with 2 tablespoons of the mushroom-cheese mixture.

3. Wipe out the skillet. Add the remaining 1 teaspoon oil and heat over medium heat. Add the chicken and sprinkle with the remaining ½ teaspoon salt and ⅛ teaspoon pepper. Cook until the chicken is browned on the outside and cooked through, 7–8 minutes on each side. Cut each chicken breast into 4 or 5 slices, transfer to a serving plate, and keep warm.

4. Add the shallot to the skillet and cook until fragrant, about 30 seconds. Add the broth and sherry; bring to a boil. Reduce the heat and simmer about 3 minutes. Meanwhile, dissolve the cornstarch in the cold water in a small bowl. Stir the cornstarch mixture into the skillet and cook, stirring constantly, until the mixture bubbles and thickens, about 1 minute. Serve the sauce over the chicken.

PER SERVING (1 stuffed chicken breast with 3 tablespoons sauce): 257 Cal, 8 g Total Fat, 2 g Sat Fat, 0 g Trans Fat, 65 mg Chol, 560 mg Sod, 14 g Carb, 1 g Fib, 27 g Prot, 43 mg Calc. *PointsPlus* value: *7*.

COOK'S TIP

Toss 2 cups cooked rice with ¼ cup toasted slivered almonds and serve with the chicken. This will increase the per serving *PointsPlus* value by *4*.

Wild Mushroom and
Goat Cheese–Stuffed
Chicken Breasts

Grilled Chicken with Raspberries and Greens

Grilled Chicken with Raspberries and Greens

Makes 4 Servings

4 (4–5-ounce) thin-sliced chicken breast cutlets

½ teaspoon dried thyme

¼ plus ⅛ teaspoon salt

¼ teaspoon black pepper

2 tablespoons raspberry vinegar

2 tablespoons finely chopped shallots

1 tablespoon all-fruit raspberry preserves

2 teaspoons extra-virgin olive oil

1 (4-ounce) package mixed salad greens

½ cup fresh raspberries

1. Sprinkle the chicken evenly with the thyme, the ¼ teaspoon salt, and ⅛ teaspoon of the pepper. Spray a nonstick ridged grill pan with nonstick spray and set over high heat. Add the chicken and cook until browned on the outside and cooked through, about 3 minutes on each side.

2. Meanwhile, combine the vinegar, shallots, preserves, oil, and the remaining ⅛ teaspoon salt and ⅛ teaspoon pepper in a large bowl. Add the greens and toss to coat with the dressing.

3. Arrange a chicken breast on each of 4 serving plates; surround each with one-fourth of the salad and garnish with the raspberries.

PER SERVING (1 piece chicken with about 2 cups salad): 184 Cal, 6 g Total Fat, 1 g Sat Fat, 0 g Trans Fat, 68 mg Chol, 286 mg Sod, 6 g Carb, 1 g Fib, 25 g Prot, 23 mg Calc.
PointsPlus value: *4*.

COOK'S TIP

Chicken and fruit has always been a winning flavor combination, and this elegant entree takes full advantage of the tempting flavor of ripe summer berries. Raspberry vinegar and a touch of raspberry preserves give the dressing a sweet-tart taste that bursts with berry flavor.

Know Your Bird

Last year 8 billion chickens were eaten—that's an impressive 134 million each day—while 45 million turkeys were enjoyed during the Thanksgiving holiday. Whether you like breast meat or leg meat, one thing is for sure: Americans love chicken and turkey—and for good reason. Its mild flavor lends itself to all manner of cooking, including roasting, frying, grilling, braising, sautéing, stir-frying, and broiling; it's reasonably priced; and provides good-for-you lean protein. To get the most flavorful and healthful chicken or turkey, look for a brand that boasts a 100 percent vegetarian diet and birds raised without the use of antibiotics. Keep in mind that poultry is never given hormones, regardless of how they are raised or what a label states. Some producers incorporate marigold petals into their feed, which turns chicken skin yellow. This does not indicate a bird that is healthier or better quality. Confused about all the various types of chickens and turkeys that are available? Use our easy-to-follow shopping guide.

Fresh: Turkey or chicken that's never been stored below 26°F. Best purchased no more than 2 days before roasting.

Frozen: Turkey or chicken that's been stored at 0°F or below.

Basted or Self-Basted: Turkey injected with or marinated in a butter or fat solution, often with salted broth and/or seasonings, so brining is not recommended.

Natural: Turkey or chicken not treated or injected with artificial flavors, colors, or preservatives.

Free-Range: Turkey or chicken that's been allowed access to the outdoors for about half of their growing time.

Organic: A turkey or chicken raised under USDA certified organic practices, fed only certified organic feed, and never treated with antibiotics.

Kosher: Turkey or chicken prepared under rabbinical supervision. Part of the koshering process is salting these birds, so brining is not recommended. Sold fresh and frozen.

Heritage: These turkeys are the ancestors of the common broad-breasted turkeys that are readily available. Because these beautifully plumed birds take up to twice as long as standard turkeys to reach their market weight, they are more expensive. Their names include Narragansett, Bourbon Red, Standard Bronze, and Jersey Buff. Leaner and with less breast meat, their flavor is richer. They benefit from being brined. For more information, go to www.heritageturkeyfoundation.org.

Chicken Breasts with Cremini Mushroom Sauce

Makes 4 Servings

4 (5-ounce) skinless boneless chicken breasts

½ teaspoon salt

¼ teaspoon black pepper

2 teaspoons extra-virgin olive oil

12 ounces cremini mushrooms, thickly sliced

⅓ cup dry white wine

⅓ cup reduced-sodium chicken broth

2 teaspoons all-purpose flour

2 large garlic cloves, minced

2 teaspoons chopped fresh rosemary

2 tablespoons chopped fresh flat-leaf parsley

1. Sprinkle the chicken with the salt and pepper. Heat 1 teaspoon of the oil in a large nonstick skillet over medium heat. Add the chicken and cook until lightly browned, about 4 minutes on each side. Transfer the chicken to a plate.

2. Add the remaining 1 teaspoon oil to the skillet. Add the mushrooms and cook, stirring often, until the mushrooms are browned, about 5 minutes.

3. Whisk together the wine, broth, and flour in a small bowl until smooth. Add to the skillet along with the garlic. Cook, stirring constantly, until the sauce bubbles and thickens, about 1 minute. Return the chicken to the skillet, turning to coat with the sauce; sprinkle with the rosemary. Reduce the heat and simmer, covered, turning the chicken occasionally, until cooked through, about 5 minutes. Sprinkle with the parsley.

PER SERVING (1 piece chicken with generous ⅓ cup sauce): 237 Cal, 7 g Total Fat, 2 g Sat Fat, 0 g Trans Fat, 86 mg Chol, 423 mg Sod, 7 g Carb, 1 g Fib, 34 g Prot, 28 mg Calc. *PointsPlus* value: *6.*

COOK'S TIP

Round out the meal by serving steamed whole green beans and cooked whole wheat penne or other tubular pasta for soaking up all the tasty sauce (1 cup cooked whole wheat penne per serving will increase the *PointsPlus* by *4*).

Crunchy Oven-Fried Chicken with Herb Gravy

Makes 4 Servings

½ cup plus 2 tablespoons all-purpose flour

1⅓ cups cornflake crumbs

2 large egg whites, lightly beaten

2 (½-pound) bone-in chicken breast halves, skinned

2 (¼-pound) chicken drumsticks, skinned

2 (5-ounce) bone-in chicken thighs, skinned

½ teaspoon salt

¼ cup fat-free buttermilk

½ teaspoon hot pepper sauce, or to taste

1 tablespoon butter

1 cup reduced-sodium chicken broth

½ teaspoon dried thyme or rosemary

⅛ teaspoon black pepper

1. Preheat the oven to 375°F. Line a large shallow baking pan with foil. Place a wire rack in the pan; spray the rack with nonstick spray.

2. Place ½ cup of the flour and the cornflake crumbs on separate sheets of wax paper. Put the egg whites in a shallow bowl.

3. Put the chicken in a large bowl; sprinkle with the salt. Whisk together the buttermilk and hot sauce in a glass measure; pour over the chicken and turn to coat.

4. Coat the chicken, one piece at a time, with the flour, then dip into the beaten egg whites, allowing the excess to drip off. Coat the chicken with the cornflake crumbs, pressing lightly so they adhere. Place the chicken on the prepared rack; lightly spray with nonstick spray. Bake until the chicken is golden brown and cooked through, about 45 minutes (do not turn).

5. Meanwhile, to make the gravy, melt the butter in a small saucepan over medium heat. Whisk in the remaining 2 tablespoons flour; cook, whisking constantly, 1 minute. Gradually whisk in the chicken broth until smooth. Cook, whisking constantly, until the gravy bubbles and thickens, about 2 minutes. Stir in the thyme and black pepper. Divide the chicken among 4 plates and serve with the gravy.

PER SERVING (¼ of chicken with ¼ cup gravy)**: 310 Cal, 11 g Total Fat, 4 g Sat Fat, 0 g Trans Fat, 91 mg Chol, 635 mg Sod, 20 g Carb, 1 g Fib, 32 g Prot, 48 mg Calc.**
PointsPlus value: *8.*

COOK'S TIP

Serve the chicken with a mix of steamed green beans, strips of red bell peppers, and yellow and green summer squash.

Osso Buco–Style Chicken

Makes 6 Servings

See cover for photo.

2 teaspoons extra-virgin olive oil

6 (7-ounce) whole chicken legs, skinned

1 onion, chopped

1 carrot, chopped

1 celery stalk, chopped

3 garlic cloves, minced

1 teaspoon dried oregano

⅛ teaspoon red pepper flakes

½ cup reduced-sodium chicken broth

1 (28-ounce) can crushed tomatoes

½ teaspoon salt

1. Heat the oil in a large deep nonstick skillet or Dutch oven over medium-high heat. Add 3 chicken legs and cook until browned, about 4 minutes on each side. Transfer the chicken to a plate. Repeat to brown the remaining chicken.

2. Add the onion, carrot, celery, garlic, oregano, and pepper flakes to the skillet. Cook, stirring occasionally, until the vegetables begin to soften, about 4 minutes. Pour in the broth, stirring constantly to scrape the brown bits from the bottom of the pan. Stir in the tomatoes, salt, and chicken; bring to a boil. Reduce the heat to medium-low and simmer, covered, until the chicken is cooked through and very tender, about 40 minutes.

PER SERVING (1 whole chicken leg with ½ cup sauce): 267 Cal, 11 g Total Fat, 3 g Sat Fat, 0 g Trans Fat, 96 mg Chol, 522 mg Sod, 13 g Carb, 3 g Fib, 31 g Prot, 73 mg Calc.
PointsPlus value: 7.

COOK'S TIP

Gremolata, a mixture of chopped parsley, grated lemon zest, and minced garlic is the traditional garnish for osso buco—braised veal shanks. To prepare it, combine ¼ cup finely chopped fresh parsley, the grated zest of ½ lemon, and 1 minced garlic clove.

Grilled Chicken Salad with Pears and Gorgonzola

Makes 6 Servings

1 pound skinless boneless chicken breasts, lightly pounded

¾ teaspoon salt

½ teaspoon black pepper

2 tablespoons apple cider vinegar

1 tablespoon extra-virgin olive oil

2 teaspoons honey

1 teaspoon Dijon mustard

4 cups loosely packed mixed salad greens

1 small fennel bulb, trimmed and thinly sliced

1 ripe Bosc pear, cored and chopped

6 tablespoons coarsely chopped toasted walnuts

3 tablespoons crumbled Gorgonzola cheese

1. Sprinkle the chicken with ½ teaspoon of the salt and the pepper. Spray a nonstick ridged grill pan with nonstick spray and set over medium-high heat. Add the chicken and cook until browned on the outside and cooked through, about 4 minutes on each side. Transfer the chicken to a cutting board; let rest for about 5 minutes. Cut the chicken, on the diagonal, into ¼-inch-thick slices.

2. Meanwhile, to make the dressing, whisk together the vinegar, oil, honey, mustard, and the remaining ¼ teaspoon salt in a large bowl until blended. Add the chicken, salad greens, fennel, and pear; toss to coat.

3. Divide the salad among 6 plates; top evenly with the walnuts and sprinkle with the cheese. Serve at once.

PER SERVING (1⅓ cups salad, 1 tablespoon walnuts, and ½ tablespoon cheese): 220 Cal, 11 g Total Fat, 2 g Sat Fat, 0 g Trans Fat, 49 mg Chol, 446 mg Sod, 12 g Carb, 3 g Fib, 20 g Prot, 79 mg Calc.
PointsPlus value: *6.*

COOK'S TIP

Aromatic, crunchy fennel and sweet, juicy pears contrast nicely with the distinctive taste of Gorgonzola cheese. For the best flavor, let the cheese come to room temperature before serving. Gorgonzola is our first choice here, but you can substitute any good blue-veined cheese, including Danish blue, Maytag Blue, or Roquefort.

**Grilled Chicken Salad with
Pears and Gorgonzola**

Easy Chicken Pad Thai

Makes 4 Servings

6 ounces rice stick noodles

⅓ cup ketchup

1 tablespoon sugar

1 tablespoon Asian fish sauce

½ teaspoon Sriracha

2 teaspoons Asian (dark) sesame oil

1 large egg, lightly beaten

1 cup diced cooked chicken breast

½ small red onion, thinly sliced

1 large garlic clove, minced

½ cup loosely packed fresh cilantro leaves

2 tablespoons finely chopped unsalted peanuts

1. Cook the noodles according to the package directions; drain. Rinse under cold running water and drain again.

2. Meanwhile, stir together the ketchup, sugar, fish sauce, and Sriracha in a small bowl until blended.

3. Heat 1 teaspoon of the oil in a large nonstick skillet over medium heat. Add the egg and cook, stirring and breaking up the curds, just until set, about 2 minutes; transfer to a small plate.

4. Heat the remaining 1 teaspoon oil in the skillet. Add the chicken, onion, and garlic; cook, stirring, until the onion begins to soften, 2–3 minutes. Add the noodles and cook, tossing constantly, until heated through, 1–2 minutes. Stir in the ketchup mixture and the egg; cook, tossing, until heated through, about 1 minute longer. Divide the pad Thai among 4 plates and sprinkle evenly with the cilantro and peanuts.

PER SERVING (1¼ cups): 324 Cal, 8 g Total Fat, 2 g Sat Fat, 0 g Trans Fat, 82 mg Chol, 834 mg Sod, 47 g Carb, 2 g Fib, 15 g Prot, 39 mg Calc.
PointsPlus value: *8.*

COOK'S TIP

Enjoy even more of this pad Thai by adding 1 cup or more of mung bean sprouts to the skillet along with the egg in step 4.

Chicken and Mushroom Bread Pizza

Makes 4 Servings

1 tablespoon extra-virgin
    olive oil

1 shallot, finely chopped

1 (10-ounce) package baby
    bella or white mushrooms,
    thinly sliced

⅛ teaspoon black pepper

1½ cups finely shredded cooked
    chicken breast

1 (8-ounce) loaf Italian bread,
    split

¼ cup (1 ounce) grated
    Parmesan cheese

2 tablespoons chopped fresh
    flat-leaf parsley

1 teaspoon white truffle oil

1. Preheat the oven to 350°F.

2. Heat the extra-virgin olive oil in a large nonstick skillet over medium heat. Add the shallot and cook, stirring frequently, until softened, about 3 minutes. Increase the heat to medium-high. Add the mushrooms and pepper and cook, stirring frequently, until the mushrooms are very soft, 4–5 minutes. Remove the pan from the heat and stir in the chicken.

3. Pull out some of the bread from the center of the bread halves, if desired. Place the bread on a large baking sheet. Top each bread half evenly with the chicken mixture, then sprinkle evenly with the cheese. Bake until heated through, about 20 minutes. Sprinkle with the parsley and drizzle with the truffle oil. Cut each bread in half, making a total of 4 pieces and serve at once.

PER SERVING (1 piece): 329 Cal, 11 g Total Fat, 3 g Sat Fat, 0 g Trans Fat, 48 mg Chol, 488 mg Sod, 32 g Carb, 3 g Fib, 25 g Prot, 146 mg Calc.
PointsPlus value: *8.*

COOK'S TIP

White truffle oil, with its unique aroma, makes this pizza very special and very elegant with no effort. Though it is a bit pricey, you only need a little. Here, the oil is drizzled over the pizza just before serving so its intoxicating aroma can be appreciated. The oil is also great over mashed potatoes, grilled mushrooms, risotto, and eggs.

Mediterranean Lemon Chicken with Artichokes and Orzo

Mediterranean Lemon Chicken with Artichokes and Orzo

Makes 6 Servings

6 ounces orzo

2 ounces reduced-fat feta cheese

8 pitted Kalamata olives, sliced

6 (½-pound) whole chicken legs, skinned

¾ teaspoon salt

¼ plus ⅛ teaspoon black pepper

1 (1¼-pound) can artichoke hearts, drained and quartered

3 garlic cloves, minced

1½ teaspoons fresh oregano leaves, or ½ teaspoon dried

1 cup reduced-sodium chicken broth

2 tablespoons lemon juice

1. Cook the orzo according to the package directions, omitting the salt, if desired; drain and transfer to a large bowl. Stir in the cheese and olives; cover and keep warm.

2. Sprinkle the chicken with the salt and pepper. Spray a large nonstick skillet with nonstick spray and set over medium-high heat. Add the chicken and cook until browned, 3–4 minutes on each side. Transfer the chicken to a plate.

3. Add the artichoke hearts, garlic, and oregano to the skillet; cook, stirring constantly, until fragrant, about 1 minute. Return the chicken to the skillet and add the broth and lemon juice; bring to a boil. Reduce the heat and simmer, covered, until the chicken is cooked through, about 20 minutes.

4. Transfer the chicken to a plate. Pour 1 cup of the artichoke sauce over the orzo and toss well. Divide the orzo among 6 plates and place 1 chicken leg on each plate. Serve with the remaining sauce.

PER SERVING (1 chicken leg, ½ cup orzo mixture, and scant ¼ cup sauce): 365 Cal, 10 g Total Fat, 4 g Sat Fat, 0 g Trans Fat, 91 mg Chol, 864 mg Sod, 32 g Carb, 5 g Fib, 36 g Prot, 127 mg Calc. *PointsPlus* value: *9.*

COOK'S TIP

Lemon juice really makes this dish. For additional lemon flavor—and if you have the time—grate the zest from the lemon before you juice it and stir the zest into the orzo just before serving.

Chicken Paprikash

Makes 4 Servings

1 pound skinless boneless
    chicken breasts, cut into
    ½-inch pieces

¾ teaspoon salt

¼ teaspoon black pepper

4 teaspoons unsalted butter

2 celery stalks, chopped

2 carrots, chopped

1 onion, chopped

1 garlic clove, minced

3 tablespoons all-purpose flour

1½ cups reduced-sodium
    chicken broth

½ cup dry white wine

1 tablespoon paprika

½ cup fat-free sour cream

1. Sprinkle the chicken with ½ teaspoon of the salt and ⅛ teaspoon of the pepper. Melt 2 teaspoons of the butter in a large nonstick skillet over medium-high heat. Add the chicken and cook, turning occasionally, until browned and cooked through, about 5 minutes. Transfer the chicken to a plate.

2. Melt the remaining 2 teaspoons butter in the same skillet. Add the celery, carrots, onion, and garlic; cook, stirring occasionally, until softened, about 6 minutes. Add the flour and cook, stirring constantly, until the flour is golden, about 1 minute. Stir in the broth, wine, paprika, and remaining ¼ teaspoon salt and ⅛ teaspoon pepper; bring to a boil. Reduce the heat and simmer, uncovered, until the mixture bubbles and thickens and the vegetables are tender, about 5 minutes. Add the chicken and simmer, stirring occasionally, until heated through, about 2 minutes. Remove the skillet from the heat and stir in the sour cream.

PER SERVING (1 cup): 273 Cal, 5 g Total Fat, 3 g Sat Fat, 0 g Trans Fat, 87 mg Chol, 608 mg Sod, 19 g Carb, 3 g Fib, 31 g Prot, 92 mg Calc.
PointsPlus value: *7.*

COOK'S TIP

You'll want to soak up every bit of the sauce in this dish, so serve it with egg noodles or high-fiber bread (½ cup cooked egg noodles per serving will increase the *PointsPlus* value by *3,* while a slice of high-fiber bread per serving will increase the *PointsPlus* value by *2*).

Chicken, Shrimp, and Kielbasa Paella

Makes 6 Servings

1 tablespoon extra-virgin
    olive oil

2 (¾-pound) bone-in chicken
    breast halves skinned and
    cut in half crosswise

½ pound extra-large shrimp,
    peeled and deveined

¼ pound turkey kielbasa, cut
    into ¼-inch-thick slices

1 onion, chopped

1 green bell pepper, chopped

3 garlic cloves, minced

1 (14½-ounce) can diced
    tomatoes, drained

1¼ cups reduced-sodium
    chicken broth

¾ cup long-grain white rice

8 small pimiento-stuffed green
    olives, sliced

½ teaspoon saffron threads,
    crushed

⅛ teaspoon cayenne

3 tablespoons chopped fresh
    cilantro (optional)

1. Heat the oil in a large nonstick skillet over medium-high heat. Add the chicken and cook until browned, 3–4 minutes on each side. Transfer the chicken to a plate. Add the shrimp to the skillet and cook until browned, 1½ minutes on each side; transfer to a separate plate. Add the kielbasa to the skillet and cook until browned, about 3 minutes on each side; transfer to the plate with the chicken.

2. Add the onion, bell pepper, and garlic to the skillet; cook, stirring occasionally, until softened, about 4 minutes. Add the tomatoes, broth, rice, olives, saffron, and cayenne; bring to a boil. Add the chicken and kielbasa; return to a boil. Reduce the heat and simmer, covered, about 15 minutes.

3. Add the shrimp to the skillet and simmer, covered, until the chicken and kielbasa are cooked through and the shrimp are opaque in the center, about 7 minutes. Fluff the mixture with a fork and stir in the cilantro, if using.

PER SERVING (1⅓ **cups**): 299 Cal, 8 g Total Fat, 2 g Sat Fat, 0 g Trans Fat, 94 mg Chol, 587 mg Sod, 27 g Carb, 2 g Fib, 29 g Prot, 59 mg Calc.
PointsPlus value: *7.*

COOK'S TIP

This famous saffron-infused Valencian rice dish is rich with chicken, seafood, sausages, and flavorful seasonings. If you like paella, it might be worthwhile investing in a paella pan—a shallow round pan with splayed sides and brightly colored handles—to cook and serve this classic.

Porcini Chicken

Porcini Chicken

Makes 4 Servings

½ ounce dried porcini
  mushrooms

1 cup hot water

4 (4–5-ounce) thin-sliced
  chicken breast cutlets

½ teaspoon salt

¼ teaspoon black pepper

3 tablespoons minced shallots

½ cup dry red wine

½ tablespoon unsalted butter

1. Combine the mushrooms and the water in a small bowl; let soak about 20 minutes. Using a slotted spoon, lift the mushrooms from the liquid, rinse thoroughly, and coarsely chop. Line a strainer with a paper towel. Pour the mushroom liquid through the strainer; reserve ½ cup of the liquid.

2. Sprinkle the chicken with the salt and pepper. Spray a large nonstick skillet with nonstick spray (preferably olive oil spray) and set over high heat. Add the chicken and cook until lightly browned, about 1 minute on each side. Reduce the heat to medium. Sprinkle the chicken with the shallots; spray with the nonstick spray. Cook until the chicken is browned on the outside and cooked through, about 3 minutes longer on each side. Transfer the chicken and shallots to a serving platter; cover and keep warm.

3. Add the chopped mushrooms to the skillet and cook, stirring constantly, about 30 seconds. Add the reserved mushroom liquid and bring to a boil, scraping any browned bits from the bottom of the pan, until the liquid has almost evaporated. Add the wine and boil until reduced by half, about 2 minutes. Remove the pan from the heat; stir in the butter until melted. Serve the sauce with the chicken.

PER SERVING (1 piece chicken with 2 tablespoons sauce): 218 Cal, 5 g Total Fat, 2 g Sat Fat, 0 g Trans Fat, 82 mg Chol, 367 mg Sod, 6 g Carb, 1 g Fib, 30 g Prot, 28 mg Calc.
PointsPlus value: *5.*

COOK'S TIP

If you love the taste of mushrooms, dried porcinis are a must ingredient to have on hand. Soaking the mushrooms brings out all their wonderful meaty texture and woodsy flavor, while the soaking liquid becomes an important component of the sauce.

Chicken Salad with Figs, Prosciutto, and Pine Nuts

Makes 4 Servings

2 tablespoons balsamic vinegar

1 tablespoon extra-virgin
    olive oil

1 teaspoon honey

1 teaspoon Dijon mustard

¼ teaspoon black pepper

⅛ teaspoon salt

¾ pound skinless boneless
    chicken breasts, lightly
    pounded

6 cups mixed salad greens

4 fresh figs, cut lengthwise into
    quarters

2 ounces thinly sliced
    prosciutto

1 tablespoon toasted pine nuts

1. To make the dressing, whisk together the vinegar, oil, honey, mustard, pepper, and salt in a medium bowl until blended; set aside.

2. Spray a nonstick ridged grill pan with nonstick spray and set over medium-high heat. Add the chicken and cook until browned on the outside and cooked through, about 4 minutes on each side. Transfer the chicken to a cutting board; let rest for about 5 minutes. Cut the chicken, on the diagonal, into ¼-inch-thick slices.

3. Place the greens on a large serving platter. Arrange the figs around the greens. Top the greens with the chicken and prosciutto, then sprinkle with the pine nuts. Drizzle the salad with the dressing and serve at once.

PER SERVING (1½ cups)**: 230 Cal, 9 g Total Fat, 2 g Sat Fat, 0 g Trans Fat, 60 mg Chol, 385 mg Sod, 14 g Carb, 4 g Fib, 24 g Prot, 70 mg Calc.**
PointsPlus value: *6.*

COOK'S TIP

This is a wonderful late summer/early autumn salad to prepare when fresh figs are in season. Take advantage of the amazing array of salad greens now available in specialty markets and in many supermarkets for this dish.

Chicken Salad with Figs, Prosciutto, and Pine Nuts

Baked Beans with Chicken Sausage

Makes 6 Servings

¾ pound chicken sausages, thinly sliced

1 onion, chopped

1 green bell pepper, chopped

2 garlic cloves, minced

1 jalapeño pepper, seeded and finely chopped

2 (15½-ounce) cans pinto beans, rinsed and drained

1 (14½-ounce) can reduced-sodium chicken broth

1 (6-ounce) can reduced-sodium tomato paste

2 tablespoons apple cider vinegar

2 tablespoons honey

1 tablespoon Dijon mustard

1 teaspoon paprika

¼ teaspoon salt

¼ teaspoon black pepper

½ teaspoon liquid smoke (optional)

1. Preheat the oven to 375°F.

2. Heat a large nonstick skillet over medium heat. Add the sausage and cook, turning frequently, until browned, about 2 minutes. Using a slotted spoon, transfer the sausage pieces to a 2-quart baking dish. Drain the fat from the skillet.

3. Return the skillet to medium heat; add the onion and bell pepper. Cook, stirring frequently, until softened, about 3 minutes. Add the garlic and jalapeño pepper; cook, stirring constantly, until fragrant, about 30 seconds. Add the beans, broth, and tomato paste; cook, stirring constantly until they create a smooth sauce. Stir in the vinegar, honey, mustard, paprika, salt, black pepper, and liquid smoke, if using. Pour the contents of the skillet into the baking dish with the sausage.

4. Cover and bake until bubbling and somewhat thickened, about 1 hour and 30 minutes, stirring every 30 minutes. Uncover and let stand for about 5 minutes before serving.

PER SERVING (1¼ cups): 313 Cal, 8 g Total Fat, 2 g Sat Fat, 0 g Trans Fat, 33 mg Chol, 841 mg Sod, 42 g Carb, 10 g Fib, 20 g Prot, 77 mg Calc.
PointsPlus value: *8.*

COOK'S TIP

The battle rages over liquid smoke—some people won't touch it while others swear by it. Truth is, it can give casseroles, such as this one, a pleasant smoky edge. There are many brands on the market. Look for one without preservatives or artificial flavors—one that is simply made from hickory or mesquite smoke distillate and water.

Chicken, Cilantro, and Cucumber Wraps

Makes 4 Servings

2 cups shredded cooked
    chicken breast

½ cup finely chopped
    cucumber

¼ cup low-fat mayonnaise

¼ cup chopped fresh cilantro

1 teaspoon minced peeled fresh
    ginger

1 teaspoon Asian (dark)
    sesame oil

¼ teaspoon salt

⅛ teaspoon black pepper

4 (8-inch) tomato or whole
    wheat flour tortillas

1. Combine the chicken, cucumber, mayonnaise, cilantro, ginger, oil, salt, and pepper in a medium bowl; toss until well mixed. Let stand for 10 minutes to allow the flavors to blend.

2. Toast the tortillas in a dry large nonstick skillet over medium heat, about 1 minute on each side.

3. Divide the chicken filling evenly among the tortillas and roll up. Cut the rolls in half on a slight diagonal.

PER SERVING (1 wrap): 239 Cal, 6 g Total Fat, 1 g Sat Fat, 0 g Trans Fat, 57 mg Chol, 517 mg Sod, 21 g Carb, 3 g Fib, 24 g Prot, 23 mg Calc.
PointsPlus value: *6.*

COOK'S TIP

Cilantro stems are very flavorful, so finely chop them and add them to the leaves. They also make a tasty addition to marinades, dressings, and sauces.

**Chicken and Quinoa
Salad with Dried Fruit**

Chicken and Quinoa Salad with Dried Fruit

Makes 6 Servings

3 tablespoons seasoned rice vinegar

2 tablespoons mirin (rice wine)

1 tablespoon soy sauce

2 teaspoons minced peeled fresh ginger

1 teaspoon Asian (dark) sesame oil

2 cups water

1 cup quinoa

1 pound skinless boneless chicken thighs

½ cup finely chopped scallions

½ cup chopped fresh cilantro

½ cup chopped pitted dates

¼ cup dried currants

½ teaspoon salt

½ teaspoon black pepper

1. To make the dressing, whisk together the vinegar, mirin, soy sauce, ginger, and oil in a small bowl until blended; set aside.

2. Bring the water to a boil in a medium saucepan; stir in the quinoa. Reduce the heat and simmer, covered, until all of the liquid has been absorbed, about 20 minutes. Transfer the quinoa to a large bowl; let cool about 10 minutes.

3. Spray a large nonstick skillet with nonstick spray and set over medium-high heat. Add the chicken and cook, turning occasionally, until browned on the outside and cooked through, about 10 minutes. Transfer the chicken to a cutting board; let rest for about 5 minutes. Cut the chicken into ¾-inch pieces.

4. Add the chicken to the quinoa. Stir in the scallions, cilantro, dates, currants, salt, and pepper. Drizzle with the dressing and toss well to coat.

PER SERVING (scant 1 cup): 266 Cal, 8 g Total Fat, 2 g Sat Fat, 0 g Trans Fat, 50 mg Chol, 483 mg Sod, 29 g Carb, 3 g Fib, 18 g Prot, 38 mg Calc.
PointsPlus value: 7.

COOK'S TIP

An ancient grain, quinoa (KEEN-wah) has a light, delicate taste and can be used instead of other grains. Considered to be a "superfood," it contains all the essential amino acids, making it a great source of complete protein. You'll find quinoa in most supermarkets.

Chicken-Prosciutto Bundles

Makes 4 Servings

4 (5-ounce) skinless boneless chicken breasts

4 (½-inch-thick) slices part-skim mozzarella cheese (½-ounce each)

12 fresh basil leaves

¼ teaspoon black pepper

8 thin slices prosciutto (about 4 ounces)

1 teaspoon extra-virgin olive oil

1. Preheat the oven to 400°F.

2. Make a pocket in the side of each chicken breast by inserting a sharp paring knife into the thickest part, then gently cutting back and forth to make a small pocket in the side. Do not cut through to the back or the sides of the breasts. Enlarge the pockets gently with your fingers. Stuff each pocket with 1 slice cheese and 3 basil leaves. Sprinkle the chicken with the pepper and wrap 2 slices prosciutto around each stuffed chicken breast half.

3. Heat the oil in a large ovenproof skillet over medium-high heat. Add the chicken and cook until lightly browned, about 3 minutes on each side. Transfer the chicken in the skillet to the oven and bake until cooked through, 12–15 minutes.

PER SERVING (1 piece chicken): 267 Cal, 10 g Total Fat, 4 g Sat Fat, 0 g Trans Fat, 107 mg Chol, 514 mg Sod, 1 g Carb, 0 g Fib, 40 g Prot, 124 mg Calc.
PointsPlus value: *6.*

COOK'S TIP

Prosciutto adds rich flavor to this dish. For the best flavor, choose prosciutto that is imported from Italy, such as prosciutto di Parma. Have the prosciutto cut into paper-thin slices in the deli department of the supermarket or buy it presliced.

Tarragon Chicken Salad with Orange Mayonnaise

Makes 4 Servings

¼ cup fat-free mayonnaise

2 teaspoons chopped fresh tarragon

1½ teaspoons Dijon mustard

1½ teaspoons apple cider vinegar

⅛ teaspoon salt

⅛ teaspoon black pepper

1 navel orange

2 cups shredded cooked chicken breast

1 cup seedless green grapes, halved

1 celery stalk, thinly sliced

¼ cup very thinly sliced red onion

2 tablespoons chopped walnuts

8 Boston or butter lettuce leaves

1. To make the dressing, stir together the mayonnaise, tarragon, mustard, vinegar, salt, and pepper in a large bowl. Grate ½ teaspoon zest from the orange and stir it into the dressing. Remove all the peel and white pith from the orange. Slice the orange, then cut each slice in quarters.

2. Add the chicken, grapes, orange pieces, celery, onion, and walnuts to the dressing; stir until mixed well. Divide the lettuce among 4 plates. Spoon the chicken salad onto the lettuce.

PER SERVING (about 1 cup chicken salad with 2 lettuce leaves): 183 Cal, 6 g Total Fat, 1 g Sat Fat, 0 g Trans Fat, 50 mg Chol, 394 mg Sod, 15 g Carb, 3 g Fib, 19 g Prot, 53 mg Calc. *PointsPlus* value: *5.*

COOK'S TIP

This recipe is our flavorful twist on a Waldorf chicken salad, which was created in the late 1890s by Oscar Tschirky, the maître d'hotel at the Waldorf Hotel (now the Waldorf-Astoria). The original recipe didn't contain nuts, but once they were added, the variation became a mainstay. This salad is usually made with apples but grapes are a welcome change.

Moroccan Chicken Kebabs

Makes 4 Servings

1 tablespoon lemon juice

2 teaspoons grated peeled
   fresh ginger

1½ teaspoons ground cumin

1 teaspoon ground coriander

¼ teaspoon ground cinnamon

Pinch of cayenne

1½ pounds skinless boneless
   chicken thighs, cut into
   2-inch pieces

2 small zucchini, cut into
   12 (1½-inch) pieces

8 cherry tomatoes

½ teaspoon salt

1. Combine the lemon juice, ginger, cumin, coriander, cinnamon, and cayenne in a zip-close plastic bag; add the chicken. Squeeze out the air and seal the bag; turn to coat the chicken. Refrigerate, turning the bag occasionally, for at least 1 hour or up to 4 hours.

2. Spray a broiler rack with extra-virgin olive oil nonstick spray; preheat the broiler. Alternately thread the chicken and vegetables onto 4 (8-inch) metal skewers; sprinkle both sides evenly with the salt and spray with extra-virgin olive oil nonstick spray. Broil the kebabs 4 inches from the heat, turning occasionally, until the chicken is cooked through and browned, 10–12 minutes.

PER SERVING (1 kebab): 263 Cal, 13 g Total Fat, 4 g Sat Fat, 0 g Trans Fat, 112 mg Chol, 399 mg Sod, 4 g Carb, 1 g Fib, 32 g Prot, 28 mg Calc.
PointsPlus value: *7*.

COOK'S TIP

Serve the kebabs on a bed of whole wheat couscous (½ cup cooked whole wheat couscous per serving will increase the *PointsPlus* value by *3*).

Tomato and Red Wine–Braised Chicken Legs

Makes 4 Servings

4 (½-pound) whole chicken legs, skinned

¾ teaspoon salt

¼ teaspoon black pepper

1 teaspoon extra-virgin olive oil

2 garlic cloves, minced

1 (28-ounce) can Italian-seasoned crushed tomatoes

½ cup dry red wine

3 tablespoons chopped fresh flat-leaf parsley

2 teaspoons grated orange zest

8 ounces pappardelle or extra-wide noodles

1. Sprinkle the chicken with ½ teaspoon of the salt and ⅛ teaspoon of the pepper. Heat the oil in a large nonstick skillet over medium-high heat. Add the chicken and cook until browned, 3–4 minutes on each side. Transfer the chicken to a plate.

2. Add the garlic to the skillet and cook, stirring constantly, until fragrant, about 30 seconds. Add the tomatoes and wine; bring to a boil. Reduce the heat and simmer, uncovered, about 5 minutes. Return the chicken to the skillet and add the remaining ¼ teaspoon salt and ⅛ teaspoon pepper; return to a boil. Reduce the heat and simmer, covered, until the chicken is cooked through and pulls easily from the bones, 35–40 minutes.

3. Transfer the chicken to a plate; cover with foil to keep warm. Return the tomato mixture in the skillet to a boil. Reduce the heat to medium and cook, uncovered, until slightly thickened, about 8 minutes. Return the chicken to the skillet, then stir in the parsley and orange zest.

4. Meanwhile, cook the pasta according to the package directions, omitting the salt, if desired; drain. Divide the pasta among 4 plates, then top with a chicken leg and the sauce.

PER SERVING (1 cup pasta, 1 chicken leg, and ½ cup sauce): 467 Cal, 8 g Total Fat, 2 g Sat Fat, 0 g Trans Fat, 156 mg Chol, 823 mg Sod, 56 g Carb, 6 g Fib, 38 g Prot, 110 mg Calc. *PointsPlus* value: *12*.

COOK'S TIP

Fresh orange zest adds piquancy to this robust stew, which is easily doubled with half of it popped into the freezer for another time. The chicken and sauce will keep in the refrigerator for up to 3 days or in the freezer for up to 3 months. If frozen, let the chicken and sauce thaw overnight in the refrigerator before gently reheating.

make-ahead dishes

Chili Verde

Makes 6 Servings

2 teaspoons canola oil

1 large onion, chopped

2 green bell peppers, chopped

3 garlic cloves, minced

1 jalapeño pepper, seeded and minced

¾ pound skinless boneless chicken breast, cut into ½-inch pieces

2 teaspoons dried oregano

1 teaspoon sugar

1 teaspoon ground cumin

¼ teaspoon salt

1 pound fresh tomatillos, chopped

1 (4½-ounce) can chopped green chiles

½ cup reduced-sodium chicken broth

1 (15½-ounce) can cannellini (white kidney) beans, rinsed and drained

6 tablespoons fat-free sour cream

6 tablespoons finely chopped red onion

1½ cups baked tortilla chips

1. Heat the oil in a large nonstick Dutch oven over medium-high heat. Add the onion, bell peppers, garlic, and jalapeño pepper; cook, stirring frequently, until softened, about 10 minutes. Add the chicken and cook, turning occasionally, until browned, about 6 minutes.

2. Add the oregano, sugar, cumin, and salt; cook, stirring constantly, until fragrant, about 1 minute. Stir in the tomatillos, chiles, and broth; bring to a boil. Reduce the heat and simmer, uncovered, until the flavors are blended and the chili thickens slightly, about 20 minutes. Stir in the beans; return to a boil. Reduce the heat and simmer until heated through, about 1 minute.

3. Serve the chili in bowls; top with the sour cream and red onion and serve with the chips.

PER SERVING (scant 1 cup chili with 1 tablespoon each sour cream and red onion, and ¼ cup tortilla chips): 240 Cal, 5 g Total Fat, 1 g Sat Fat, 0 g Trans Fat, 35 mg Chol, 407 mg Sod, 30 g Carb, 7 g Fib, 20 g Prot, 88 mg Calc.
PointsPlus value: *6.*

COOK'S TIP

Tomatillos are small green tomatoes with papery husks (coverings) that can be found in Latin American markets and in the produce section of some supermarkets. If you can't find fresh tomatillos, substitute 2 (11-ounce) cans tomatillos, drained and broken up. If using canned, omit the salt in the recipe.

Seriously Spicy Chicken Chili

Makes 6 Servings

2 dried ancho chile peppers

1 cup boiling water

¼ pound chorizo sausage, thinly sliced

1 large onion, chopped

3 celery stalks, chopped

2 garlic cloves, chopped

1 (28-ounce) can Italian peeled tomatoes, broken up

1 pound skinless boneless chicken thighs, cut into ½-inch pieces

1 cup fresh or frozen corn kernels

1 teaspoon ground cumin

½ teaspoon sugar

½ teaspoon salt

1–2 habañero peppers, seeded and minced

2 tablespoons chopped fresh cilantro

2 cups hot cooked white rice

6 tablespoons light sour cream

6 tablespoons chopped red onion or scallions

1. Soak the ancho chiles in 1 cup of boiling water in a bowl, about 30 minutes. Drain and discard the liquid; finely chop the chiles and set aside.

2. Heat a nonstick Dutch oven over medium heat. Add the chorizo and cook until browned, about 5 minutes. Add the onion, celery, and garlic; cook, stirring occasionally, until softened, about 6 minutes.

3. Add the tomatoes, chicken, corn, cumin, sugar, salt, habañero pepper, and the ancho chiles; bring to a boil. Reduce the heat and simmer, partially covered, until the flavors are blended and the chili thickens slightly, about 40 minutes. Stir in the cilantro.

4. Serve the chili in bowls with the rice; top with the sour cream and red onion.

PER SERVING (1 cup chili, ⅓ cup rice, and 1 tablespoon each sour cream and onion): 361 Cal, 14 g Total Fat, 5 g Sat Fat, 0 g Trans Fat, 64 mg Chol, 900 mg Sod, 34 g Carb, 4 g Fib, 26 g Prot, 120 mg Calc. *PointsPlus* value: *9.*

COOK'S TIP

If you like your chili bordering on incendiary, this recipe is for you. The combination of spicy chorizo, mild ancho chiles, and spicy-hot habañero chiles gives this zesty dish a unique blend of flavors. Be very careful not to touch your face, eyes, or other tender areas of your body when handling chiles, as they can burn and irritate.

Cincinnati 5-Way Chili

Makes 6 Servings

1 teaspoon canola oil

1 onion, chopped

3 garlic cloves, chopped

1 tablespoon chili powder

1 teaspoon ground cumin

¼ teaspoon ground allspice

1 pound ground skinless
   turkey breast

1 (16-ounce) jar mild chunky
   salsa

1 (8-ounce) can tomato sauce

½ ounce bittersweet chocolate,
   grated

½ pound spaghetti

1 (15½-ounce) can red kidney
   beans, rinsed and drained

6 tablespoons chopped
   red onion

6 tablespoons shredded
   reduced-fat Monterey Jack
   cheese

1. Heat the oil in a nonstick Dutch oven over medium-high heat. Add the onion and garlic; cook, stirring frequently, until golden, about 7 minutes. Stir in the chili powder, cumin, and allspice; cook, stirring constantly, until fragrant, about 1 minute. Add the turkey and cook, breaking it up with a wooden spoon, until browned, about 5 minutes.

2. Add the salsa, tomato sauce, and chocolate; bring to a boil. Reduce the heat and simmer, partially covered, until the flavors are blended and the chili thickens slightly, about 20 minutes.

3. Meanwhile, cook the spaghetti according to the package directions omitting the salt, if desired; drain. Put the beans in a microwavable bowl; cover and microwave on High until heated through, about 2 minutes. Divide the spaghetti among 6 plates. Spoon the chili evenly over the spaghetti, top with the beans, then sprinkle with the onion and cheese.

PER SERVING (about ⅔ cup spaghetti, ¾ cup chili, ¼ cup beans, and 1 tablespoon each onion and cheese): 385 Cal, 5 g Total Fat, 2 g Sat Fat, 0 g Trans Fat, 55 mg Chol, 934 mg Sod, 54 g Carb, 7 g Fib, 31 g Prot, 124 mg Calc.
PointsPlus value: *9.*

COOK'S TIP

Traditionally, Cincinnati 5-way chili is served on an oval plate on a bed of spaghetti and topped with chili, red kidney beans, chopped onion, and shredded cheese. Cincinnati chili parlors also serve it plain (1-way), with cheese (2-way), with onions and cheese (3-way), or with spaghetti, onions, and cheese (4-way).

Chicken and Vegetable Chili

Makes 6 Servings

1 tablespoon extra-virgin
 olive oil

1 pound ground skinless
 chicken breast

1 large onion, chopped

2 garlic cloves, minced

1 jalapeño pepper, seeded and
 minced

1 (28-ounce) can crushed
 tomatoes

½ cup water

1 small eggplant, diced

2 zucchini, diced

1–2 teaspoons chili powder

1 teaspoon ground cumin

1 teaspoon salt

1 teaspoon sugar

½ teaspoon dried oregano

6 tablespoons light sour cream

4 scallions, thinly sliced

1½ cups baked tortilla chips

2 cups shredded romaine
 lettuce

2 cups chopped tomatoes

1. Heat the oil in a nonstick Dutch oven over medium heat. Add the chicken and cook, breaking it up with a wooden spoon, until browned, about 5 minutes. Add the onion, garlic, and jalapeño pepper; cook, stirring frequently, until softened and fragrant, about 4 minutes.

2. Add the tomatoes, water, eggplant, zucchini, chili powder, cumin, salt, sugar, and oregano; bring to a boil. Reduce the heat and simmer, covered, stirring occasionally, until the vegetables are well softened and the flavors are blended, about 40 minutes.

3. Divide the chili among 6 shallow bowls; top evenly with the sour cream and a few sliced scallions. Serve the chili with the chips, lettuce, and tomatoes in bowls on the side.

PER SERVING (generous 1 cup chili, 1 tablespoon sour cream, ¼ cup tortilla chips, and ⅓ cup lettuce and tomato): 231 Cal, 6 g Total Fat, 2 g Sat Fat, 0 g Trans Fat, 56 mg Chol, 683 mg Sod, 25 g Carb, 6 g Fib, 22 g Prot, 108 mg Calc. *PointsPlus* value: **6.**

COOK'S TIP

Here's a basic chili that is stretched with lots of good-for-you vegetables and nicely seasoned with chili powder and jalapeño pepper, the most popular chile pepper in North America. They are medium-hot and readily available in the produce section of supermarkets.

Corn Bread–Topped Red Chili

Makes 6 Servings

2 teaspoons canola oil

1 large onion, chopped

1 red bell pepper, chopped

2 garlic cloves, minced

1 red jalapeño pepper, seeded and chopped

¾ pound skinless boneless chicken breasts, cut into ½-inch pieces

2 teaspoons chipotle chile powder

1 teaspoon dried oregano

1 (28-ounce) can Italian peeled tomatoes

1 (15½-ounce) can red kidney beans

⅔ cup yellow cornmeal

⅓ cup all-purpose flour

2 teaspoons baking powder

1 teaspoon sugar

¼ teaspoon salt

¼ cup fat-free milk

¼ cup fat-free egg substitute

¼ cup (1 ounce) shredded sharp Cheddar cheese

1. Heat the oil in a nonstick Dutch oven over medium-high heat. Add the onion, bell pepper, garlic, and jalapeño pepper; cook, stirring frequently, until softened, about 8 minutes. Add the chicken and cook, turning occasionally, until lightly browned, about 8 minutes.

2. Add the chile powder and oregano; cook, stirring constantly, until fragrant, about 1 minute. Stir in the tomatoes; bring to a boil. Reduce the heat and simmer, covered, until the flavors are blended and the chili thickens slightly, about 20 minutes. Rinse and drain the beans, then stir into the chili and cook until heated through. Transfer the mixture to a 2-quart shallow baking dish.

3. Preheat the oven to 400°F.

4. To make the corn bread, combine the cornmeal, flour, baking powder, sugar, and salt in a medium bowl. Combine the milk and egg substitute in a small bowl. Stir the milk mixture into the cornmeal mixture until just blended. Stir in the cheese. Spoon the batter in 6 spoonfuls on top of the casserole. Bake, uncovered, until the chili is bubbly and the corn bread is golden, about 15 minutes.

PER SERVING (about ¾ cup chili with 1 piece corn bread): 304 Cal, 6 g Total Fat, 2 g Sat Fat, 0 g Trans Fat, 39 mg Chol, 670 mg Sod, 40 g Carb, 7 g Fib, 23 g Prot, 203 mg Calc.
PointsPlus value: *7.*

COOK'S TIP

You can make the chili without the topping up to 2 days ahead; keep it in the refrigerator. When you're ready to serve the chili, reheat it in a saucepan and transfer to a baking dish. Make the corn bread batter, spoon it on top of the hot chili, and bake as directed.

**Corn Bread–Topped
Red Chili**

Easy Chili con Queso

Makes 4 Servings

1 teaspoon canola oil

1 large onion, chopped

1–2 teaspoons chili
    seasoning mix

1 (14½-ounce) can diced
    tomatoes

2 cups fresh or frozen
    corn kernels

1 cup chopped cooked chicken

4 (6-inch) flour tortillas

½ cup (2 ounces) shredded
    reduced-fat Monterey Jack
    cheese

1. Heat the oil in a large nonstick saucepan over medium heat. Add the onion and cook, stirring frequently, until softened, about 5 minutes. Add the chili seasoning and cook, stirring constantly, until fragrant, about 1 minute. Add the tomatoes; bring to a boil. Reduce the heat and simmer, uncovered, until the flavors are blended, about 3 minutes. Add the corn and chicken; return to a simmer and cook, about 2 minutes.

2. Meanwhile, spray a 7-inch nonstick skillet with nonstick spray and set over medium-high heat. Add the tortillas, one at a time, and cook until lightly toasted, 1–2 minutes on each side. Cut each tortilla into 4 triangles.

3. Remove the saucepan from the heat and add the cheese. Stir until the cheese melts. Serve the chili with the toasted tortilla triangles.

PER SERVING (1 cup chili with 4 tortilla triangles): 290 Cal, 9 g Total Fat, 3 g Sat Fat, 0 g Trans Fat, 40 mg Chol, 459 mg Sod, 36 g Carb, 4 g Fib, 19 g Prot, 179 mg Calc.
PointsPlus value: *8.*

COOK'S TIP

If you don't want to take the time to toast tortillas, serve this chili with low-fat baked tortilla chips instead. One ounce of low-fat baked tortilla chips per serving will increase the *PointsPlus* value by *3.*

Chili Pronto

Makes 4 Servings

1 (14½-ounce) can diced tomatoes with green chiles

1 (10-ounce) package frozen diced green bell peppers

1 (9-ounce) package frozen mixed vegetables

1 (4½-ounce) can chopped mild green chiles

1 tablespoon chili or taco seasoning mix

1½ cups chopped cooked chicken

¼ cup fat-free sour cream

2 scallions (white and light green portions only), thinly sliced

2 cups baked tortilla chips

1. Combine the tomatoes, bell peppers, mixed vegetables, chiles, and chili seasoning in a nonstick saucepan; bring to a boil. Reduce the heat and simmer, uncovered, until the flavors are blended and the vegetables are softened, about 10 minutes. Add the chicken and cook, stirring occasionally, until heated through, about 3 minutes.

2. Divide the chili among 4 bowls. Top with the sour cream and scallions and serve with the chips.

PER SERVING (scant 1 cup chili, 1 tablespoon sour cream, and ½ cup tortilla chips): 235 Cal, 4 g Total Fat, 1 g Sat Fat, 0 g Trans Fat, 46 mg Chol, 635 mg Sod, 30 g Carb, 6 g Fib, 20 g Prot, 124 mg Calc. *PointsPlus* value: *6.*

COOK'S TIP

Canned and frozen products plus already cooked chicken and packaged tortilla chips make this chili a breeze to assemble. Chili and taco seasonings—tasty blends of chile peppers, salt, cumin, oregano, and garlic—can be used interchangeably. They can be found in 1- or 2-ounce packages in the Mexican section of the supermarket.

Mediterranean
Chicken Casserole

Mediterranean Chicken Casserole

Makes 6 Servings

3 (¾-pound) bone-in chicken breast halves, skinned and cut crosswise in half

1 (14½-ounce) can no-salt-added diced tomatoes

1 cup reduced-sodium chicken broth

2 fennel bulbs, trimmed and thinly sliced (about 4 cups)

10 pitted green olives, rinsed and chopped

1 garlic clove, minced

2 teaspoons chopped fresh rosemary

¼ teaspoon salt

¼ teaspoon black pepper

⅛ teaspoon saffron threads

3 tablespoons yellow cornmeal

1. Preheat the oven to 350°F.

2. Spray a Dutch oven or large flameproof casserole dish with nonstick spray and set over medium-high heat. Add the chicken breasts and brown for about 2 minutes on each side.

3. Add the tomatoes and broth to the Dutch oven; bring to a boil, scraping up any browned bits from the bottom of the pot. Add the fennel, olives, garlic, rosemary, salt, pepper, and saffron. Stir, making sure chicken breasts are partially submerged in liquid.

4. Cover the Dutch oven and bake 35 minutes. Uncover and stir in the cornmeal until it is incorporated into the sauce. Continue baking until an instant-read thermometer inserted in a breast registers 165°F and the sauce is slightly thickened, about 10 minutes longer. Serve the chicken with the vegetables and sauce.

PER SERVING (1 piece chicken with ¾ cup vegetables and sauce): **217 Cal, 5 g Total Fat, 1 g Sat Fat, 0 g Trans Fat, 74 mg Chol, 429 mg Sod, 12 g Carb, 4 g Fib, 30 g Prot, 79 mg Calc.** *PointsPlus* value: *5.*

COOK'S TIP

To trim fresh fennel, remove the feathery fronds and any thick stalks that protrude from the bulb (save for vegetable stock, if you like). Trim about ¼ inch off the bottom of the bulb, then slice it.

Chicken Eggplant Parmesan

Makes 4 Servings

4 (¼-pound) skinless boneless chicken breasts

2 ounces fat-free mozzarella cheese, cut into 4 long, thin slices

1 small onion, chopped

1 garlic clove, minced

1 (8-ounce) eggplant, cut into ½-inch chunks

3 plum tomatoes, chopped

1 tablespoon dry Marsala wine

2 teaspoons chopped fresh oregano

1 teaspoon chopped fresh thyme

½ teaspoon salt

¼ teaspoon black pepper

¼ teaspoon red pepper flakes (optional)

4 tablespoons grated Parmesan cheese

1. Preheat the oven to 350°F. Spray a 1½-or 2-quart baking dish with nonstick spray.

2. Make a pocket in the side of each chicken breast by inserting a sharp paring knife into the thickest part, then gently cutting back and forth to make a small pocket in the side. Do not cut through to the back or the sides of the breasts. Place 1 slice of mozzarella cheese in each pocket. Place the chicken in the baking dish.

3. Spray a large nonstick skillet with nonstick spray and set over medium heat. Add the onion and cook, stirring frequently, until slightly softened, about 2 minutes. Add the garlic and cook 15 seconds. Add the eggplant and cook, stirring frequently, until it begins to soften, about 4 minutes.

4. Add the tomatoes, wine, oregano, thyme, salt, black pepper, and red pepper flakes, if using, to the skillet. Cook, stirring frequently, just until the tomatoes begin to break down, about 2 minutes. Pour the mixture over the chicken. Cover and bake 30 minutes. Uncover, baste the chicken with any juices in the pan, and continue baking, uncovered, basting every 5 minutes, until the chicken is cooked through, about 15 minutes longer. Serve the chicken with the vegetables and sauce; sprinkle each serving with 1 tablespoon of Parmesan cheese.

PER SERVING (1 piece chicken with ½ cup vegetables and sauce and 1 tablespoon Parmesan): 200 Cal, 4 g Total Fat, 2 g Sat Fat, 0 g Trans Fat, 69 mg Chol, 536 mg Sod, 8 g Carb, 3 g Fib, 30 g Prot, 286 mg Calc.
PointsPlus value: *5.*

COOK'S TIP

Marsala is a fortified wine from Sicily. It's available in two forms: Dry, which is slightly bitter but very woodsy, and sweet, which is primarily used as an after-dinner drink. If you don't have any Marsala on hand, substitute dry sherry.

Chicken and Mushroom Casserole

Makes 6 Servings

6 (¼-pound) skinless boneless chicken breasts

¾ pound cremini or white mushrooms, thinly sliced

2 scallions, thinly sliced

2 tablespoons dry vermouth

1 teaspoon chopped fresh thyme

¼ teaspoon salt

¼ teaspoon black pepper

1 cup brown rice

2 tablespoons dried cranberries

1 (14½-ounce) can reduced-sodium chicken broth

1. Preheat the oven to 350°F.

2. Spray a Dutch oven or large flameproof casserole dish with nonstick spray and set over medium heat. Add the chicken breasts in one layer, working in batches if necessary, and cook until browned on one side, about 2 minutes. Transfer the chicken to a plate.

3. Add the mushrooms and scallions to the Dutch oven; cook, stirring frequently, until the mushrooms give off their liquid and it reduces to a glaze, about 4 minutes. Add the vermouth and simmer for 10 seconds, scraping up any browned bits from the bottom of the pan.

4. Add the thyme, salt, and pepper; cook, stirring constantly, until fragrant, about 10 seconds. Add rice and cranberries, stir once, then stir in broth. Add the chicken breasts, browned side up, and bring to a simmer.

5. Remove the Dutch oven from the heat, cover, and bake until the chicken is cooked through and the rice is tender but still toothsome, about 55 minutes.

PER SERVING (1 piece chicken with ¾ cup rice and vegetables): 277 Cal, 4 g Total Fat, 1 g Sat Fat, 0 g Trans Fat, 63 mg Chol, 179 mg Sod, 29 g Carb, 2 g Fib, 28 g Prot, 35 mg Calc. *PointsPlus* value: *7.*

COOK'S TIP

Look no further than this classic chicken casserole for satisfying your family and impressing guests. The brown rice adds a nutty taste to the dish, while the dried cranberries contribute a sparkly finish.

Chicken Shepherd's Pie

Chicken Shepherd's Pie

Makes 6 Servings

3 large Yukon Gold potatoes (about 1½ pounds), peeled and quartered

¾ cup fat-free milk

1 tablespoon Dijon mustard

¼ teaspoon black pepper

1 medium onion, chopped

¾ pound ground skinless chicken breast

1½ tablespoons all-purpose flour

2 tablespoons white Worcestershire sauce

1 teaspoon finely chopped fresh sage

½ teaspoon crushed green peppercorns

¾ cup reduced-sodium chicken broth

1 (10-ounce) package frozen peas and carrots, thawed

¼ teaspoon paprika

1. Bring the potatoes, with enough water to cover, to a boil in a large pot. Reduce the heat and simmer, covered, until the potatoes are tender when pierced with a fork, about 12 minutes. Drain and place in a medium bowl. Add the milk, mustard, and black pepper. Mash with a potato masher or an electric mixer on medium speed until creamy, about 4 minutes by hand or 2 minutes with a mixer; set aside.

2. Preheat the oven to 350°F.

3. Spray a large nonstick skillet with nonstick spray and set over medium heat. Add the onion and cook, stirring frequently, until softened, about 2 minutes. Add the chicken and cook, breaking it up with a wooden spoon, until browned, about 4 minutes.

4. Sprinkle the flour over the chicken mixture. Stir well and cook, just until the flour is absorbed, about 30 seconds. Stir in the Worcestershire sauce, sage, and crushed green peppercorns; cook until fragrant, about 10 seconds. Stir in the broth and bring to a boil. Reduce the heat and simmer until the mixture bubbles and thickens, about 1 minute. Stir in the peas and carrots. Pour the mixture into a 9-inch square baking dish.

5. Spoon or pipe the mashed potatoes over the chicken mixture. Sprinkle with the paprika. Place the baking dish on a rimmed baking sheet and bake until bubbling and heated through, about 40 minutes. Let stand for about 5 minutes before serving.

PER SERVING (1 cup): 208 Cal, 1 g Total Fat, 0 g Sat Fat, 0 g Trans Fat, 38 mg Chol, 249 mg Sod, 31 g Carb, 4 g Fib, 19 g Prot, 77 mg Calc.
PointsPlus value: *5.*

COOK'S TIP

Yukon Gold potatoes are a great choice for the topping to this comfort food classic. These potatoes have a medium amount of starch, buttery flavor, and a rich yellow color.

Chicken and Potato Casserole

Makes 4 Servings

1 (¾-pound) baking potato,
  preferably a russet potato,
  peeled

1 small onion, chopped

1 celery stalk, chopped

1 garlic clove, minced

¾ pound ground skinless
  chicken breast

2 tablespoons paprika

½ teaspoon salt

¼ teaspoon black pepper

½ cup reduced-sodium
  chicken broth

½ cup fat-free sour cream

1. Fill a large bowl with cool water. Cut the potato in half lengthwise. Using a vegetable peeler, make long thin "noodles" from the cut sides of the potato, letting the strips fall into the water.

2. Bring a pot of water to a boil. Drain the potato noodles and add them to the pot. Cook just until they lose their crunchy edge, no more than 2 minutes. Drain and refresh under cool water.

3. Preheat the oven to 350°F. Spray a 1-quart shallow baking dish with nonstick spray.

4. Spray a large nonstick skillet with nonstick spray and set over medium heat. Add the onion and celery; cook, stirring frequently, until slightly softened, about 2 minutes. Add the garlic and cook 15 seconds. Add the chicken and cook, breaking it up with a wooden spoon, until browned, about 2 minutes. Add the paprika, salt, and pepper, then pour in the broth, scraping up any browned bits from the bottom of the skillet. Bring to a boil; reduce the heat and simmer 1 minute. Remove from heat and stir in the sour cream.

5. Place one-third of the potato noodles in the baking dish, making one overlapping layer. Add one-third of the chicken mixture; spread over the potatoes. Repeat the layering two more times, using the remaining potatoes and chicken mixture. Bake until lightly browned and bubbling, about 40 minutes. Let stand for about 5 minutes before serving.

PER SERVING (scant 1 cup): 215 Cal, 4 g Total Fat, 1 g Sat Fat, 0 g Trans Fat, 52 mg Chol, 444 mg Sod, 22 g Carb, 3 g Fib, 23 g Prot, 98 mg Calc.
PointsPlus value: *5.*

COOK'S TIP

Potatoes make great "noodles." Just slice them into thin strips with a vegetable peeler, then parboil for a few minutes and voilà. Here, they're layered in a paprika-laced casserole that is reminiscent of paprikash, the famous Hungarian dish.

Chicken and Mushroom Tetrazzini

Makes 4 servings

6 ounces whole wheat spaghetti

½ pound ground skinless chicken breast

8 ounces mixed mushrooms, such as cremini, oyster, and white, sliced

1 small onion, chopped

1 large garlic clove, minced

1½ tablespoons all-purpose flour

1¼ cups reduced-sodium chicken broth

¼ cup dry white wine or dry vermouth

2 teaspoons chopped fresh thyme

½ teaspoon salt

¼ teaspoon black pepper

⅛ teaspoon freshly grated nutmeg

6 tablespoons fat-free sour cream

2 tablespoons chopped fresh flat-leaf parsley

¼ cup grated Parmesan cheese

1. Cook the spaghetti according to the package directions omitting the salt, if desired. Drain and set aside.

2. Meanwhile, preheat the oven to 375°F. Spray a 1-quart baking dish with nonstick spray.

3. Spray a large nonstick skillet with nonstick spray and set over medium heat. Add the chicken and cook, breaking it up with a wooden spoon, until browned, about 4 minutes. Using a slotted spoon, transfer the chicken to a medium bowl. Wipe out the skillet.

4. Spray the skillet with nonstick spray. Add the mushrooms and cook, stirring, until they give off their liquid and it has reduced by half, about 4 minutes. Add the onion and garlic and cook, stirring, until softened, about 5 minutes. Return the chicken to the skillet; sprinkle with the flour. Cook, stirring constantly, just until the flour is no longer visible, about 30 seconds.

5. Stir in the broth, wine, thyme, salt, pepper, and nutmeg; bring to a boil. Reduce the heat and simmer until the sauce has thickened slightly, about 1 minute. Remove the skillet from the heat and stir in the sour cream and parsley. Add the pasta and cheese and toss until mixed well.

6. Transfer the chicken-pasta mixture to the baking dish. Bake until the top is lightly browned and the filling is heated through, about 20 minutes. Let stand for about 5 minutes before serving.

PER SERVING (scant 1 cup): 277 Cal, 2 g Total Fat, 1 g Sat Fat, 0 g Trans Fat, 40 mg Chol, 563 mg Sod, 39 g Carb, 4 g Fib, 26 g Prot, 141 mg Calc.
PointsPlus value: *7.*

COOK'S TIP

Save some prep time by buying sliced mushrooms and grated Parmesan cheese.

Chicken Noodle Casserole

Makes 6 Servings

½ pound no-yolk egg noodles

3 tablespoons all-purpose flour

1 cup reduced-sodium
chicken broth

2 teaspoons canola oil

1 small onion, finely chopped

2 cups fat-free milk

1 tablespoon Dijon mustard

1 tablespoon chopped fresh
tarragon

½ teaspoon salt

¼ teaspoon black pepper

1 (10-ounce) package
frozen peas

2 cups chopped cooked
chicken

½ cup (2 ounces) shredded
reduced-fat Cheddar or
Swiss cheese

1. Preheat the oven to 350°F. Spray a 2-quart high-sided baking dish with nonstick spray.

2. Cook the noodles according to the package directions, omitting the salt. Drain and set aside.

3. Meanwhile, whisk the flour and ½ cup of the broth in a small bowl until the flour dissolves.

4. Heat the oil in a large saucepan over medium heat. Add the onion and cook, stirring frequently, until softened, about 3 minutes. Stir in the milk and the remaining ½ cup broth; bring the mixture to a simmer. Whisk in the flour mixture; cook, stirring constantly, until the sauce bubbles and thickens, about 3 minutes. Stir in the mustard, tarragon, salt, and pepper.

5. Remove the pan from the heat and stir in the noodles, peas, chicken, and cheese. Pour the mixture into the baking dish. Bake until bubbling and golden brown, about 40 minutes. Let stand for about 5 minutes before serving.

PER SERVING (1⅓ cups): 343 Cal, 6 g Total Fat, 1 g Sat Fat, 0 g Trans Fat, 42 mg Chol, 543 mg Sod, 44 g Carb, 4 g Fib, 28 g Prot, 200 mg Calc.
PointsPlus value: *9.*

COOK'S TIP

Here's an old-fashioned family favorite: Chicken, peas, and noodles all bound together in a creamy sauce. No one will ever think it's something you made for your "diet"—and that's because it's not diet food. It's good, homey fare prepared so you can stay on track with your good food choices.

Chicken Noodle Casserole

Buttermilk Biscuit–Topped Potpie

Makes 5 Servings

1½ cups reduced-sodium chicken broth

½ cup fat-free half-and-half

2 tablespoons all-purpose flour

1 tablespoon country-style Dijon mustard

¼ teaspoon black pepper

Pinch of cayenne

1 tablespoon unsalted butter

1 small red onion, chopped

4 celery stalks, diced

2 garlic cloves, minced

½ teaspoon dried savory or thyme

2 cups frozen mixed vegetables (corn, carrots, peas, and green beans), thawed

1½ cups diced cooked chicken breast

1 (6-ounce) package refrigerated buttermilk biscuits

1. Preheat the oven to 425°F. Spray a 3-quart shallow baking dish with nonstick spray.

2. Whisk together the broth, half-and-half, flour, mustard, black pepper, and cayenne in a glass measure until blended.

3. Melt the butter in a large nonstick skillet over medium heat. Add the onion, celery, garlic, and savory; cook, stirring, until softened, about 5 minutes. Stir in the mixed vegetables and chicken and cook until heated through, about 3 minutes. Add the broth mixture and cook, stirring constantly, until the sauce bubbles and thickens, about 3 minutes.

4. Pour the chicken mixture into the baking dish. Arrange the biscuits on top, spacing them evenly. Bake until the filling is bubbly and the biscuits are golden brown, 10–12 minutes.

PER SERVING (generous 1 cup chicken with vegetables and 1 biscuit): 306 Cal, 10 g Total Fat, 3 g Sat Fat, 2 g Trans Fat, 42 mg Chol, 757 mg Sod, 35 g Carb, 6 g Fib, 20 g Prot, 105 mg Calc. *PointsPlus* value: *8.*

COOK'S TIP

Adding about 1 cup of sliced mushrooms—any kind you like—to the skillet along with the onion in step 3 adds deep, earthy flavor to this American classic without increasing the *PointsPlus* value.

Cutting Chicken

With a sharp boning knife and a few minutes, you can custom-butcher your bird and save money too! When whole chickens go on sale, buy several. Pack the cut-up parts into recipe- or meal-size portions, and seal in zip-close plastic freezer bags. Label, date, and freeze up to 9 months.

CUTTING UP A WHOLE CHICKEN

- To cut up a chicken, place it, breast side up, on a cutting board. With a boning knife, cut through the skin between the thigh and body. Bend the leg back until the joint pops. Cut through the joint, separating the whole leg portion from the body. To separate the drumstick from the thigh, cut through the skin just above the knee joint, then cut them apart. Repeat.

- To remove a wing, pull it away from the body. Cut through the skin between the wing and body. Bend the wing back until the joint pops. Cut through the joint to separate the wing from the body. Repeat.

- To separate the breast from the back, using a knife or kitchen scissors, cut along the ribs on each side of the bird, separating the breast from the back of the bird.

- To cut the breast in half, use a knife or kitchen scissors to cut lengthwise through the breastbone. Place the breast, skin side down, on the board with the wider end facing you. With the tip of the knife, cut through the white cartilage at the top of the breast. Pick up the breast and bend it back, exposing the hard triangular-shaped center bone, then pull it out and cut the breast in half.

- To cut the back into thigh portions, hold the back in both hands, skin facing up, and bend the ends in toward the center until the bones crack; cut the back in half. Cut along each side of the backbone; discard or save for stock.

BONING CHICKEN BREAST HALVES

- Place the breast, skin side down, on the cutting board. Slide the knife under the flat part of the breastbone. Use short strokes to cut just under the bone until you get to the other side. With the tip of the knife, cut around the shoulder joint (where the wing was attached).

- To remove the wishbone, with your fingers feel along the top edge of the meat for a thin, short bone (half of the wishbone). With the tip of the knife, free the tip of the bone, then scrape along the bone to separate it from the meat.

- To finish, cut through the tissue where the bone is still attached to the meat. Separate the ribs and wishbone from the meat. Pull off the skin, if desired.

BONING CHICKEN THIGHS

- Place a thigh, skin side down, on a cutting board. Cut along one side of the bone, using short strokes to separate the meat from the bone. Turn the thigh around and repeat on the other side.

- To finish, slide the knife under the bone to free the meat from the bone. Cut around the bone at each end, cutting away any cartilage. Turn the thigh over and remove the skin, if desired.

Easy Chicken Cassoulet

Makes 8 Servings

8 (5-ounce) bone-in skinless chicken thighs

6 ounces Canadian bacon, diced

2 cups baby carrots

2 celery stalks, chopped

1 large leek, cleaned and thinly sliced

2 (15½-ounce) cans cannellini (white kidney) beans, rinsed and drained

2 cups reduced-sodium chicken or vegetable broth

¼ cup water

1 tablespoon finely chopped fresh thyme

¼ teaspoon black pepper

2 bay leaves

⅛ teaspoon cayenne (optional)

½ teaspoon lemon juice

1. Preheat the oven to 350°F.

2. Spray a large Dutch oven or flameproof casserole dish with nonstick spray and set over medium heat. Working in batches if necessary, add the chicken and brown, about 2 minutes on each side. Transfer the chicken to a plate.

3. Add the Canadian bacon to the Dutch oven and cook until lightly browned, about 1 minute. Add the carrots, celery, and leek; cook, stirring frequently, until softened, about 4 minutes. Add the beans, broth, water, thyme, black pepper, bay leaves, and cayenne, if using; bring to a simmer.

4. Remove the Dutch oven from the heat; add the chicken and any accumulated juices, nestling the chicken among the vegetables. Cover and bake until the chicken is almost falling off the bone and the sauce is somewhat thickened, about 1 hour and 30 minutes.

5. Discard the bay leaves. Transfer 1 cup of the vegetable and bean mixture to a food processor; pulse until smooth. Stir this puree back into the Dutch oven to thicken the sauce. Stir in the lemon juice.

PER SERVING (1 chicken thigh with ¾ cup vegetables and sauce): 310 Cal, 10 g Total Fat, 3 g Sat Fat, 0 g Trans Fat, 68 mg Chol, 465 mg Sod, 23 g Carb, 6 g Fib, 32 g Prot, 113 mg Calc. *PointsPlus* value: *8.*

COOK'S TIP

Our delicious cassoulet was inspired by the classic French version, which usually takes hours—or even days—to prepare. Cassoulet is often made with a combination of meats; we use chicken thighs and Canadian bacon which, with the fresh vegetables and herbs, lend well-rounded flavor to this casserole.

Curried Chicken and Green Bean Casserole

Makes 4 Servings

¾ pound skinless boneless chicken thighs, cut into 1½-inch pieces

2 teaspoons unsalted butter

1 large onion, thinly sliced

2 teaspoons curry powder

1 (14½-ounce) can reduced-sodium vegetable broth

1 (5-ounce) can fat-free evaporated milk

2 tablespoons all-purpose flour

1 (10-ounce) package frozen cut green beans, thawed

2 tablespoons plain dry bread crumbs

1. Preheat the oven to 375°F. Spray a 1½-quart shallow baking dish or gratin dish with nonstick spray.

2. Spray a large nonstick skillet with nonstick spray and set over medium heat. Add the chicken and cook, turning occasionally, until lightly browned, about 3 minutes. Transfer the chicken to a bowl.

3. Melt the butter in the same skillet over low heat. Add the onion and cook, stirring frequently, until golden, about 10 minutes. Sprinkle the curry powder over the onion and cook until fragrant, about 15 seconds. Add the broth and bring to a simmer, scraping up any browned bits from the bottom of the skillet.

4. Whisk the evaporated milk and flour in a small bowl, then stir some of the hot broth from the skillet into the flour mixture. Return the mixture to the skillet. Cook, stirring constantly, until the mixture bubbles and thickens. Add the chicken, any accumulated juices, and the green beans to the skillet; mix well.

5. Transfer the chicken mixture to the baking dish, sprinkle with the bread crumbs, and bake until cooked through and bubbling, about 45 minutes.

PER SERVING (generous 1 cup): **250 Cal, 9 g Total Fat, 3 g Sat Fat, 0 g Trans Fat, 59 mg Chol, 239 mg Sod, 19 g Carb, 3 g Fib, 23 g Prot, 178 mg Calc.**
PointsPlus value: *6.*

COOK'S TIP

The chicken and green bean casserole that so many of us grew up with has been given a makeover thanks to the addition of flavorful curry powder. Fat-free evaporated milk, which replaces the cream or cream soup typically used, adds a creamy richness to the sauce. Serve with a simple salad of lettuce, tomatoes, and radishes.

Easy Chicken Lasagna

Makes 9 Servings

1 pound ground skinless
chicken breast

½ pound cremini or white
mushrooms, thinly sliced

1 (26-ounce) jar fat-free
marinara sauce

1 (15-ounce) container fat-free
ricotta cheese

2 cups (8 ounces) shredded
part-skim mozzarella
cheese

2 large egg whites, lightly
beaten

½ teaspoon freshly grated
nutmeg

1 (8-ounce) can no-salt-added
tomato sauce

1 (9-ounce) package no-boil
lasagna noodles

¼ cup grated Parmigiano-
Reggiano cheese

1. Preheat the oven to 375°F.

2. Spray a large nonstick skillet with nonstick spray and set over medium heat. Add the chicken and cook, breaking it up with a wooden spoon, until lightly browned, about 1 minute. Add the mushrooms and cook until they give off their liquid and it reduces by half, about 4 minutes. Stir in the marinara sauce and bring the mixture to a simmer. Remove the skillet from the heat and set aside.

3. Combine the ricotta cheese, mozzarella cheese, egg whites, and nutmeg in a medium bowl.

4. Spread the tomato sauce evenly across the bottom of a 9 × 13-inch baking pan. Place 5 of the lasagna noodles over the sauce in one layer. Top with one-third of the chicken mixture, then spread half the cheese mixture over the chicken mixture. Repeat the layering one more time, then top with the remaining 5 noodles and the remaining one-third chicken mixture. Sprinkle the Parmigiano-Reggiano over the top.

5. Cover and bake the lasagna 45 minutes. Uncover and bake until bubbling and lightly browned on top, about 10 minutes longer. Let stand for about 5 minutes before serving.

PER SERVING (⅑ of lasagna): 340 Cal, 7 g Total Fat, 3 g Sat Fat, 0 g Trans Fat, 54 mg Chol, 553 mg Sod, 36 g Carb, 2 g Fib, 33 g Prot, 342 mg Calc.
PointsPlus value: *9.*

COOK'S TIP

Parmigiano-Reggiano is a long-aged, carefully crafted cheese from northern Italy, famed for its buttery flavor and slightly grainy texture. Look for wedges sold with the rind intact and stamped with the name Parmigiano-Reggiano. Avoid grated Parmesan cheese sold in jars, as it usually contains additives.

Easy Chicken Lasagna

other birds

*turkey, cornish hen,
quail, and duck*

Roast Turkey with Onion Gravy

Makes 12 Servings

1 (9½-pound) turkey with giblets

6 tablespoons packed fresh sage leaves

8 fresh flat-leaf parsley sprigs

8 fresh thyme sprigs

3 onions, cut into ½-inch slices

3 cups reduced-sodium chicken broth

1 tablespoon water

2 teaspoons cornstarch

¼ teaspoon salt

¼ teaspoon black pepper

1. Preheat the oven to 350°F.

2. Loosen the skin around the turkey breast by running your fingers between the skin and the meat. Make a 1-inch slit on each thigh and each drumstick; run your fingers between the skin and the meat to loosen the skin. Slip 1 tablespoon of the sage leaves, 1 parsley sprig, and 1 thyme sprig into each slit; then slip 1 tablespoon of the sage leaves, 2 parsley sprigs, and 2 thyme sprigs under the skin on each side of breast.

3. Place the turkey in a large roasting pan. Arrange the giblets, neck, and onion slices around the turkey. Drizzle the turkey and onions with 1 cup of the broth.

4. Roast until an instant-read thermometer inserted in a thigh registers 165°F, about 2 hours, basting with additional broth every 20 minutes. When the broth runs out, use the pan juices to baste the turkey. Transfer the turkey to a carving board and let stand for about 10 minutes before carving.

5. Meanwhile, discard the giblets and neck from the pan. Using a slotted spoon transfer the onions to a cutting board; roughly chop them. Stir the browned bits on the bottom of the pan to dissolve them. Strain the pan juices into a measuring cup, skim off any visible fat, and add enough water to equal 1½ cups. Pour into a saucepan, add the chopped onions, and heat until simmering.

6. Stir the water and cornstarch in a small bowl until dissolved; stir in some of the hot pan juices. Return all to the saucepan and cook, stirring constantly, until the mixture bubbles and thickens. Stir in the salt and pepper; serve with turkey. Remove the skin before eating.

PER SERVING (2 slices white turkey and 1 slice dark turkey, with about 3 tablespoons gravy): 228 Cal, 4 g Total Fat, 1 g Sat Fat, 0 g Trans Fat, 131 mg Chol, 262 mg Sod, 3 g Carb, 1 g Fib, 42 g Prot, 38 mg Calc.
PointsPlus value: *5.*

COOK'S TIP

Nothing says Thanksgiving better than our juicy roast turkey, especially when accompanied by gravy made from the baked onions and pan drippings.

Thanksgiving Turkey on the Grill

Makes 12 Servings, plus leftovers

4 garlic cloves, minced

2 tablespoons chopped
    fresh sage

1 tablespoon paprika

1 tablespoon extra-virgin
    olive oil

1½ teaspoons salt

½ teaspoon black pepper

1 (10-pound) turkey, giblets
    discarded

1. Spray the grill rack with nonstick spray; prepare the grill for indirect cooking and maintain a medium-hot fire.

2. Combine the garlic, sage, paprika, oil, salt, and pepper in a small bowl; mix well. Loosen the skin around the turkey breast by running your fingers between the skin and the meat. Make a 1-inch slit on each thigh and each drumstick; run your fingers between the skin and meat to loosen the skin. Rub the garlic mixture under the skin on each side of the breast and the legs. Tuck the wing tips underneath the turkey and tie the legs together with kitchen string to help hold the shape of the bird during grilling.

3. Place the turkey on the indirect heat section of the grill rack (away from the heat source), cover the grill, and grill until an instant-read thermometer inserted in a thigh registers 165°F, about 3 hours. Transfer the turkey to a carving board and let stand for about 10 minutes before carving. Remove the skin before eating.

PER SERVING (2 slices white turkey and 1 slice dark turkey): 185 Cal, 5 g Total Fat, 2 g Sat Fat, 0 g Trans Fat, 97 mg Chol, 265 mg Sod, 0 g Carb, 0 g Fib, 33 g Prot, 27 mg Calc. *PointsPlus* value: *4.*

COOK'S TIP

Turkey is a snap to cook on a grill, and the best part is that it frees up your oven for other dishes. Rubbed with garlic, sage, and paprika, this turkey has a deep golden color and a smoky herbed flavor. You'll have enough to serve 12 people with leftovers for another day. Refrigerate any leftovers promptly and keep no more than 3 days.

Southwestern Turkey Breast

Makes 10 Servings

1½ tablespoons chili powder

1 teaspoon ground cumin

1 tablespoon canola oil or
   pumpkin seed oil

2 teaspoons lime juice

1 (5-pound) turkey breast

¼ cup reduced-sodium chicken
   broth, if necessary

1. Adjust the racks to divide the oven into thirds. Preheat the oven to 350°F. Spray a large roasting pan with nonstick spray.

2. Mix the chili powder and cumin in a small bowl; stir in the oil and lime juice until the mixture forms a thick paste.

3. Loosen the skin around the turkey breast by running your fingers between the skin and the meat, starting at the tips of the breast halves. Once the skin is loosened, divide the spice mixture between the two halves and spread it liberally onto the meat and pat the skin back into place. Place the turkey breast in the roasting pan.

4. Roast in the lower third of the oven, basting with pan juices every 20 minutes, until an instant-read thermometer inserted in the breast registers 165°F, about 2 hours. If the pan juices dry out before the turkey is cooked through, use the broth to baste the bird occasionally. Transfer the turkey breast to a carving board and let stand for about 10 minutes before carving. Remove the skin before eating.

PER SERVING (2 slices): 191 Cal, 3 g Total Fat, 1 g Sat Fat, 0 g Trans Fat, 107 mg Chol, 93 mg Sod, 1 g Carb, 0 g Fib, 38 g Prot, 24 mg Calc.
PointsPlus value: *4.*

COOK'S TIP

Pumpkin seed oil is a staple in Mexican cooking and is often used in Tex-Mex dishes. It's sometimes called by its Spanish name pepitá oil. Just a small amount adds a distinctive slightly smoky flavor.

Whole Turkey Breast with Zesty Cranberry Relish

Makes 12 Servings

1 tablespoon extra-virgin
   olive oil

4 garlic cloves, minced

1 tablespoon chopped fresh
   oregano

1 tablespoon salt

½ teaspoon black pepper

1 (7-pound) turkey breast
   with ribs

1 ¼ cups sugar

1 cup orange juice

⅔ cup water

½ cup chopped sweet onion,
   such as Vidalia

¼ teaspoon red pepper flakes

1 (12-ounce) bag fresh or frozen
   cranberries

2 teaspoons grated lime zest

1. Spray the grill rack with nonstick spray; prepare the grill for indirect cooking and maintain a medium fire.

2. Combine the oil, garlic, oregano, salt, and black pepper in a small bowl; mix well. Loosen the skin around the turkey breast by running your fingers between the skin and the meat, starting at the tips of the breast halves. Once the skin is loosened, divide the spice mixture between the two halves and spread it liberally onto the meat, and pat the skin back into place.

3. Place the turkey breast, skin side up, on the indirect heat section of the grill rack (away from the heat source), cover the grill, and grill until an instant-read thermometer inserted in the breast registers 165°F, 2½–3 hours.

4. Meanwhile, combine the sugar, orange juice, water, onion, and red pepper flakes in a medium saucepan; bring to a boil. Add the cranberries and return to a boil. Reduce the heat and simmer, stirring occasionally, until the mixture thickens slightly and the cranberries pop, about 15 minutes. Remove from the heat and stir in the lime zest. Let the mixture cool about 30 minutes, then chill until ready to serve.

5. Transfer the turkey breast to a carving board and let stand for about 10 minutes before carving. Remove the skin before eating. Serve with the relish.

PER SERVING (2 slices turkey with ⅓ cup relish): 348 Cal, 3 g Total Fat, 1 g Sat Fat, 0 g Trans Fat, 138 mg Chol, 288 mg Sod, 29 g Carb, 2 g Fib, 49 g Prot, 34 mg Calc.
PointsPlus value: *8*.

COOK'S TIP

A ¼ teaspoon red pepper flakes may not seem like a lot but it adds quite a zing to this relish. For a less spicy finish, reduce the amount to ⅛ teaspoon. You can make the relish ahead and store it in the refrigerator in a covered container for up to 2 weeks.

Slow-Cooker Ham and Cheese-Stuffed Turkey Breast

Makes 4 Servings

1 red onion, chopped

½ cup dry white wine

½ teaspoon salt

1 teaspoon extra-virgin olive oil

2 cups chopped fresh spinach leaves

2 large garlic cloves, minced

3 tablespoons dried currants

1 skinless boneless turkey breast half (about 1½ pounds)

¼ teaspoon black pepper

4 very thin slices baked ham (about ½-ounce each)

3 tablespoons grated Grana Padano cheese

1. Set aside ¾ cup of the onion. Combine the remaining onion, wine, and ¼ teaspoon of the salt in a 5- or 6-quart slow cooker.

2. Heat the oil in a large nonstick skillet over medium heat. Add the reserved onion and cook, stirring, until softened, about 5 minutes. Add the spinach and garlic; cook, stirring, until the spinach is tender and liquid has evaporated, about 3 minutes. Stir in the currants. Remove the skillet from heat and let the filling cool for about 10 minutes.

3. Place the turkey, skinned side up, on a cutting board. Holding a sharp knife parallel to the board and starting at one long side, cut three-quarters of the way through and open the breast up like a book. Place a sheet of plastic wrap over the turkey. With a meat mallet or rolling pin, gently pound it to a ½-inch thickness.

4. Sprinkle the turkey with the remaining ¼ teaspoon salt and and the pepper. Arrange the slices of ham over the turkey, overlapping them if needed and leaving a ½-inch border. Spread the spinach mixture over the ham and sprinkle with the cheese. Starting at a narrow end, roll up the turkey, jelly-roll fashion. Tie it with kitchen string at 1-inch intervals.

5. Transfer the turkey roll to the slow cooker. Cover and cook until the turkey is fork-tender, 3–4 hours on high or 6–8 hours on low. Transfer the roll to a cutting board and let stand for 5 minutes before slicing. Remove the string and cut the turkey into 12 slices. Serve with the sauce.

PER SERVING (3 slices turkey and ⅓ cup sauce): 290 Cal, 6 g Total Fat, 2 g Sat Fat, 0 g Trans Fat, 127 mg Chol, 585 mg Sod, 11 g Carb, 2 g Fib, 46 g Prot, 108 mg Calc. *PointsPlus* value: *7*.

COOK'S TIP

If you have not tried Grana Padano cheese, this is the perfect time to taste one of Italy's most popular grating cheeses. It is a bit milder than Parmesan, but they are pretty much interchangeable. It can be found in cheese shops and in specialty food stores.

Thai Turkey Stew

Makes 6 Servings

1 (13½-ounce) can light (reduced-fat) coconut milk

2 tablespoons packed light brown sugar

2 tablespoons reduced-sodium soy sauce

1 tablespoon Asian fish sauce

2 teaspoons Thai curry paste, hot or mild or 2 teaspoons curry powder

1 pound skinless boneless turkey breast, cut into 1-inch pieces

2 scallions, cut into 1-inch pieces

1 (1-pound) cauliflower, trimmed and cut into florets

1 green bell pepper, chopped

1 (10-ounce) package frozen okra, thawed

1 cup fresh shelled peas, or frozen peas, thawed

1 tablespoon water

2 teaspoons cornstarch

1. Preheat the oven to 400°F.

2. Whisk the coconut milk, sugar, soy sauce, fish sauce, and curry paste in a 3-quart baking dish with a tight-fitting lid or a clay Chinese stew pot.

3. Add the turkey, scallions, cauliflower, bell pepper, okra, and peas; mix well. Cover and bake until the sauce is bubbling and the turkey is cooked through, about 55 minutes.

4. Stir the water and cornstarch in a small bowl until dissolved; stir in some of the juices from the baking dish. Return all to the baking dish and stir. Continue baking, uncovered, until slightly thickened, about 10 minutes longer. Let stand for 5 minutes before serving.

PER SERVING (generous 1 cup): 237 Cal, 7 g Total Fat, 5 g Sat Fat, 0 g Trans Fat, 50 mg Chol, 393 mg Sod, 23 g Carb, 6 g Fib, 24 g Prot, 86 mg Calc.
PointsPlus value: *6.*

COOK'S TIP

Coconut milk is made from fresh coconut flesh that is steeped in water, then pressed. Light, or reduced-fat, coconut milk is simply the second pressing of the same coconut solids, so it contains much less fat and helps to keep the *PointsPlus* value low in this stew.

Turkey and Bell Pepper Roulades

Makes 4 Servings

4 teaspoons extra-virgin olive oil

1 small red bell pepper, cut into thin strips

1 small green bell pepper, cut into thin strips

1 onion, thinly sliced

½ teaspoon salt

¼ teaspoon black pepper

4 (¼-pound) turkey breast cutlets

1 cup reduced-sodium chicken broth

1 tablespoon lemon juice

1 teaspoon Dijon mustard

1 teaspoon Worcestershire sauce

¼ cup light sour cream

1. Heat 2 teaspoons of the oil in a large nonstick skillet. Add the red and green bell peppers, the onion, ¼ teaspoon of the salt, and ⅛ teaspoon of the black pepper; cook, stirring occasionally, until softened, about 5 minutes. Remove the skillet from the heat and let cool about 10 minutes.

2. Gently pound the turkey cutlets to a ¼-inch thickness with a meat mallet or heavy saucepan. Sprinkle with the remaining ¼ teaspoon salt and ⅛ teaspoon black pepper and arrange on a work surface with the short sides nearest you. Divide the bell pepper mixture into 4 portions and place each portion crosswise on the side of the turkey closest to you. Roll up, jelly-roll style, and secure each with a wooden pick.

3. Wipe out the skillet, add the remaining 2 teaspoons oil, and heat over medium-high heat. Add the turkey rolls and cook, turning occasionally, until browned, about 4 minutes. Add the broth, lemon juice, mustard, and Worcestershire sauce; bring to a boil. Reduce the heat and simmer, covered, until the turkey is cooked through, about 7 minutes. Transfer the turkey rolls to a serving plate and keep warm. Increase the heat to high and boil the mixture in the skillet rapidly until slightly reduced, about 4 minutes. Remove the skillet from the heat and stir in the sour cream. Serve the sauce with the turkey rolls.

PER SERVING (1 turkey roll with ¼ cup sauce): 215 Cal, 8 g Total Fat, 2 g Sat Fat, 0 g Trans Fat, 81 mg Chol, 516 mg Sod, 6 g Carb, 1 g Fib, 29 g Prot, 43 mg Calc.
PointsPlus value: *5.*

COOK'S TIP

Roulades—stuffed and rolled thin slices of meat—are surprisingly easy to assemble and make a wonderful presentation. Serve these with whole wheat couscous that has been tossed with orange zest and lemon zest (½ cup cooked whole wheat couscous per serving will increase the *PointsPlus* value by *3*).

Turkey Cutlets Parmesan

Makes 4 Servings

4 (¼-pound) turkey breast cutlets

2 large egg whites

⅓ cup Italian seasoned dry bread crumbs

3 tablespoons all-purpose flour

1 tablespoon extra-virgin olive oil

2 ⅔ cups fat-free tomato-basil sauce

½ cup shredded part-skim mozzarella cheese

¼ cup grated Parmesan cheese

1. Gently pound the turkey cutlets to a scant ¼-inch thickness with a meat mallet or heavy saucepan.

2. Lightly beat the egg whites in a medium bowl. Spread the bread crumbs on a plate. Spread the flour on a second plate. Working with 1 piece of turkey at a time, dip both sides into the flour; shake off the excess flour. Then dip the turkey into the egg whites and then into the bread crumbs to coat; set aside. Repeat with remaining cutlets, flour, egg whites, and bread crumbs.

3. Heat the oil in a large nonstick skillet over medium-high heat. Add the coated turkey cutlets and cook until browned and cooked through, about 3 minutes on each side. Reduce the heat and pour the pasta sauce over the cutlets. Top each cutlet with 2 tablespoons of the mozzarella cheese and 1 tablespoon of the Parmesan cheese. Cover and simmer until the sauce is hot and the cheese melts, about 4 minutes.

PER SERVING (1 cutlet with about ⅓ cup sauce)**: 318 Cal, 9 g Total Fat, 4 g Sat Fat, 0 g Trans Fat, 88 mg Chol, 666 mg Sod, 20 g Carb, 1 g Fib, 37 g Prot, 232 mg Calc.**
PointsPlus value: *8.*

COOK'S TIP

Turkey cutlets are more delicate than chicken cutlets, so they require more care when being pounded. Place the cutlets between two pieces of wax paper or plastic wrap and, with a firm but gentle motion, pound the cutlets in an outward motion from the center.

Turkey Fajitas with Nectarine Salsa

Makes 4 Servings

1 large red onion

4 nectarines, about 1 pound, pitted and cut into ¼-inch dice

2 small jalapeño peppers, seeded and minced

1 tablespoon chopped fresh cilantro

1 tablespoon lime juice

¾ teaspoon salt

3 teaspoons extra-virgin olive oil

¾ pound turkey breast cutlets, cut into 2 × ¼-inch strips

¼ teaspoon black pepper

2 assorted color bell peppers, seeded and cut into thin strips

4 (8-inch) fat-free flour tortillas

1. To make the nectarine salsa, finely chop ¼ of the red onion and place in a medium bowl. Slice the remaining ¾ onion and set aside. To the chopped onion, add the nectarines, 1 of the jalapeños, the cilantro, lime juice, and ¼ teaspoon of the salt; mix well.

2. Heat 1 teaspoon of the oil in a large nonstick skillet over medium-high heat. Add the turkey; sprinkle with the black pepper and the remaining ½ teaspoon salt. Cook, stirring occasionally, until browned and cooked through, about 4 minutes. Transfer the turkey to a plate.

3. Heat the remaining 2 teaspoons oil in the same skillet over medium-high heat. Add the reserved sliced onion, remaining jalapeño, and the bell peppers; cook, stirring occasionally, until softened and light golden, about 8 minutes. Add the turkey and cook until heated through, about 1 minute.

4. Meanwhile, warm the tortillas according to the package directions. Divide the turkey mixture evenly among the tortillas (about ¾ cup filling on each) and top with salsa (about ½ cup on each). Roll up and serve at once.

PER SERVING (1 fajita): 370 Cal, 5 g Total Fat, 1 g Sat Fat, 0 g Trans Fat, 56 mg Chol, 946 mg Sod, 55 g Carb, 5 g Fib, 26 g Prot, 83 mg Calc.
PointsPlus value: *9.*

COOK'S TIP

Salsa is best made and served within a few hours. However, if you would like to make it ahead, chop the fruit and vegetables the night before and store them separately in the refrigerator. Just before serving, combine them and toss with the lime juice, cilantro, and salt.

**Turkey Fajitas with
Nectarine Salsa**

Turkey Cutlet Tostadas with Tomatillo-Lime Salsa

Makes 4 Servings

6 tomatillos (about ¾ pound),
   papery husks removed and
   tomatillos rinsed

½ jalapeño pepper, seeded

¼ cup chopped fresh cilantro

2 tablespoons lime juice

½ teaspoon salt

4 (¼-pound) turkey cutlets

4 (6-inch) corn tortillas

1 cup loosely packed thinly
   sliced romaine lettuce

1. Spray the grill rack with nonstick spray; prepare the grill for a medium-high fire.

2. To make the salsa, place the tomatillos on the grill rack and grill, turning often, until softened and lightly charred, 6–8 minutes. Put the jalapeño into a food processor and pulse until minced. Add the tomatillos and pulse until chopped. Add the cilantro, lime juice, and ¼ teaspoon of the salt; pulse just until mixed. Transfer the salsa to a small bowl.

3. Sprinkle the turkey cutlets with the remaining ¼ teaspoon salt and lightly spray with nonstick spray. Place on the grill rack and grill, turning once, until well marked and cooked through, about 8 minutes. Transfer the cutlets to a cutting board. Let cool for about 5 minutes; thinly slice or coarsely chop.

4. Place the tortillas on the grill rack and grill until warmed through, about 30 seconds on each side. Place 1 tortilla on each of 4 plates. Top each with ¼ cup romaine, one-fourth of the turkey, and 2 tablespoons salsa.

PER SERVING (1 tostada): **208 Cal, 2 g Total Fat, 1 g Sat Fat, 0 g Trans Fat, 75 mg Chol, 748 mg Sod, 18 g Carb, 3 g Fib, 29 g Prot, 47 mg Calc.**
PointsPlus value: *5.*

COOK'S TIP

Indulge your taste buds by topping each tostada with diced avocado, chopped fresh tomato, and grated reduced-fat Monterey Jack cheese (⅛ of an avocado, diced, and 1 ounce of reduced-fat Monterey Jack cheese for each serving will increase the *PointsPlus* value by *3*).

Barbecue-Glazed Turkey Meat Loaf

Makes 6 Servings

1¼ pounds ground skinless turkey breast

⅓ cup seasoned dry bread crumbs

¼ cup (1 ounce) shredded reduced-fat Cheddar cheese

¼ cup minced onion

1 large egg, lightly beaten

1 teaspoon dried oregano

¼ teaspoon salt

¼ teaspoon black pepper

2 tablespoons ketchup

2 teaspoons packed brown sugar

2 teaspoons Worcestershire sauce

1 teaspoon spicy brown mustard

1. Fold a 24-inch length of foil in half lengthwise. Fit into the bottom and up the sides of a 5- or 6-quart slow cooker insert.

2. Put the turkey, bread crumbs, cheese, onion, egg, oregano, salt, and pepper in a medium bowl; mix with your hands until well combined. Shape the mixture into a loaf and place on the foil in the slow cooker.

3. Cover the slow cooker and cook until the meat loaf juices run clear or an instant-read thermometer inserted in the center of the meat loaf registers 165°F, 3–4 hours on high or 6–8 hours on low.

4. Combine the ketchup, sugar, Worcestershire sauce, and mustard in a small bowl. Spoon the mixture over the meat loaf, and spread it smooth. Cover the slow cooker and cook until the glaze is heated through, about 30 minutes longer. With the help of the foil, lift the meat loaf from the slow cooker and transfer to a platter. Discard the foil and cut the meat loaf into 6 slices.

PER SERVING (1 slice meat loaf): 162 Cal, 2 g Total Fat, 1 g Sat Fat, 0 g Trans Fat, 99 mg Chol, 332 mg Sod, 8 g Carb, 0 g Fib, 25 g Prot, 71 mg Calc.
PointsPlus value: *4.*

COOK'S TIP

To make fresh bread crumbs, leave 2 or 3 slices of whole wheat bread out on the countertop overnight. Break the bread into pieces, then pulse in a food processor or a mini food processor just until crumbs form.

Slow-Cooker Turkey Meatballs with Mustardy Sour Cream Sauce

Makes 6 Servings

3 slices firm white bread, torn into pieces

1 pound ground skinless turkey breast

⅓ cup finely chopped onion

1 large egg

2 tablespoons Dijon mustard

½ teaspoon salt

¼ teaspoon black pepper

½ cup reduced-sodium chicken broth

1 tablespoon steak sauce

½ cup fat-free sour cream

1. Preheat the oven to 450°F. Spray a large rimmed baking sheet with nonstick spray.

2. Put the bread into a food processor or blender and pulse until it forms fine crumbs. Combine the bread crumbs, turkey, onion, egg, 1 tablespoon of the mustard, the salt, and pepper in a large bowl. With damp hands, form the mixture into 36 meatballs. Place the meatballs on the baking sheet. Bake until lightly browned, about 15 minutes.

3. Transfer the meatballs to a 5- or 6-quart slow cooker. Mix together the broth, the remaining 1 tablespoon mustard, and the steak sauce in a glass measure; pour over the meatballs. Cover and cook until the meatballs are firm and cooked through and the sauce has thickened slightly, 1–2 hours on high or 2–4 hours on low.

4. Just before serving, stir in sour cream until blended.

PER SERVING (6 meatballs with 2 tablespoons sauce): 150 Cal, 2 g Total Fat, 0 g Sat Fat, 0 g Trans Fat, 43 mg Chol, 558 mg Sod, 10 g Carb, 0 g Fib, 22 g Prot, 58 mg Calc.
PointsPlus value: *4.*

COOK'S TIP

Serve these tasty and tender meatballs over quinoa (½ cup cooked quinoa for each serving will increase the *PointsPlus* value by *3*).

North African Turkey Kebabs

Makes 4 Servings

1 pound ground skinless turkey
    breast

2 garlic cloves, minced

2 tablespoons chopped
    fresh cilantro

1 tablespoon lemon juice

2 teaspoons grated peeled
    fresh ginger

1 teaspoon ground coriander

1 teaspoon hot pepper sauce

¾ teaspoon ground cumin

¾ teaspoon salt

¼ teaspoon ground cinnamon

1. Spray the grill rack with nonstick spray; prepare the grill for a medium-hot fire.

2. Combine the turkey, garlic, cilantro, lemon juice, ginger, coriander, hot pepper sauce, cumin, salt, and cinnamon in a large bowl; mix well. Divide the mixture into 4 equal portions. Roll each portion into a cylinder 5 inches long and 1½ inches in diameter. Chill 30 minutes. Insert a skewer, lengthwise, into the center of each cylinder.

3. Place the kebabs on the grill rack and grill, turning every 3 minutes, until the turkey is cooked through, 12–15 minutes.

PER SERVING (1 kebab): 132 Cal, 1 g Total Fat, 0 g Sat Fat, 0 g Trans Fat, 75 mg Chol, 502 mg Sod, 2 g Carb, 0 g Fib, 27 g Prot, 27 mg Calc.
PointsPlus value: *3*.

COOK'S TIP

To get a head start on this recipe, make the cylinders of turkey the day before and refrigerate them covered until ready to grill. Added bonus—the flavors will have a chance to develop so these kebabs will taste even better.

Slow-Cooked Smoky Turkey Picadillo

Makes 4 Servings

1 small onion, chopped

2 large garlic cloves, minced

1 (14½-ounce) can diced
    tomatoes, drained

1 red bell pepper, chopped

3 tablespoons tomato paste

2 tablespoons packed light
    brown sugar

2 tablespoons chipotle
    chile powder

2 teaspoons unsweetened
    cocoa

2 teaspoons ground cumin

¾ teaspoon salt

2 (1-pound) bone-in skinless
    turkey thighs

2 tablespoons cornmeal

1½ cups frozen corn kernels,
    thawed

3 tablespoons dark raisins,
    chopped

1 tablespoon hot pepper sauce,
    such as Frank's Red Hot

1. Spray a medium nonstick skillet with extra-virgin olive oil nonstick spray and set over medium heat. Add the onion and garlic and cook, stirring, until softened, about 5 minutes.

2. Combine the tomatoes, bell pepper, tomato paste, brown sugar, chile powder, cocoa, cumin, salt, and onion mixture in a 5- or 6-quart slow cooker. Put the turkey on top. Cover and cook until the turkey is fork-tender, 3–4 hours on high or 6–8 hours on low.

3. Using a slotted spoon, transfer the turkey to a plate and let stand until cool enough to handle, about 20 minutes.

4. Meanwhile, slowly add the cornmeal to the slow cooker, stirring, until blended. Stir in the corn, raisins, and pepper sauce. Cover and cook on high until the mixture simmers and thickens and the corn is tender, about 20 minutes.

5. Remove and discard the bones from the turkey; cut the turkey meat into bite-size pieces. Return the turkey pieces to the slow cooker. Cover and cook just until heated through, about 5 minutes. Ladle the picadillo into 4 large bowls.

PER SERVING (1½ cups picadillo): 371 Cal, 7 g Total Fat, 2 g Sat Fat, 0 g Trans Fat, 140 mg Chol, 920 mg Sod, 40 g Carb, 6 g Fib, 41 g Prot, 99 mg Calc.
PointsPlus value: *9*.

COOK'S TIP

Serve this picadillo the classic way—over hot cooked brown rice. And for a hit of bright flavor, top each serving with a generous dollop of fat-free salsa and some coarsely chopped fresh cilantro (½ cup cooked brown rice for each serving will increase the *PointsPlus* value by *3*).

Bacon-Cheddar Turkey Burgers

Makes 4 Servings

3 tablespoons fat-free mayonnaise

1 tablespoon ketchup

2 slices Canadian bacon, cut into small pieces

1 pound ground skinless turkey breast

3 slices fat-free sharp Cheddar cheese, cut into small pieces

1 teaspoon Worcestershire sauce

¼ teaspoon salt

⅛ teaspoon black pepper

1. Spray a broiler rack with canola nonstick spray; preheat the broiler.

2. Meanwhile, combine the mayonnaise and ketchup in a small bowl; set aside.

3. Spray a large nonstick skillet with canola nonstick spray and set over medium heat. Add the bacon and cook, stirring occasionally, until the bacon browns and starts to become crisp, about 5 minutes. Transfer to a large bowl and let cool completely.

4. Add the turkey, cheese, Worcestershire sauce, salt, and pepper to the bacon in the large bowl. Form into 4 patties. Place the patties on the broiler rack and broil, 5 inches from the heat, until an instant-read thermometer inserted in the side of each patty registers 165°F, 6 minutes on each side. Top each burger with 1 tablespoon of the mayonnaise mixture.

PER SERVING (1 burger): 167 Cal, 2 g Total Fat, 1 g Sat Fat, 0 g Trans Fat, 82 mg Chol, 636 mg Sod, 4 g Carb, 0 g Fib, 32 g Prot, 53 mg Calc.
PointsPlus value: *4.*

COOK'S TIP

Serve these burgers on multigrain buns and you'll increase the per-serving *PointsPlus* value by *2.*

Turkey-Mushroom Pot Stickers with Dipping Sauce

Makes 25 Servings

⅓ cup lime juice

3 tablespoons cold water plus more for steaming

1 tablespoon Asian fish sauce

1 tablespoon sugar

1 scallion, finely chopped

Pinch of red pepper flakes

1 cup finely chopped napa or savoy cabbage

2 cups boiling water

½ pound ground skinless turkey breast

6 shiitake mushrooms, stems discarded, caps finely chopped

1 large egg white

2 tablespoons finely chopped fresh cilantro

2 tablespoons reduced-sodium soy sauce

2 teaspoons Asian (dark) sesame oil

1 teaspoon cornstarch

⅛ teaspoon black pepper

50 (3 to 3½-inch) round wonton wrappers

1. To make the dipping sauce, combine the lime juice, 3 tablespoons cold water, the fish sauce, sugar, half of scallion, and the red pepper flakes in a small bowl.

2. Put the cabbage into a strainer. Slowly pour the boiling water over the cabbage. When the cabbage is cool enough to handle, squeeze out the excess water. Combine the cabbage, turkey, mushrooms, egg white, cilantro, soy sauce, oil, cornstarch, black pepper, and the remaining half scallion in a bowl until blended.

3. Line a baking sheet with parchment paper. To make the dumplings, place 10 wrappers on a work surface (keep the remaining wrappers covered with a damp paper towel so they don't dry out) and place 1 rounded measuring teaspoon of the cabbage mixture in the center of each wrapper. Lightly brush the edges of the wrappers with water. Fold the wrappers in half and press the edges together to seal. Place the dumplings on the baking sheet and cover with plastic wrap. Repeat with the remaining wrappers and filling, to make a total of 50 dumplings.

4. Spray a large nonstick skillet with nonstick spray and set over medium-high heat. Arrange half of the dumplings in the skillet. Cook until golden on the bottom, about 2 minutes. Add ¼ cup cold water. Reduce the heat and steam, covered, until cooked through, about 4 minutes. Uncover and cook until the water evaporates, about 4 minutes longer. Transfer the dumplings to a baking sheet and keep warm. Repeat with the remaining dumplings and ¼ cup more cold water. Serve the dumplings with the dipping sauce.

PER SERVING (2 dumplings with 1 teaspoon dipping sauce): 66 Cal, 1 g Total Fat, 0 g Sat Fat, 0 g Trans Fat, 14 mg Chol, 82 mg Sod, 10 g Carb, 0 g Fib, 4 g Prot, 8 mg Calc.
PointsPlus value: *2.*

COOK'S TIP

These classic dumplings are a cinch to make when using wonton wrappers. They can be filled and shaped ahead of time, then covered and refrigerated overnight or frozen for up to 3 months.

Turkey Sausage and Mushroom Risotto

Makes 6 Servings

5–6 cups reduced-sodium chicken broth

3 teaspoons extra-virgin olive oil

¾ pound turkey sausage, casings removed, sausage crumbled

½ pound white mushrooms, sliced

1 teaspoon dried oregano

¾ cup Madeira wine

1 shallot, chopped

3 garlic cloves, minced

1½ cups Arborio rice

⅓ cup grated Parmesan cheese

¼ teaspoon black pepper

1. Bring the broth to a boil in a medium saucepan. Reduce the heat and keep at a simmer.

2. Heat 1 teaspoon of the oil in a large nonstick skillet over medium-high heat. Add the sausage meat and cook, breaking up the sausage with a wooden spoon, until browned and cooked through, about 5 minutes. Add the mushrooms and oregano; cook, stirring frequently, until the mushrooms are tender, about 4 minutes. Add ¼ cup of the Madeira and cook until it is absorbed, about 1 minute. Transfer the mixture to a bowl.

3. Heat the remaining 2 teaspoons oil in the same skillet over medium-high heat. Add the shallot and garlic; cook, stirring constantly, until fragrant, about 1 minute. Add the rice and cook, stirring, until it is lightly toasted, about 2 minutes. Add the remaining ½ cup Madeira and stir until it is almost absorbed, about 1 minute. Add the broth, 1 cup at a time, stirring until it is absorbed before adding more, until the rice is just tender. The cooking time should be about 20 minutes from the first addition of broth. Add the sausage mixture, cheese, and pepper; cook, stirring, until heated through, about 1 minute. Serve at once.

PER SERVING (1 cup): 404 Cal, 12 g Total Fat, 2 g Sat Fat, 0 g Trans Fat, 38 mg Chol, 511 mg Sod, 49 g Carb, 2 g Fib, 21 g Prot, 71 mg Calc.
PointsPlus value: *11.*

COOK'S TIP

Mushrooms lend a delicate, earthy taste to this sumptuous risotto. While we used white mushrooms, feel free to substitute fresh shiitakes (remove the stems) or creminis for even richer flavor.

Three-Herb and Lemon Roasted Cornish Hens

Makes 4 Servings

1 tablespoon finely chopped
   fresh flat-leaf parsley

2 teaspoons finely chopped
   fresh rosemary

2 teaspoons finely chopped
   fresh thyme

Grated zest of 1 small lemon

2 garlic cloves, minced

2 teaspoons extra-virgin
   olive oil

½ teaspoon salt

¼ teaspoon black pepper

2 (1½-pound) Cornish
   game hens

1. Preheat the oven to 400°F.

2. Mix together all of the ingredients except for the hens in a small bowl. Using kitchen shears, cut along each side of the backbone of the hens; discard the backbones. Turn the hens, breast side up, and open flat. With the palm of your hand, flatten the breasts slightly. With your fingers, gently loosen the skin on the breasts and thighs. Spread the herb mixture over the meat under the skin, then press the skin back into place.

3. Spray a large heavy ovenproof skillet with nonstick spray and set over medium-high heat. Add the hens, skin side down, and cook until browned, about 5 minutes; do not turn. Using tongs, gently turn the hens over.

4. Put the skillet into the oven and roast the hens until an instant-read thermometer inserted into a thigh registers 165°F, about 25 minutes longer. Transfer the hens to a cutting board and let stand for 10 minutes. Cut the hens in half and arrange on a small serving platter. Remove the skin before eating.

PER SERVING (½ **Cornish hen): 210 Cal, 8 g Total Fat, 2 g Sat Fat, 0 g Trans Fat, 146 mg Chol, 378 mg Sod, 1 g Total Carb, 0 g Fib, 32 g Prot, 25 mg Calc.**
PointsPlus value: *5.*

COOK'S TIP

Poussin (poo-SA), which is French for baby chickens, are plump, tender, about the same size as Cornish game hens, and work equally well in this recipe. If you don't see them in the poultry case, ask your butcher to special order them for you. They are rather special, making them a good choice for an important occasion.

Roasted Orange-Herb Game Hens

Makes 4 Servings

⅓ cup minced shallots

1 tablespoon dried fines herbes

2 teaspoons grated orange zest

¼ teaspoon salt

¼ teaspoon black pepper

2 (1½-pound) Cornish game hens, halved

1 cup reduced-sodium chicken broth

¾ cup orange juice

1. Preheat the oven to 450°F. Combine the shallots, fines herbes, orange zest, salt, and pepper in a small bowl. Transfer 1 tablespoon of the herb mixture to another small bowl; set aside.

2. With your fingers, gently loosen the skin from the breast meat of each hen half. Rub the 1 tablespoon herb mixture into the meat, under the skin, of each of the hen halves, then press the skin back into place.

3. Place the hens in a roasting pan and roast for 10 minutes. Add the broth. Roast, basting the hens twice with the broth, until an instant-read thermometer inserted in a thigh registers 165°F, about 20 minutes longer.

4. Transfer the hens to a platter; cover loosely with foil and keep warm. Place the roasting pan directly on top of two burners over high heat. Add the orange juice and the remaining herb mixture; bring to a boil, scraping any browned bits from the bottom of the pan. Reduce the heat and simmer until the sauce has reduced to about 1 cup, about 4 minutes. Serve the hens with the sauce. Remove the skins from the hens before eating.

PER SERVING (½ **Cornish game hen with** ¼ **cup sauce**): 237 Cal, 6 g Total Fat, 2 g Sat Fat, 0 g Trans Fat, 159 mg Chol, 366 mg Sod, 6 g Carb, 1 g Fib, 37 g Prot, 45 mg Calc. *PointsPlus* value: *5.*

COOK'S TIP

If shallots are not available in your market, substitute ⅓ cup minced onion and 1 teaspoon minced garlic.

Cranberry-Braised Cornish Hens

Cranberry-Braised Cornish Hens

Makes 4 Servings

2 (1 ¼-pound) Cornish game hens, skinned

1 small onion, finely chopped

1 garlic clove, minced

⅓ cup canned whole-berry cranberry sauce

¼ cup dry vermouth

1 tablespoon orange marmalade

1 bay leaf

1 teaspoon chopped fresh thyme

½ teaspoon salt

¼ teaspoon black pepper

2 teaspoons water

1 teaspoon cornstarch

1. Preheat the oven to 350°F.

2. Tie the legs of each hen together with kitchen twine. Tie the twine twice around the whole body of each hen. Spray a Dutch oven or 2½-quart flameproof casserole dish with nonstick spray and set over medium heat. Add the hens and brown on all sides, about 4 minutes. Transfer the hens to a plate.

3. Add onion and garlic to the Dutch oven; cook, stirring frequently, until softened, about 2 minutes. Stir in the cranberry sauce, vermouth, and marmalade; cook, stirring occasionally, until the marmalade melts. Stir in the bay leaf, thyme, salt, and pepper. Reduce the heat and simmer, uncovered, stirring occasionally, about 5 minutes.

4. Return the hens, breast side up, to the Dutch oven. Baste once with some of the mixture in the Dutch oven, then cover and bake until an instant-read thermometer inserted in a thigh registers 165°F, about 45 minutes. Transfer the hens to a carving board; let stand for about 5 minutes. Remove the twine then cut the hens in half.

5. Skim any visible fat from the sauce in the Dutch oven. Discard the bay leaf. Place the Dutch oven over medium heat and bring to a simmer.

6. Stir the water and cornstarch in a small bowl until dissolved; stir in some of the hot juices from the Dutch oven. Return to the Dutch oven and cook, stirring constantly, until the mixture bubbles and thickens. Serve the sauce with the hens.

PER SERVING (½ hen with 2 tablespoons sauce): **225 Cal, 4 g Total Fat, 1 g Sat Fat, 0 g Trans Fat, 122 mg Chol, 370 mg Sod, 14 g Carb, 1 g Fib, 27 g Prot, 21 mg Calc.**
PointsPlus value: *5.*

COOK'S TIP

If you tie kitchen string around the legs and a couple of times around the body of each Cornish hen, it will help the hens retain their round shape as they bake.

Cornish Hens au Vin

Makes 4 Servings

2 (1¼-pound) Cornish game hens, halved and skinned

2 garlic cloves, minced

2 tablespoons all-purpose flour

½ teaspoon salt

¼ teaspoon black pepper

1 slice thick-cut bacon, chopped

3 shallots, chopped

3 carrots, cut into ½-inch chunks

1 cup frozen whole small onions

1 cup reduced-sodium chicken broth

⅓ cup dry white wine

¾ pound small red or white potatoes, scrubbed and halved

½ pound fresh white or baby bella mushrooms, halved

¼ cup chopped fresh flat-leaf parsley

2 tablespoons chopped fresh marjoram, or 2 teaspoons dried

1. Rub the hens with the garlic then sprinkle with the flour, salt, and pepper; set aside. Heat a large nonstick Dutch oven over medium-high heat. Add the bacon and cook, stirring occasionally, until browned, about 5 minutes; transfer to paper towels to drain.

2. Add the hens, 2 halves at a time, to the Dutch oven and cook over medium-high heat until lightly browned, about 3 minutes on each side. Transfer to a plate and set aside.

3. Add the shallots to the Dutch oven and cook, stirring frequently, until golden, about 3 minutes. Add the carrots and onions; cook, stirring occasionally, about 2 minutes. Add the broth, wine, and potatoes; bring to a boil, stirring to scrape the browned bits from the bottom of the Dutch oven. Return the hens to the Dutch oven. Reduce the heat and simmer, covered, about 20 minutes. Add the mushrooms and simmer until the hens are cooked through and the vegetables are tender, about 15 minutes longer. Stir in the parsley, marjoram, and bacon just before serving.

PER SERVING (½ **Cornish hen with generous 1 cup vegetables and sauce): 333 Cal, 6 g Total Fat, 2 g Sat Fat, 0 g Trans Fat, 124 mg Chol, 475 mg Sod, 31 g Carb, 4 g Fib, 33 g Prot, 67 mg Calc.** *PointsPlus* value: *8.*

COOK'S TIP

Use poultry scissors or a very sharp knife to cut the hens in half. After pulling off the skin, be sure to remove as much of the excess fat as possible.

Apricot and Mustard–Glazed Cornish Hens

Makes 4 Servings

¼ cup plus 1 tablespoon apricot preserves

2 tablespoons country-style Dijon mustard

1 large garlic clove, minced

¼ teaspoon black pepper

⅛ teaspoon salt

2 (1¼-pound) Cornish game hens

1 cup reduced-sodium chicken broth

2 shallots, minced

2 teaspoons chopped fresh rosemary

2 teaspoons unsalted butter

1. Preheat the oven to 450°F. Spray a shallow roasting pan with nonstick spray.

2. Combine ¼ cup of the preserves, the mustard, garlic, ⅛ teaspoon of the pepper, and the salt in a small bowl. With your fingers, gently loosen the skin on the breasts of the hens; spread the preserve mixture over the meat under the skin. Press the skin back into place. Tie the legs of each hen together with kitchen string and tuck the wings under.

3. Place the hens in the roasting pan and roast until an instant-read thermometer inserted into the thickest part of a thigh registers 165°F, about 1 hour.

4. Transfer the hens to a small serving platter; cover loosely with foil and keep warm. Set the roasting pan directly over two burners over high heat. Add the broth, shallots, rosemary, the remaining 1 tablespoon preserves, and the remaining ⅛ teaspoon pepper; bring to boil, scraping any browned bits from the bottom of the pan. Reduce the heat and simmer until the sauce has reduced to about ½ cup, 4–5 minutes. Remove the pan from the heat and swirl in the butter until blended.

5. Split each hen in half and serve with the sauce. Remove the skin before eating.

PER SERVING (½ hen with 2 tablespoons sauce): 228 Cal, 6 g Total Fat, 2 g Sat Fat, 0 g Trans Fat, 103 mg Chol, 412 mg Sod, 19 g Carb, 1 g Fib, 23 g Prot, 36 mg Calc.
PointsPlus value: *6.*

COOK'S TIP

Round out your meal by serving steamed asparagus and cooked jasmine rice tossed with grated orange zest and chopped fresh parsley (½ cup cooked jasmine rice for each serving will increase the *PointsPlus* value by *3*).

Butterflied Cornish Hens with Crushed Pepper and Garlic

Makes 4 Servings

1 tablespoon chopped fresh
    flat-leaf parsley

1 large garlic clove, minced

2 teaspoons extra-virgin
    olive oil

½ teaspoon red pepper flakes

½ teaspoon salt

2 (1½-pound) Cornish
    game hens

1. Spray the grill rack with extra-virgin olive oil nonstick spray; prepare the grill for a medium-hot fire.

2. Meanwhile, combine all of the ingredients except the hens in a small bowl; set aside.

3. Using kitchen shears, cut along each side of the backbones of the hens; discard the backbones. Turn the hens, breast side up and open flat, then use the palm of your hand to flatten the breasts slightly. With your fingers, gently loosen the skin on the breasts and thighs. Rub half of the parsley mixture over the meat under the skin of each hen, then press the skin back into place; tuck the wings under.

4. Place the hens, skin side down, on the grill rack and grill until the skin is deep golden and crispy, about 15 minutes. Turn the hens and grill until an instant-read thermometer inserted into a thigh registers 165°F, about 15 minutes longer. Transfer the hens to a cutting board and let stand for about 5 minutes. Using poultry shears or kitchen scissors, cut each hen in half by cutting along the breastbone. Remove the skin before eating.

PER SERVING (½ game hen): **224 Cal, 8 g Total Fat, 2 g Sat Fat, 0 g Trans Fat, 159 mg Chol, 391 mg Sod, 1 g Carb, 0 g Fib, 35 g Prot, 24 mg Calc.**
PointsPlus value: *5.*

COOK'S TIP

This dish can also easily be made indoors. Prepare the hens as directed and preheat the oven to 500°F. Put the hens, skin side down, in a very large heavy skillet that has been sprayed with nonstick spray and weight with another heavy skillet. Cook over high heat until deep golden, about 8 minutes, then turn. Transfer to the oven until cooked, about 20 minutes.

Peppered Orange Quail

Makes 4 Servings

2 tablespoons molasses

1 tablespoon grated
   orange zest

1 teaspoon balsamic vinegar

¾ teaspoon cracked
   black pepper

4 (¼-pound) semi-boneless
   quail, thawed, skin removed,
   and split open down
   the back

½ teaspoon salt

1. Spray the grill rack with nonstick spray; prepare the grill for a medium-hot fire.

2. Combine the molasses, orange zest, vinegar, and pepper in a zip-close plastic bag; add the quail. Squeeze out the air and seal the bag; turn to coat the quail. Refrigerate, turning the bag occasionally, for about 15 minutes.

3. Lift the quail from the marinade and sprinkle with the salt. Discard the marinade. Place the quail on the grill rack and grill until cooked through, about 5 minutes on each side.

PER SERVING (1 quail): 168 Cal, 7 g Total Fat, 2 g Sat Fat, 0 g Trans Fat, 64 mg Chol, 369 mg Sod, 4 g Carb, 0 g Fib, 23 g Prot, 47 mg Calc.
PointsPlus value: *4.*

COOK'S TIP

Don't feel like grilling? Broil the quail instead. Spray the broiler rack with nonstick spray and preheat the broiler. Place the quail on the broiler rack and broil 4 or 5 inches from the heat until cooked through, about 5 minutes on each side.

Pan-Seared Quail with Dried Cranberry Chutney

Pan-Seared Quail with Dried Cranberry Chutney

Makes 4 Servings

4 (5-ounce) whole quail

5 tablespoons sugar

2 tablespoons reduced-sodium soy sauce

½ teaspoon five-spice powder

3 teaspoons canola oil

1 small onion, finely chopped

1 tablespoon grated peeled fresh ginger

1 cup orange juice

½ cup dried cranberries

½ cup dried pitted tart cherries

½ teaspoon salt

¼ teaspoon black pepper

1. Using a sharp knife, split each quail along the backbone and press down on the breasts to flatten; remove the skin. Combine 1 tablespoon of the sugar, the soy sauce, and five-spice powder in a zip-close plastic bag. Add the quail. Squeeze out the air and seal the bag; turn to coat the quail. Refrigerate, turning the bag occasionally, for at least 2 hours or up to overnight.

2. To make the chutney, heat 1 teaspoon of the oil in a medium nonstick skillet over medium heat. Add the onion and ginger; cook, stirring frequently, until softened, about 3 minutes. Add the remaining 4 tablespoons sugar, the orange juice, cranberries, and cherries; bring to a boil. Reduce the heat and simmer, stirring occasionally, until thickened, about 8 minutes. Stir in ¼ teaspoon of salt and ⅛ teaspoon of pepper.

3. Remove the quail from the marinade and pat dry with paper towels. Discard the marinade. Sprinkle the quail with the remaining ¼ teaspoon salt and ⅛ teaspoon pepper. Heat the remaining 2 teaspoons oil in a large nonstick skillet over medium heat. Add the quail and cook, breast side down, for 5 minutes. Turn the quail over and reduce the heat to medium-low. Cover the skillet and simmer until the quail is cooked through, about 8 minutes. Serve with the chutney.

PER SERVING (1 quail with ¼ cup chutney): 392 Cal, 11 g Total Fat, 3 g Sat Fat, 0 g Trans Fat, 64 mg Chol, 635 mg Sod, 51 g Carb, 3 g Fib, 25 g Prot, 64 mg Calc.
PointsPlus value: *10.*

COOK'S TIP

Quail are small game birds that are tender and flavorful. You can buy them at many butcher shops and online at www.dartagnan.com. Removing the skin on the quail helps cut the fat in the recipe. Keep in mind that the skin on the wing tips will not come off, so discard them, if you like.

Sautéed Duck with Pears and Apples

Makes 4 Servings

4 (4–5-ounce) skinless
    boneless duck breasts

¾ teaspoon salt

¼ teaspoon black pepper

4 teaspoons unsalted butter

2 pears, peeled, cored, and cut
    into ½-inch cubes

1 Golden Delicious apple,
    peeled, cored, and cut into
    ½-inch pieces

1 tablespoon sugar

½ teaspoon dried thyme

¼ cup brandy

¾ cup apple juice

⅓ cup prepared duck demi-
    glace

2 teaspoons cornstarch

1 tablespoon cold water

1. Sprinkle the duck with ½ teaspoon of the salt and ⅛ teaspoon of the pepper. Melt 2 teaspoons of the butter in a large nonstick skillet over medium-high heat. Add the duck and cook until browned and just cooked through, about 4 minutes on each side. Cut each duck breast into 4 slices, transfer to a plate, and keep warm.

2. Wipe out the skillet and melt the remaining 2 teaspoons butter. Add the pears, apple, sugar, and thyme; cook, stirring frequently, until the fruit is light golden, about 4 minutes. Add the brandy and cook 1 minute. Add the apple juice and demi-glace; bring to a boil. Reduce the heat and simmer, uncovered, until slightly thickened, about 4 minutes.

3. Dissolve the cornstarch in the water; add to the skillet, stirring constantly. Cook and stir until the mixture bubbles and thickens, about 1 minute. Stir in the remaining ¼ teaspoon salt and ⅛ teaspoon pepper. Serve the sauce with the duck breasts.

PER SERVING (1 duck breast with generous ⅓ cup sauce): 370 Cal, 11 g Total Fat, 5 g Sat Fat, 0 g Trans Fat, 119 mg Chol, 622 mg Sod, 31 g Carb, 4 g Fib, 29 g Prot, 23 mg Calc.
PointsPlus value: *10.*

COOK'S TIP

This flavorful fall dish lends itself perfectly to being served with a side of creamy mashed cooked butternut or acorn squash. You can find demi-glace in specialty food stores and in the meat department of some supermarkets.

Sautéed Duck with Pears and Apples

Duck Breasts with Raspberry-Thyme Sauce

Makes 4 Servings

1 (6-ounce) container fresh
    raspberries

2 tablespoons sugar

2 tablespoons apple cider
    vinegar

1 teaspoon Dijon mustard

½ teaspoon salt

4 (5-ounce) skinless boneless
    duck breasts

1 tablespoon chopped
    fresh thyme

¼ teaspoon black pepper

1 teaspoon canola oil

1. Combine the raspberries, sugar, and vinegar in a small saucepan. Bring to a boil; reduce the heat and simmer, stirring occasionally, just until the berries are softened, about 3 minutes. Stir in the mustard and a pinch of the salt. Remove the saucepan from the heat.

2. Sprinkle the duck with the thyme, the remaining salt, and the pepper. Heat the oil in a large heavy nonstick or cast-iron skillet over medium-high heat. Add the duck skinned side down and cook 3 minutes on each side for medium-rare or to the desired doneness. Transfer the duck to a cutting board and keep warm.

3. Add the raspberry sauce to the skillet and bring to a simmer, stirring to scrape up any browned bits from the bottom of the pan. Pour the sauce into a sauceboat.

4. Cut the duck crosswise into ¼-inch slices and serve with the sauce.

PER SERVING (1 duck breast with about 2 tablespoons sauce): 187 Cal, 6 g Total Fat, 2 g Sat Fat, 0 g Trans Fat, 87 mg Chol, 386 mg Sod, 9 g Total Carb, 2 g Fib, 23 g Prot, 19 mg Calc. *PointsPlus* value: *4.*

COOK'S TIP

To dress up this dish, garnish each plate with a few berries along with a fresh thyme sprig. If you like, substitute other berries such as blackberries or blueberries for the raspberries—or use a combination.

Hoisin Duck Tacos with Cucumber Salsa

Makes 4 Servings

3 tablespoons hoisin sauce

2 tablespoons sake or
white wine

4 (5–6-ounce) skinless
boneless duck breasts

1 cucumber, peeled, seeded,
and cut into ¼-inch dice

½ red bell pepper, cut into
¼-inch dice

1 scallion, chopped

1 tablespoon reduced-sodium
soy sauce

2 teaspoons rice vinegar

1½ teaspoons sugar

½ teaspoon salt

4 (6-inch) corn tortillas

⅛ small head napa cabbage,
shredded, about 1 cup

1. Combine the hoisin sauce and sake in a zip-close plastic bag; add the duck. Squeeze out the air and seal the bag; turn to coat the duck. Refrigerate, turning the bag occasionally, for at least 1 hour or up to overnight.

2. Spray the grill rack with nonstick spray; prepare the grill for a medium-hot fire.

3. To make the salsa, combine the cucumber, bell pepper, scallion, soy sauce, vinegar, sugar, and salt in a medium bowl; mix well.

4. Wipe the excess marinade from the duck and place the duck on the grill rack. Discard the marinade. Grill the duck until cooked through, 4–5 minutes on each side. Let stand for about 5 minutes, then thinly slice the duck across the grain.

5. Warm the tortillas directly on the grill rack, about 30 seconds on each side. Place a tortilla on each of 4 plates; top each tortilla with ¼ cup cabbage and 1 sliced duck breast. Serve with the salsa.

PER SERVING (1 taco with ⅓ cup salsa): 302 Cal, 8 g Total Fat, 2 g Sat Fat, 0 g Trans Fat, 110 mg Chol, 739 mg Sod, 24 g Carb, 2 g Fib, 31 g Prot, 35 mg Calc.
PointsPlus value: *8.*

COOK'S TIP

East meets West in this combination of ingredients, where Asian flavors take center stage and are gathered together in tortillas.

Slow-Cooker Duck and White Bean Chili

Makes 6 Servings

1 pound skinless boneless duck breasts, cut into ½-inch pieces

Grated zest and juice of 1 tangerine

6 carrots, sliced

1 small red onion, quartered and sliced

1 (14½-ounce) can fire-roasted diced tomatoes

1 (8-ounce) can no-salt-added tomato sauce

1 (15½-ounce) can navy or great northern beans, rinsed and drained

2 tablespoons chili powder

2 teaspoons ground cumin

1 teaspoon dried oregano

¼ cup chopped fresh cilantro (optional)

1. Spray a large nonstick skillet with nonstick spray and set over medium heat. Add half of the duck and cook, turning occasionally, until lightly browned, about 4 minutes. Transfer the duck to a 5- or 6-quart slow cooker. Repeat with the remaining duck.

2. Add the tangerine juice to the skillet. Bring to a boil, scraping up the browned bits from the bottom of the pan. Pour the tangerine juice mixture into the slow cooker. Stir in the carrots, onion, tomatoes, tomato sauce, beans, tangerine zest, chili powder, cumin, and oregano. Cover and cook until the duck and vegetables are tender, 4–5 hours on high or 8–10 hours on low. Divide the chili among 6 bowls and sprinkle with the cilantro, if using.

PER SERVING (about 1 cup): 318 Cal, 5 g Total Fat, 1 g Sat Fat, 0 g Trans Fat, 81 mg Chol, 589 mg Sod, 50 g Carb, 11 g Fib, 23 g Prot, 151 mg Calc.
PointsPlus value: *8.*

COOK'S TIP

Here's an upscale chili that is perfect company fare. Serve it on your best dishes accompanied by a bowl of whole wheat orzo (½ cup of cooked pasta for each serving will increase the *PointsPlus* value by *3*).

Hoisin Duck Stir-Fry

Makes 4 Servings

⅔ cup reduced-sodium chicken broth

¼ cup hoisin sauce

2 tablespoons reduced-sodium soy sauce

3 teaspoons cornstarch

4 teaspoons Asian (dark) sesame oil

1 pound skinless boneless duck breasts, cut into thin strips

3 scallions, chopped

1 tablespoon grated peeled fresh ginger

½ pound fresh green beans, trimmed

1 cup cherry tomatoes, halved

1. Combine the broth, hoisin sauce, soy sauce, and cornstarch in a small bowl; mix well.

2. Heat a large nonstick skillet or wok over medium-high heat until a drop of water sizzles. Pour in 2 teaspoons of the oil and swirl to coat the pan, then add the duck and stir-fry until browned and cooked through, about 4 minutes. Transfer the duck to a plate.

3. Heat the remaining 2 teaspoons oil in the same skillet. Add the scallions and ginger; stir-fry until fragrant, about 30 seconds. Add the green beans and stir-fry until crisp-tender, about 3 minutes. Add the tomatoes and stir-fry 1 minute. Add the duck and the broth mixture. Cook, stirring constantly, until the mixture bubbles and thickens, about 1 minute.

PER SERVING (1 cup): 232 Cal, 7 g Total Fat, 1 g Sat Fat, 0 g Trans Fat, 66 mg Chol, 659 mg Sod, 16 g Carb, 3 g Fib, 27 g Prot, 61 mg Calc.
PointsPlus value: *6.*

COOK'S TIP

This versatile stir-fry is delicious when prepared with duck, but it also lends itself well to lean pork tenderloin, boneless and skinless chicken breasts or thighs, or shrimp.

Turkey Talk

There's nothing like the savory aroma of roasting turkey filling your home on Thanksgiving day to create—and bring back—fond memories of family and friends coming together. Follow these guidelines to help keep you confident and relaxed in the kitchen

THREE WAYS TO SAFELY THAW TURKEY

In the Refrigerator

Leave the turkey in its original wrapping and place in a pan to catch any drips. Allow 24 hours thawing time for every 4 to 5 pounds. Once thawed, keep the turkey refrigerated; cook within 2 days.

In Cold Water

Leave the turkey in its original wrapping and place, breast side down, in a sink or deep vessel. Add enough cold water to completely cover. Plan on 30 minutes thawing time per pound, changing the water about every 30 minutes to keep the turkey well chilled. Be sure to roast the turkey right after it has thawed.

In the Microwave

Remove the turkey from its original wrapping and place in a microwavable dish to catch any drips. Follow the manufacturer's instructions for timing and power levels. Roast the turkey immediately after thawing, as some of the meat may have warmed enough to begin being cooked.

COOKING TIMES AND TEMPS

The secret to cooking up a moist turkey is roasting it thoroughly but not too much, keeping in mind that an unstuffed turkey cooks faster and more evenly than a stuffed turkey. As a plus, baking the stuffing (sometimes referred to a dressing) separately gives the stuffing a tempting crisp and browned crust.

Turkey is safely cooked when the internal temperature reaches 165°F. Use an instant-read thermometer inserted into the thickest part of the thigh, not touching any bone. (Don't count on the accuracy of those plastic pop-up indicators.) Once done, tent the bird loosely with foil and let it stand for 20 minutes or a bit longer before carving, so the juices have a chance to redistribute within the meat.

APPROXIMATE TURKEY ROASTING TIMES (unstuffed, 325°F oven)

SIZE	TIME
2 to 3 pounds (breast half)	50 minutes to 1 hour
4 to 8 pounds (breast)	1½ to 3¼ hours
8 to 12 pounds (whole turkey)	2¾ to 3 hours
12 to 14 pounds (whole turkey)	3 to 3¾ hours
14 to 18 pounds (whole turkey)	3¾ to 4¼ hours
18 to 20 pounds (whole turkey)	4¼ to 4½ hours
20 to 24 pounds (whole turkey)	4½ to 5 hours

Duck Tzimmes

Makes 8 Servings

2 (4-ounce) fully cooked duck legs confit

5 large carrots, cut into 1-inch pieces

1 pound sweet potatoes, peeled and cut into 1-inch pieces

1 cup pitted prunes, quartered

½ cup dried cherries

¼ cup reduced-sodium chicken broth

3 tablespoons honey

½ teaspoon salt

½ teaspoon ground cinnamon

¼ teaspoon garlic powder

1. Adjust the racks to divide the oven into thirds. Preheat the oven to 350°F. Spray a 9 × 13-inch baking pan with nonstick spray.

2. Remove any white fat and all the skin from the duck legs confit. Pull off the meat and shred with your hands or two forks. You should have about 1½ cups of meat. Place the meat in a large bowl and combine with the carrots, sweet potatoes, prunes, and cherries.

3. Whisk the broth, honey, salt, cinnamon, and garlic powder in a small bowl until smooth. Pour over the duck and vegetables; toss to coat. Pour this mixture and any juices into the baking pan.

4. Cover the pan with foil and bake in the lower third of the oven, tossing every 15 minutes, until the vegetables are tender, about 1 hour and 10 minutes. Let stand, uncovered, for about 5 minutes before serving.

PER SERVING (1 cup): 228 Cal, 3 g Total Fat, 1 g Sat Fat, 0 g Trans Fat, 33 mg Chol, 253 mg Sod, 42 g Carb, 5 g Fib, 11 g Prot, 51 mg Calc.
PointsPlus value: *6.*

COOK'S TIP

Tzimmes is a traditional Jewish dish of prunes, sweet potatoes, and brisket, usually eaten at Rosh Hashanah—the Jewish New Year. It's fairly sweet as it symbolizes the hope for a sweet New Year. We've replaced the brisket with duck confit—a French extravagance of duck legs preserved in duck fat.

Ginger Duck and Wild Rice Salad

Ginger Duck and Wild Rice Salad

Makes 4 Servings

2 tablespoons reduced-sodium
   soy sauce

2 tablespoons orange juice

1 tablespoon red-wine vinegar

1 tablespoon honey

1 teaspoon Asian (dark)
   sesame oil

1 (6-ounce) box long-grain and
   wild rice mix, spice packet
   discarded

1 teaspoon canola oil

2 teaspoons minced peeled
   fresh ginger

1 garlic clove, minced

½ pound skinless boneless
   duck breasts, cut into
   2 x ¼-inch strips

¼ cup dried cranberries

4 scallions, thinly sliced on the
   diagonal

2 tablespoons coarsely
   chopped toasted pecans

1. To make the dressing, whisk together the soy sauce, orange juice, vinegar, honey, and sesame oil in a small bowl until blended; set aside.

2. Prepare the rice according to the package directions, discarding the spice packet. Transfer the rice to a large bowl; set aside.

3. Heat the canola oil in a large nonstick skillet over medium heat. Add the ginger and garlic; cook, stirring frequently, until fragrant, about 1 minute. Add the duck and cook over medium-high heat, turning occasionally, until browned on the outside and cooked through, about 6 minutes.

4. Add the duck mixture to the rice. Stir in the cranberries, scallions, and pecans. Drizzle with the dressing and toss well to coat.

PER SERVING (1¼ **cups**): 326 Cal, 6 g Total Fat, 1 g Sat Fat, 0 g Trans Fat, 33 mg Chol, 294 mg Sod, 51 g Carb, 3 g Fib, 18 g Prot, 33 mg Calc.
PointsPlus value: *8.*

COOK'S TIP

Fresh duck is available from late spring to early winter. However, you can substitute thawed frozen duck or skinless boneless chicken thighs if you like. Alternatively, you can use leftover turkey in this recipe by stirring 1 cup chopped cooked turkey into the salad along with the dressing.

Dry and Liquid Measurement Equivalents

TEASPOONS	TABLESPOONS	CUPS	FLUID OUNCES
3 teaspoons	1 tablespoon		½ fluid ounce
6 teaspoons	2 tablespoons	⅛ cup	1 fluid ounce
8 teaspoons	2 tablespoons plus 2 teaspoons	⅙ cup	
12 teaspoons	4 tablespoons	¼ cup	2 fluid ounces
15 teaspoons	5 tablespoons	⅓ cup minus 1 teaspoon	
16 teaspoons	5 tablespoons plus 1 teaspoon	⅓ cup	
18 teaspoons	6 tablespoons	¼ cup plus 2 tablespoons	3 fluid ounces
24 teaspoons	8 tablespoons	½ cup	4 fluid ounces
30 teaspoons	10 tablespoons	½ cup plus 2 tablespoons	5 fluid ounces
32 teaspoons	10 tablespoons plus 2 teaspoons	⅔ cup	
36 teaspoons	12 tablespoons	¾ cup	6 fluid ounces
42 teaspoons	14 tablespoons	1 cup minus 2 tablespoons	7 fluid ounces
45 teaspoons	15 tablespoons	1 cup minus 1 tablespoon	
48 teaspoons	16 tablespoons	1 cup	8 fluid ounces

Metric Conversions

If you are converting the recipes in this book to metric measurements, use the following chart as a guide.

VOLUME

¼ teaspoon	1 milliliter
½ teaspoon	2 milliliters
1 teaspoon	5 milliliters
1 tablespoon	15 milliliters
2 tablespoons	30 milliliters
3 tablespoons	45 milliliters
¼ cup	60 milliliters
⅓ cup	80 milliliters
½ cup	120 milliliters
⅔ cup	160 milliliters
¾ cup	175 milliliters
1 cup	240 milliliters
1 quart	950 milliliters

LENGTH

1 inch	25 millimeters
1 inch	2.5 centimeters

OVEN TEMPERATURE

250°F	120°C
275°F	140°C
300°F	150°C
325°F	160°C
350°F	180°C
375°F	190°C
400°F	200°C
425°F	220°C
450°F	230°C
475°F	250°C
500°F	260°C
525°F	270°C

WEIGHT

1 ounce	30 grams
¼ pound	120 grams
½ pound	240 grams
1 pound	480 grams

PointsPlus value Index

Index